D0350727

THE MONSTER OF
THE MADIDI

THE MONSTER OF THE MADIDI

SEARCHING FOR THE GIANT
APE OF THE BOLIVIAN
JUNGLE 🦋 SIMON CHAPMAN

AURUM PRESS

First published in Great Britain
2001 by Aurum Press Ltd
25 Bedford Avenue, London WC1B 3AT

Design by Geoff Green

A catalogue record for this book is available from the British Library.

ISBN 1 85410 749 6

1 3 5 7 9 10 8 6 4 2
2001 2003 2005 2004 2002

Typeset in 10.5/13.5pt Adobe Caslon
by M Rules

Printed in Great Britain by MPG Books Ltd, Bodmin

To Carolyn, who understands my tree frog dreams

Contents

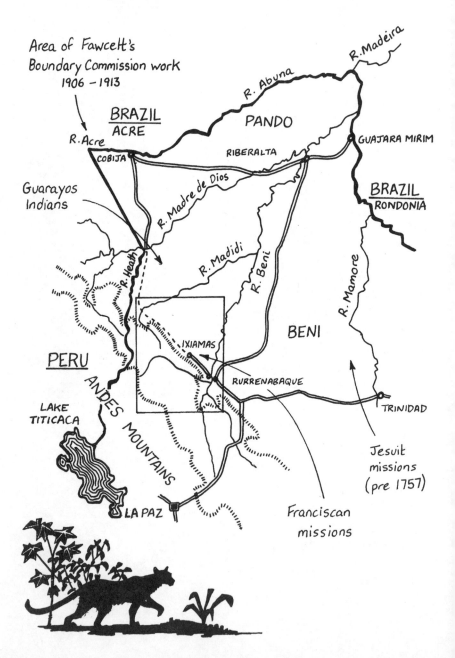

Northern Bolivia

Area of Fawcett's
Boundary Commission work
1906 – 1913

BRAZIL
ACRE

R. Acre

COBIJA

R. Abuna

PANDO

R. Madeira

RIBERALTA

GUAJARA MIRIM

BRAZIL
RONDONIA

Guarayos
Indians

R. Madre de Dios

R. Madidi

R. Heath

R. Beni

R. Mamore

PERU

ANDES MOUNTAINS

IXIAMAS

BENI

RURRENABAQUE

TRINIDAD

LAKE
TITICACA

LA PAZ

Franciscan
missions

Jesuit
missions
(pre 1757)

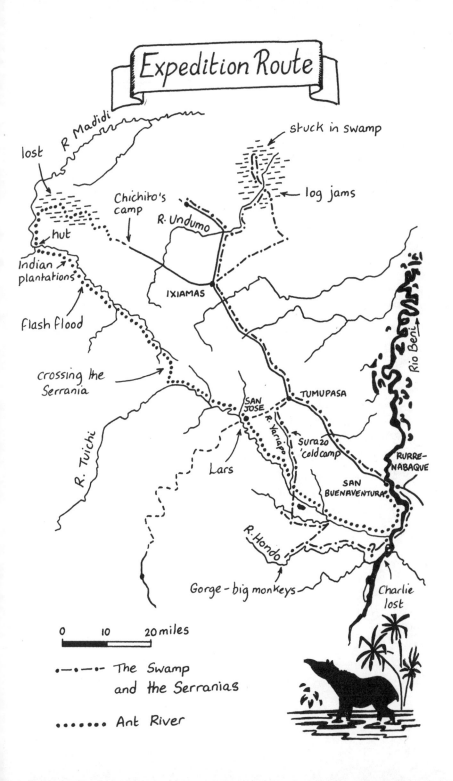

Expedition Route

R. Madidi

lost

stuck in swamp

log jams

Chichito's camp

R. Undumo

hut

Indian plantations

IXIAMAS

Flash flood

crossing the Serrania

TUMUPASA

SAN JOSE

R. Yariapo

Surazo 'cold camp'

Lars

RURRE- NABAQUE

R. Tuichi

SAN BUENAVENTURA

R. Hondo

?

Gorge - big monkeys

Charlie lost

Rio Beni

0   10   20 miles

.—.—.—. The Swamp and the Serranias

.... Ant River

Acknowledgements

Picture credits: 1, *Illustrated London News*; 2, 3, 4, 5, 6, Royal Geographical Society; all other photographs and illustrations by the author.

I would like to thank the following for their help with this book: Julian Singleton; Charlie Hruska; Lars Hafskjold; Carolyn Whitaker; the Janco brothers (Alejandro, Ignacio, Irgen, Leo, Israel (Negro), Nico and Uinma) and their father, Leoncio; Bernadino Marmani; Leoncio Navi and Justino for 'portering'; Alcide for the use of his motorboat; Chichito for the truck.

And Carolyn for always being there when I come home.

PART ONE

The Swamp and the Serranias

CHAPTER ONE

Monsters of the Madidi

CROCODILES' EYES LIGHT up when you shine a torch at them. They glow a bright orange, especially when you hold the torch as close as possible to your own eyes so that the light reflects straight back.

'It also works for birds', whispered Negro, panning the torch beam up from the stream and into a nearby bush. He gingerly crept forward and moments later returned clutching a brown, frog-mouthed bird: a nightjar whose tree-bark patterned wings he opened out to show us.

'When the light is in their eyes, they can't see and are afraid to move.' He turned to me and grinned impishly. 'Tonight we find a crocodile for you, my friend.'

Negro was nineteen, of Tacana descent. He'd grown up in this part of the Bolivian Amazon and to him it was like a playground. With his older brother Leo and a friend called Miguel, he would enthusiastically lead us off trails to show us medicinal plants, poke twigs down armadillo burrows to see if anything would come out, and make weird trilling noises to attract the attention of titi monkeys which would then trill back at him from the treetops.

At one point he insisted on swinging on a vine across a muddy chasm, only to hit a tree trunk midway and slide down 'Tom and

Jerry' fashion into the goo below. We had all made it safely across when he confided, 'A German *turista* broke her arm on the last trip here . . . but she was just unlucky.'

Our camp was in a secondary-growth thicket next to a turbulent river, which we'd ridden up in an outboard-motor-powered dugout canoe the day before. In a surprisingly short time Leo and Negro had constructed a bamboo frame and draped a plastic sheet over it to make a crude tent. As there wasn't enough room for everyone under that, I slept in another tent, a decision I felt relieved about later when a snake decided to hide amongst the sleeping bags under the shelter and had to be driven out by beating around with sticks.

We spent three days at that camp, using it as a base to explore the jungle and to make numerous (unsuccessful) fishing trips. The night walks were best of all; spotlighting the eyes of fish, caimans and tree frogs in a shallow creek that fed into the main river. My moment of glory came on the second night. I had a three-foot croc in my beam. It was partly under a bush. Its eyes shone back bright orange. I looked at Negro.

'By the tail or the neck; it makes no difference provided that you are quick.'

I opted for the tail and yanked hard. This was a mistake. The crocodile arched its back round and bit my hand. For a second it dangled by its teeth as I tried to shake it off, ripping my fingers and thudding into the bank as it scuttled back into the water. Negro was virtually falling over in fits of laughter. How could I have been so slow? Didn't I realize that I had to pull it straight up and not give it the chance to push off with its front legs? Did I want another go? He could always find me another one.

I looked at my hand, at the crescent set of puncture marks on each side that extended into a series of parallel rips as the mouth had slid down my fingers. None of the wounds were deep, though I was slightly shaken and more embarrassed than anything else. Leaving me nursing my cuts, my guide disappeared into the bushes. Just when I was beginning to lose hope of seeing him again he reappeared, torch in mouth, clutching a two-foot-long caiman in each hand. He handed one of the crocs to me and laid the other on its back, gently stroking its belly whilst talking to it in soft, loving tones, the way you might talk to a small baby. Soon the crocodile was lying still and Negro repeated the trick with the other so that the two lay next to each other, on their backs, asleep. It was easy to imagine a look of serene contentment on their faces but I rather think that this was just because of the way that crocodile mouths turn up at the ends – a crocodile smile.

𝕏

For me, a rainforest is the best place to be. Amidst the tumbling, looping cascades of vegetation, the ticking of insects, the cries of unseen animals in the treetops; that's the stuff of my daydreams. It's where I go when the humdrum reality of work and life is getting to me. I sit in the shower, close my eyes and concentrate on the sound of the water cascading off my head. I imagine a small waterfall, not much more than a trickle of water really, that funnels down a narrow gully and wells up behind a dam of pebbles and fallen leaves before spilling over onto the next level below. In my scene I'm a small animal, a tree frog perhaps, looking up at the broad leaves of the undergrowth from underneath. Some leaves are lit up in golden hues where shafts of light pierce the canopy. Mostly my world is shady and warm, very warm. My skin is damp with the cloying humidity and drops of water that are still dripping from the canopy, even though it's been some time since the rain stopped. Some splash off the leaves, momentarily causing them to twitch then flex back while a bead of moisture starts to collect on the pointed tip. In the still air above my pool hangs a cluster of tiny flies, caught by the sun whenever they pass through one of the slanting beams. They sometimes arc off into the shade for no apparent reason, but always return or are replaced by others that flit in to hover with barely perceptible movement apart from the blur of their wings.

Though the location is always the same, my waterfall changes each time I'm there. I think it depends on what mood I'm in.

Sometimes the water is gushing down the gully, on other occasions the pool has become so jammed with fallen leaves and twigs that only a trickle dribbles down to the next level. At times there is a crashing in the foliage of the canopy as a troop of monkeys passes overhead. Or I imagine I can hear the rustling of an animal foraging through the leaf litter, an armadillo or maybe an ant bird turning over dead leaves and twigs. Only occasionally do I venture away from the waterfall to see what lies over the ridge above. At the top the vegetation thins out and from there I can look straight down onto a winding river far below. It is little more than a stream rushing over a bed of grey boulders, many of which protrude from the surface, churning up frothing, white waves in their wakes. As the river nears a bend, the water becomes dark and appears still. It gathers itself in a deep pool, free of ripples, before breaking up into a mass of rivulets as it rushes over a lip of pebbles and out of my sight. Scanning upwards I can see the outline of the next ridge far above the stream – the other side of the valley. The treetops there are so far away there that they look like dark green cauliflower florets. There are more ridges beyond. They are higher, indistinct and tinged blue with the haze of distance, except in the mornings when the sun hits them full on, those rare occasions when they are not covered in mist. Those far ridges. That's where I really want to go.

❦

This is a book about jungles. Bolivian jungles. Most people think of Bolivia as a country of the Andes, where colourfully dressed Indians, descendants of the Incas, herd llamas on the high plateau, mine silver and tin, and play tunes like 'El Condor Pasa' on panpipes. While it is true that some of Bolivia is like this – most of the population are full-blood Aymara and Quechua Indians and live in the mountains – nearly half the land area is low-lying. To the east of the cordilleras, there are savannahs and rainforests. To the southeast, by the border with Paraguay, there is a vast area of virtually impenetrable thorn-scrub called the Chaco which is still scarcely explored. Further north, where the rivers drain into the Amazon basin, there are the plains of the Chiqitos and Mojos where once there were civilizations that not even the Incas could defeat. This area later became the centre of power in South America of the Jesuits. Running along the rivers here and in the far north and east are forests that still extend, more or less unbroken, except for recent deforestation, through Brazil and Peru all the way to the Atlantic.

Scarcely a third of the population of 7.4 million live in this eastern region, an area twice the size of Britain. It is mostly uninhabited and still unexplored in some places. There are jungles where spider monkeys, ocelots and jaguars live. There are lost ruins and table mountains that stick like great rocky pillars out of the greenery. There are even some tribes of uncontacted Indians that roam the interior. Bolivia is one of the increasingly few countries that still have a 'wild' frontier.

❧

I had felt drawn back to Bolivia ever since the time I first spent there whilst backpacking around South America in 1991. The one month I had allotted in my itinerary stretched into two as I hired jeeps to take me across the salt pans in the far south of the country, explored the silver mines of Potosi and trekked Inca trails from the high peaks of the cordillera to the fertile 'Yungas' valleys that lead to the jungle. Following these valleys down into the rainforest was the next logical step. I took a boat trip up the Rio Tuichi, got bitten by a crocodile and for those few days I felt I had found what I had been looking for.

I was 'hooked' by the rainforest, as I knew I would be. Not so much by the wildlife (we saw very little – just macaws and crocodiles), but by the feel of it. Here was where the Andes met the Amazon. A series of parallel hogback ridges (called Serranias) that were cut through with raging rivers made the territory inaccessible to all but a few hardy hunters and gatherers of medicinal plants. At the edges the rainforest thinned out into the marshy savannah *pampa*, so that within 30 miles you could pass from mossy cloud forest on the ridges through tropical jungles and then on to grassland or swamp. The jungle here buzzed with life. It was everywhere: in the silt-laden 'white water' rivers surging down from the Andes to the verdant *selva* on the jagged ridges of the foothills. This was a dynamic ecosystem where a storm in the mountains could cause hills to slide, islands to form in the rivers, or the land around to flood to over a man's height, literally overnight.

The Serranias captivated my guide Negro's imagination and in turn captured mine. He told of how the Incas had built roads down the ridges and traded with the settled Mojos Indians of the plains, how they had escaped into the Serranias when the Spanish came. Later these routes had been used by Franciscan missionaries who had 'civilized' the lowland tribes: the Tacana, the Araona and the Chimane, but not the Guarayos and the Toromonas, who had remained *barbaros* – literally barbarian – until the twentieth century. There had been the rubber boom, with its sudden influx of Europeans and highlanders who killed or enslaved the Indians, only to move on just as quickly when the latex could be produced cheaper elsewhere. These waves of settlers and opportunists had each in their turn swept through the Caupolican (the territory east of the Andes). Yet few had penetrated the Serranias. The ridges had remained inaccessible and pristine, home to poisonous snakes, black jaguars and, according to legend, to a giant monkey, man-sized and strong enough to rip an arm from its socket. This was the story that most fired my imagination; that of the king monkey. The *Mono Rey*.

Negro told me the legend one afternoon on our rainforest tour, just after we had been watching a troop of spider monkeys crashing noisily through the treetops. Around fifteen of them had passed through the canopy above us, attracted, Negro had said, by his ululating calls, which he told me in spider monkey meant something along the lines of, 'I've found lots of fruit. Come and get it!'

The monkeys certainly reacted when he let loose the call, screaming something like a stuck pig whilst drumming on his bottom lip so that what came out sounded like the Indian war cries you make as a child, but much more insistent, almost blood-curdling. Negro then stood back in silent self-appreciation as the trees just ahead of us erupted into similar 'food calls'. We craned our necks upwards to look at the canopy for five minutes or so as foliage shook, flakes of bark tumbled and occasionally a languorous, hairy limb reached out into a gap between the leaves. It was only when the *marimonos* had lost interest in their fruit tree or perhaps realized Negro's call was a hoax and moved off that I had a better view of them. They swung away under the branches, brachiating like gibbons, prehensile tails curling round for extra support. When they ran out of branch they leaped out into nothingness, into seemingly endless falls until, apparently effortlessly, they reached into the crown of the neighbouring tree and pulled themselves out of sight. All except one. A large male set as a rear guard by the group scurried up a diagonal limb and leaned far over towards us intruders, head bobbing low, jaw open so that I caught sight of its teeth as it coughed out 'owk owk owk'. Then it launched itself in one almighty leap into the next tree without any run up or tensing its limbs.

It was Negro who cracked the almost reverential silence that followed.

'That one, he thinks he is the *Mono Rey*', he said quietly, as if to himself.

'Yes?' I responded.

Negro continued. 'It's the king monkey, a type of giant *marimono* that lives up in the high ridges, beyond where people go. It's said to look like these, but much bigger, nearly as big as a man, and it has no tail – like an ape. It's so strong, it could throw you like a light stick or wrench your arm from its socket. It lives on the hearts of the thin palms that grow on the slopes above the main forest. It uproots whole trees and rips off the bark to get to the white pulp underneath.'

'You've seen one?' I cut in as his story tailed off. He shook his head.

'My father did, or', he continued after a pause, 'he met people that had – hunters and men that collected cinchona bark to make quinine. They told him about it. That was back when he used to trade machetes and beads with the "wild" Indians – the *barbaros* – over the mountains past the Rio Madidi.'

⁂

Normally I would shrug off a local legend like this as just a story, a little local 'colour' to enthral the tourists, but Negro's description stuck in my mind. It recalled in me the memory of a black and white photograph that I had seen years before on a television programme about unsolved mysteries. This showed the dead body of a supposedly man-sized 'ape' that had attacked an expedition in Venezuela in 1920. The 'ape' in the picture, which looked rather like a spider monkey, had been sat on a wooden crate with a stick propped under its chin to stop it falling over. I recalled that the contention had been as to whether this was a four-and-a-half-feet tall, tail-less ape as the expedition leader, a Swiss geologist called Francis de Loys, asserted, or just a fake. There was no sense of scale to the photo, no one standing in camera shot to verify the beast's size. Just de Loys' statement that his party had been attacked by two of these creatures (the other, a male, escaped) and his measurements, including the note that he had counted 32 teeth (the same as Old World apes) rather than the 36 teeth that New World spider monkeys usually have. There wasn't even any physical evidence. De Loys had attempted to skin the 'ape' and to keep its skull but 'the hardships met with by the party on their long journey across the forest, however, prevented the final preservation of either the skin or the bones'. The skin presumably went rotten. The skull was used as a salt box for a while and was thrown out after it fell to pieces. As for the rest of the carcass, rumour had it that de Loys and his party probably ate it.

  'Loys' Ape', as it became known, came to a certain notoriety in 1929 when a French anthropologist, Georges Montandon, announced its discovery to the scientific community, naming it *Ameranthropoides Loysi* in honour of his friend. He said that the features (in particular, he cited the 32 teeth) showed that great apes had evolved independently in the New World; this was his 'Ologenic theory of Evolution'. Papers were written and de Loys published the story of his encounter, along with the photograph, in the *Illustrated London News*. But de Loys and Montandon were ridiculed. There simply wasn't enough evidence. Enough for a new species of spider monkey maybe, but not the parallel evolution of a hominid ape, and certainly not from one suspect picture and an account now nearly ten years out of date. 'Loys' Ape' joined the ranks of Bigfoot and the Yeti in the realms of crypto-zoology.

Since then there had always been just enough of a trickle of new information to keep the story ticking over, and of course the photograph, though discredited, had never been disproved. There had been fossil remains of giant monkeys found in Brazil, rumours of sightings in Guyana and Peru. And now Bolivia? Negro had told me his story with no prompting, and the chance of him ever having seen the famous picture seemed remote in the extreme.

In Rurrenabaque all the guides had their *Mono Rey* stories. None had seen it themselves but many said they knew of someone who had. These eyewitnesses could never be found. An American zoologist, working on an eco-tourism project upriver, voiced my growing cynicism with the king monkey story.

'Forget it! It's just one of those local superstitions. Hell – the people at San Jose won't even walk around after dark because they're convinced of were-jaguars – shape shifters that roam the tracks out of the village at night.'

Still, this is what I did find out through local gossip and rumours, none of which I was able to confirm. The *Mono Rey* looked like a man-high, tail-less spider monkey. It lived up in the high Serranias between the lowland jungle and the main cordillera of the Andes, probably at higher altitudes than the tall rainforest. Its diet included palm hearts. It was strong enough to uproot the small palms from which these came and rip the tough outer covering off with its claws or teeth. The *Mono Rey* had shaggy, black or brown fur. Until recently, someone in Rurrenabaque had the skin of one that had been shot. A gringo scientist bought it and took it back home for DNA analysis. No results were ever reported so it may just have turned out to have belonged to a spectacled bear, which also lives in the high Andean cloud forests. Of course, it was a distinct possibility that the *Mono Rey* was just this, but I was inclined to doubt it as everyone insisted that it was truly a monkey. Its arms were longer than its legs, they said. Besides, it swung in trees and sometimes made leaps of five metres or more. Bears could never do that, people laughed.

Additionally, there was also a rather intriguing rumour that Santa Cruz zoo in eastern Bolivia had a live *Mono Rey* for a while, but it died. This last point I was never able to authenticate.

As for the area where the king monkey was supposed to live, it was generally agreed this was truly remote. The name of one river repeatedly came up: the Madidi. Apart from some prospectors from an oil company, who may have cut a trail over the watershed from the Rio Tuichi several years before, no one was known to have travelled there. Certainly the area had never been settled within living memory; the terrain was far too difficult for cultivation. And it was only comparatively recently that the *barbaros* had left the area. Even my biologist acquaintance conceded that if the *Mono Rey* existed, it was most likely to be there. He had once seen some satellite photos of the area.

'The landforms are awesome – all jagged mountains and cliffs,' he said. 'It's like a lost world over there.'

There was only one first-hand description I could find of the river's upper reaches. It had been written in 1915 by the English explorer, Major (later Colonel) Percy Harrison Fawcett. Colonel Fawcett is most well known for his mysterious disappearance, along with his son Jack, and one of Jack's friends, Raleigh Rimmel, after setting out on foot into the jungles of Brazil's Mato Grosso in search of a lost city in 1925. Fawcett had researched the eighteenth-century accounts of a band of Portuguese adventurers who claimed to have found the (silver) 'Mines of Muribeca', and he was convinced he was on the verge of a great discovery. His last letter to his wife, which he sent back with his two guides, said, 'You have no fear of any failure'. The disappearance quite caught the imagination of the public at the time and has remained a lure to many 'rescue' expeditions since. But, though it is with the Mato Grosso that his name is associated, Bolivia was where Fawcett's explorations started, when in 1906 he was employed by the country's Government to survey its precious rubber-producing territories along the borders with Peru and Brazil. He threw himself into the work. His expedition accounts, collected into the book *Exploration Fawcett* by his other son Brian, teem with encounters with 60-foot anacondas, Indian attack, even of finding a degenerate tribe of 'ape-men' in the wilds of Brazil. Against the background of steamy jungles, treacherous cut-throats and whizzing arrows, our hero always comes across as the paragon of British cool. Fawcett claimed it was his descriptions of the Ricardo-Franco hills of the Brazil–Bolivia border that led to his friend, the author Conan Doyle, writing the novel *The Lost World*, in which a party of British adventurers come across dinosaurs and ape-men on a remote South American plateau. It has been suggested that the character of Lord John Roxton, the career explorer-hunter, was at least partly based on him.

However, such flamboyant claims did not always find favour amongst the exploring 'establishment'. Even when I visited the Royal Geographical Society in 1996 to look at the maps he had made of his trips, I was advised not to take the information too seriously as it was well known that most of it was 'simply made up'.

Fawcett mentioned the Rio Madidi many times in his exploration accounts, though he only ever passed by the headwaters once. That was in 1913 when he and his assistant, Corporal Costin, set off from the Franciscan Mission settlement of Ixiamas to investigate rumours of a diamond rush. Like other travellers of his day, he did not linger long in the area that was well known as the home of the hostile Guarayos Indians. Fawcett solely mentions in passing that 'the upper reaches of the Madidi pass through deep canyons of soft, red rock, subject to perpetual landslides', though, true to his style, he speculates on the existence in the swamps further downriver of 'some mysterious and enormous beast . . . possibly a primeval monster. . . . Enormous tracks have been found and Indians there talk of a huge creature descried at times half sub-merged in the swamps.'

As for giant apes, there is no mention concerning the Madidi, but there is one sentence at the end of his 1915 report to the RGS concerning his explorations along the eastern Bolivia–Brazil border area. 'In these forests, by the way, exists an unusually large variety of the black howler [monkey], apparently unknown.'

The *Mono Rey*? I was inclined to think so, and if Fawcett believed there was something there then that was enough for me. I was dying for a chance to go back to the Bolivian jungle, and a trip to the Madidi to look for the *Mono Rey* seemed the perfect excuse.

Rurrenabaque

IN *Exploration Fawcett* the jungle town of Rurrenabaque is described as the 'Fringe of the Wilderness'. It was the Fawcetts' base for setting off into the rainforests of the Caupolican after six weeks of travelling precipitous mountain trails from La Paz with a mule train of equipment, then a hazardous journey on a balsa raft down the Rio Beni. And, I decided, Rurrenabaque would be my base to start my search for the *Mono Rey*, too. As the last town on the road and river within striking distance of the Serranias and with a guide there that I already knew, it could be the only choice.

Rurrenabaque is a jungle town still surrounded by jungle (unusual these days). The town lies at the point where the wide Rio Beni cuts through the Susi ridge: the last high ground of any consequence that the river passes before it enters the great Amazonian plain. There it joins the Madeira, which in turn joins the Amazon, and finally arrives at the Atlantic Ocean 2,500 miles later. Rurrenabaque is eighteen hours (downhill) by bus from the capital, La Paz. Two of the first four hours, which are in the daylight, are along a single lane ledge that diagonals down a sheer cliff face. You dread meeting a truck coming up, as etiquette dictates that it is the uphill vehicle that has to back right up to the edge to let the other squeeze past. Scrapes of red mud and bright green re-growth below, as well as numerous crosses along the roadside, attest to those who didn't make it. When it gets dark at 6.30 p.m., the road no longer feels as dangerous – or at least you can no longer see the sheer drops. In any case, any fear you had has long since drained away or you are too tired to care. Sometime in the middle of the night a change in atmosphere hits you. It's like having a steaming towel wrapped around your head. You think you're being stifled by the lack of ventilation, but when you step out into the darkness at one of the infrequent toilet stops it's just as hard to breathe. The only difference is that the cut-grass perfume of a million transpiring leaves replaces the stench of diesel and unwashed bodies inside. Your skin becomes covered in a film of sweat and dust so that you feel overwhelmingly grimy; not dirty exactly – dirt can be washed off. This is deeper: in your clothes, hair and skin. Once you've entered the lowlands it's a feeling that you can never entirely rid yourself of, except in the transitory purges of a shower or by swimming in a cool, clean river.

෫ඁ

I awoke nuzzling into the neck of a pretty-boy Israeli backpacker in the next seat. His bobbed haircut was just the same as my wife's. I extricated myself before he noticed. If he did, at least he had the decency to keep his eyes closed long enough for me to slide back to my side of the seat and affect an air of sleepy innocence.

It was morning. We seemed to have left the mountains behind. The land was now pancake flat with farm-plots of bananas and manioc or a secondary growth of spindly trees where fields had been left fallow. Beyond, not too far in the distance, was a darker green line that indicated the start of the primary forest. The jungle on the hills looked untouched. From time to time I could see flocks of garish blue and yellow macaws flying over them. Sometimes they came right over the road, lighting up gold in the morning sun. The bus trundled on towards the town

I remembered with a stab of stress that I was still upset at the non-arrival of my luggage. That set me off worrying again. Another couple of hours and I would have the job of explaining to Julian that the canoe still hadn't turned up. I would tell him that our entire plan would have to be changed. I knew he'd be fine about it. He would look for some alternative way of getting into the jungle. But it wasn't Julian who'd spent all his money on the boat or set all his hopes on using it to get into the Serranias.

At the time I had felt that the idea of taking a portable canoe had been a stroke of genius. As far as I was concerned, a boat consisting of a rubbery skin and a collection of aluminium poles that could be packed and carried in a rucksack load was the obvious answer to getting to a river's headwaters. I had been inspired by the English explorer, George Dyott, who had taken a somewhat similar craft on his expedition to search for Colonel Fawcett in 1928. His party had used bullocks and mules to carry the poles and skin, as well as four other canoes, until they had come to a river which, from Fawcett's notes and the position of his last known camp, Dyott had judged to be on the lost explorer's route. Then his men put the boat together and, after constructing five more boats (from the rolled-out bark of *jatoba* trees), they set off downriver. The expedition did not solve the Fawcett mystery. At an Anauqua Indian village Dyott came across a small, tin chest and an English-inscribed plaque that the Colonel may have left on a previous trip. He was told that Fawcett had been killed by a tribe called the Kalapalos, several days' journey to the east. Dyott and his party themselves received the unwelcome attentions of the local Indians. They decided to leave secretly, several nights later, after hundreds arrived at their river beach camp demanding presents and becoming increasingly hostile when none were given.

Though Dyott's trip interested me, it was his construction of the canoes that impressed me most, in particular his use of a portable boat that could be carried whenever a river was impossible to navigate. My own plan was ('would have been', I reproach myself) vaguely similar, albeit on a much smaller scale. Now all that had come to nothing, thanks to the airline. Three days ago, after forty hours of flights around what felt like much of the Spanish speaking world to get to La Paz, I had been told that my canoe was 'lost in transit'. Various computer searches had placed it in Madrid, Buenos Aires or possibly Montevideo. I had wasted three precious days getting nowhere while Julian had gone on ahead to organize the expedition. The airline people had promised to send the boat on to me when it arrived. Some hope.

⁂

Rurrenabaque lay on a sideways spur off the main highway where another road, one that would supposedly someday link with the Peruvian border, struck off. The Rio Beni was far too big to put a bridge over, so a pontoon pulled by a motor-canoe carried vehicles between the two sides. People were ferried on a different boat. The settlement on the opposite bank was a separate town called San-Buenaventura. It was in the 'La Paz' Department; Rurrenabaque was in 'The Beni'. Of the two settlements, Rurrenabaque was where all the money went and consequently where development took place. Over the past few years its collection of wood and plaster houses, laid out in the standard South American grid plan, had been gaining extra storeys. Some had been rebuilt in brick. There were piles of stones at the edges of the streets. Sometime soon, people said, the roads would get surfaced.

I was shocked to see how much things had changed in the five-and-a-half years since my crocodile-bite trip with Negro. The place had had an air of perpetual siesta then. There was one daily bus to La Paz and more cattle in the street than people. Now Rurrenabaque was positively buzzing. Battered American pick-ups with destinations – 'Reyes', 'Santa Rosa' – painted on placards in their windscreens plied the streets, honking their horns for trade. The corner where the road led down to the fish restaurants and the market stalls on the beach was now a motorcycle taxi rank. I retrieved my rucksack from the bus's roof rack and asked the young men revving their Yamahas how to get to Negro Janco's office on Commercial Street.

'That concrete hut by the phone office.'
I decided to walk it.

⚜

I was surprised and very relieved that Negro instantly recognized me when I entered the newly built office. He slapped one hand on my shoulder and shook my own vigorously with the other. Then he held it up to look for the scar.

'Simon', he said, gripping my fingers firmly. 'Come to catch more crocs?'

He slapped my shoulder again and gestured for me to sit down in front of a large, glass-topped desk that almost crossed the room. There were photos of tourists slid under the glass. Negro pointed out one that I had sent. He had obviously done well for himself. His hair was slicked back. He wore a well-cut shirt and a gold chain around his neck. And he thought my plan was stupid.

'I'd like you to know that right from the start', he said, spreading his hands across the map I had placed between us. 'You want to go looking for a huge, dangerous ape that probably isn't there at all. And if you find it, what will you do?'

'Julian's going to video it. I'll sketch it.' I knew my answer was weak. 'I know it's not likely . . .'

Negro cut me short.

'Simon, I must tell you this seriously. It's very ... difficult there.' He struggled for the right words. 'There are *tigres*. There are snakes – the *pucarara*; if it bites you, your leg – it swells up so much it bursts, then your flesh – it falls off in strips. There are stingrays in the rivers and the insects are so bad there – not just mosquitoes but *tabanos*. They can bite through tapir hide, so your soft, white skin is no problem.

'But', perhaps he could sense I was starting to glaze over, 'these are just the obvious things. The Serranias are straight up and down. You fall over and break your leg. What will you do? What if it's an open wound? It will go septic straight away, you know. I admire your spirit – I did when you picked up that crocodile.'

'Even though it bit me', I replied grumpily.

'You haven't got the experience.' He laid his hands flat on the table.

'So you won't help me', I said.

'I didn't say that', Negro retorted. He pointed his finger at the blank part of the map, the part marked 'Relief data incomplete. Limits of available vegetation information.'

'No one here knows what it's like up there. My brother Irgen might know people who do, but he went off into the jungle again and I've no idea where he is.'

'What about Ignacio?' Ignacio was another of Negro's brothers whose name I had heard mentioned.

'Trouble with the law.'

'Oh.' I thought I'd better leave it at that.

'I don't know where he is either. I really don't want to put you off', he continued, 'but if you had that folding boat that you wrote to me about I'd say you would have a much better chance of getting to the Madidi. You could motorboat to the top of the Tuichi, trek across from there – expensive maybe, but possible. But without the canoe, what would you do when you got there? You couldn't carry what you needed on foot, not even if you had lots of porters; you couldn't feed them. You can forget making your own boat. It would be impractical to hollow out a canoe from a tree trunk, and that high up there's probably not even any balsa wood to build a raft.'

Negro nudged me out of the expressionless stare that had taken hold of my face since he had started to lecture me. 'Is this the only map you've got?'

'No', I replied. 'We've got a couple of more detailed ones for the area of the headwaters. Julian managed to bribe them out of an Army sergeant in the Miraflores base in La Paz. He nearly got arrested.' The tone of my voice was flat, disinterested. I pulled out the maps from my day bag. They were marked 'Distribution authorized to the Department of Defense. Destroy as "for official use only".'

Negro looked up. 'Americano?' I nodded.

'D.E.A?'

'Quite possibly', I said.

Negro was obviously far more interested now. He took the maps and spread them out on the table, running his finger down the wiggly blue line that was the Madidi.

'You can get to the Madidi lower down', he pointed out, indicating where a road intersected the river. 'You could maybe buy a dugout or build a raft there. Of course it would mean going upstream.'

'So you'll guide us?'

He shook his head. 'I'd love to but I've got this agency to run. My name's in the *South American Handbook*. All the *turistas* want Negro now. Four days only', he smiled. 'That's my limit. I have my public to satisfy. But I'll ask around. And, I can certainly sort you out transport. A friend of mine, Chichito, runs supplies out to Ixiamas – it's a town on the way. I'm sure if you pay him, he'll take you on to the river.'

I followed Negro's directions to the hotel room where Julian was staying. Julian was sitting in the middle of one of two beds. He scarcely acknowledged my arrival and continued scooping out powdered milk from a tin into a clear plastic bag. Surrounding him were several dozen similar bags, each labelled with their contents (rice, pasta or sugar) then sealed into another. I noticed that each had been meticulously ticked off on a list in a notebook that lay on the bed by his side, along with details of each day's rations – enough for ten to twelve weeks of jungle travel – and its energy content in kilojoules. On the next page, there were other lists: fish hooks (3 sizes), fishing line (2 sizes), rope, batteries, shotgun – Brazilian ($140), shells (size 16). These were the same lists he had used on his previous expeditions, the numbers overwritten 'x three people' for this trip.

As a would-be jungle explorer, Julian made me feel like an amateur. Over the past five years he had taken himself into the rainforests of Peru, Brazil, Guyana and even Surinam (where very few tourists go), earning money in the 'dead time' in between by working on flat conversions in London. I had originally met Julian briefly during my first trip to South America but had lost touch with him until that Spring when he had rung me on the recommendation of an Australian girl he had travelled with in Brazil. She had told him that there was only one other person, apart from him, that she had encountered on her travels who was quite so obsessive about jungles.

His phone call was perfectly timed. I had been planning my expedition and wanted a companion. With his previous experience, Julian was perfectly suited. I had to admit to myself, though, that I did not know him that well. I knew he renovated old cars in his spare time and that he had made a suit of medieval armour which he wore when he fought in mock battles in the countryside close to his home in Herefordshire. And I knew he loved going to rainforests, though I wasn't that clear what his actual motivation was, apart from that he had an intense desire to experience true Amerindian culture. I noted that talking about his dream of being initiated into the trade secrets of a tribal shaman was one of the few things that really animated his normally measured speech. Perhaps he felt cheated of that aim by his experiences in Surinam, when he had flown 'upcountry' to an Indian village, found a guide (whom he described as 'the real thing'), then was refused permission to set off into the forest because the headman thought that Julian and his companion were spies from an oil company. They had to wait 30 days until the arrival of the next plane that could take them away.

Scanning my eyes over the piles of kit that Julian had so neatly laid out across the bed, and at the worn notebook with its over-written comments, it was obvious Julian was a serious explorer. His logistical savvy left me feeling slightly inadequate.

'No canoe', I said, stretching out on the bed. Julian looked up momentarily.

'I thought not', he murmured. 'You've seen Negro?' I nodded. Julian finished off pouring and double-bagging the milk powder.

He wrote down 'Milk 1kg' in indelible marker pen, ticked the list then gave me his full attention.

'What was the verdict?'

'The same as what he said to you roughly', I replied. 'But I showed him your maps and it looks like we might have some action'. Julian nodded. He started dividing up a packet of pasta tubes, then paused and said,

'I met a guy who wants to come with us. An Aussie.'

'Fair enough, but do we need him?'

'Not as such', Julian continued, 'but he's some sort of sports angler. He could provide us with food and if we've not got your canoe, space is no longer going to be a problem. Anyway, we could do with someone to share the costs.'

He left the sentence hanging as if waiting for me to cut in, but I couldn't think of an answer. I felt drained. No £1000-canoe, three days of airline hassle in La Paz, eighteen hours on a bus, a guide with a four-day limit and now some Aussie who wanted to come along for the ride. Maybe my face showed all of this.

'I can put him off if you want', Julian said, as I let my rucksack fall off my back and sank face down onto the neighbouring empty bed.

'Frankly I'm beyond caring', I spoke into the mattress. 'I'm too tired to think about it. The trip I planned is out the window anyway. If you want him, bring him – so long as he carries his own food.'

⚜

Julian had arranged to meet Charlie at a deep inlet of the river, just beyond where it passed the ridges. This was the best place for catfish, Charlie had told him. The waterfront there looked little different to a photograph of it I had seen in *Exploration Fawcett*. It had been taken in 1907, looking up the Rio Beni towards the Susi ridge. It showed some single-storey houses with palm thatch roofs and, on the 'beach' in the foreground, there were several cows. The town had grown since, and several of the buildings had acquired an extra storey. But apart from these changes and the fact that the canoes lined up along the waterfront now had outboard motors, the view was surely much as the English Major would have seen it when he first arrived in 1906.

Fawcett had been bitterly disappointed at what he had found at the time. He had spent two weeks sweating down the treacherous Mapiri trail from the Andes, losing mules of cargo down ravines, then later losing more equipment to the rapids on the Beni, all to get to this. He commented:

> The 'port' was a beach of mud covered with upturned balsas and refuse, where vultures croaked and quarrelled. Behind lay a collection of roughly framed huts, thatched with palm leaves and walled with split bamboos, clustering about a grass plaza at the foot of a lofty ridge. . . . This miserable settlement seemed scarcely fit for habitation by whites. My heart sank and I began to realise how truly primitive this river country was.

Over the years his views softened. He later was to say that Rurrenabaque was a 'metropolis' compared to the other settlements he passed through in the lowlands.

Rurrenabaque was originally the port for the Franciscan mission of Reyes, a day by mule into the grassland *pampa*. Cattle were taken upstream in exchange for food and goods such as textiles, arms, ammunition and alcoholic liquor. When Fawcett arrived in 1906 the town was thriving in its own right. This was the time of the Amazonian rubber boom, and Rurrenabaque had become something of a trading hub for the Caupolican region. Balls of 'cured' latex were taken upriver to the town of Mapiri from where they would be carried by Indian porters up through the Cordillera to La Paz. Manufactured goods were brought back on the return journey. As well as the population of Tacana and Napo Indians and a garrison of Bolivian infantry, a number of foreigners had been attracted by the new-found affluence. There were two British rubber traders: Merritt (known as 'Don Jorge') and Drew (formerly of Whitechapel), who had lived there for many years. Downriver an English engineer called Pearson ingeniously kept a small, government steam launch in working order, 'held together for the most part with wire or string'. There were also two 'impoverished' American gold prospectors. And there was a gunfighter.

Fawcett described red-haired Harvey as 'hot'. Wanted in the USA and in a 'neighbouring republic' for robbing a mining company, Harvey had a price on his head of £1000. Fawcett commented admiringly how he had turned the tables on a 'regiment' of soldiers that had pursued him, ambushing them and, when they had surrendered, tossing their guns into a river. A gunfighter is also mentioned in the account of a British Engineer called Guise, who was building a gold dredge up a tributary of the Beni at around the same time. Though Guise called his outlaw Macveigh, it has been suggested that he was, in fact, Harvey Logan, also known as 'Kid Curry', an associate of Butch Cassidy and the Sundance Kid. They too had escaped to Bolivia. They were killed in a shoot-out in San Vicente, in the south of the country, in 1908.

Ninety years later Rurrenabaque was teeming with outsiders again. There were timber men from Santa Cruz and Brazil, 'sport' fishermen from La Paz and oil men from Texas ('Stretch' from Houston even looked the part in cowboy boots and Stetson hat). The 'oileys' were working on an exploratory rig in the jungle over the Susi ridge. Everything had to be flown in using the shiny red and white 'Super-Puma' helicopter that buzzed the town from time to time. There was even a man constructing a dredge to sift for gold in the sediment of the Beni. He had brought a Guyanese crew with him who were reputedly so tough that the local youths wouldn't go near them. When they brawled they fought with machetes.

But the biggest group of foreigners by far were tourists. Spurred by favourable comments about 'value for money' jungle trips in their bible, the *South American Handbook*, backpackers from Germany, Australia, England and Israel were filling Rurrenabaque's cheaper hotels. Of these, the Israelis were the most numerous. They had come to experience the jungle where their countryman,

Yossi Ghinsberg, had famously got lost in the scene of his best-selling book, *Back from Tuichi.*[1]

His adventure had taken place in 1985. Ghinsberg had set off with two other backpackers and an Austrian guide to trek over the Serranias to the Rio Colorado where the 'wild' Toromonas Indians were reputed to live. The guide 'talked big' though clearly knew nothing of the terrain, and Ghinsberg began to question his motives (it turned out later that he was 'wanted' by Interpol). The group argued and split. The Austrian and one of the party, who had badly infected feet, opted to return (they were never seen again), while Ghinsberg and his remaining companion, an American, built a balsa wood raft and set off down the Rio Tuichi. When the raft became stuck on some rocks at a rapid the American leaped to shore and Ghinsberg floated on. Now it was a question of survival. Ghinsberg struck out overland and was soon hopelessly lost. For three weeks he wandered in no particular direction, living off what berries and birds' eggs he managed to find. He came down with a fever and was only dimly aware of what was happening to him as he was severely bitten by insects and injured through numerous falls. By the time rescue came, after the American had reached Rurrenabaque and alerted the authorities, he was said to have been near to death.

There were plans to make a film about the story. The gossip was that the Hollywood film star Emilio Estevez was to play the lead role. A film crew had been to Rurrenabaque shortly before I arrived. Production had been about to start, but then everything ended very quickly and the Americans pulled out. The town was buzzing with rumours. The producer had been taking cocaine, people said. The only way out of jail and a huge scandal had been

---

1   It is ironic that while the story of Ghinsberg's 1985 trip is remembered in Rurrenabaque and has given rise to the tourist industry there, no consciousness of Fawcett remains amongst the people. He has given his name to an airline in Peru (Aviacion Faucett) where he did not even explore, but in Rurrenabaque, which was the base for his surveying work from 1906 to 1913, people have no knowledge of him, the old stories having long been overgrown by newer ones.

to pay a hefty bribe. The producer had handed over his aeroplane and the film had been shelved.

☙

We found Charlie, a gangly man of around 40 in cut-off shorts and a T-shirt that read 'Merida Beach Club', at the end of the water-front where a deep inlet had been scoured out by the river as it flowed out of the gorge. He was fishing with a long, flexible rod, casting a spinner into the centre of the pool and reeling it back in short bursts so that the silver fish shape flickered up and down as it raced towards him. There was a mop-haired Bolivian squatting on a log nearby, chipping in occasionally as Charlie gave what appeared to be a fairly continuous commentary to his fishing.

By the time we reached him, he had a hook up. 'Pfzeeeeez', the fishing line sung as it spun the reel and went taut, speeding upstream then doubling back on itself and zigzagging across the current.

'It's big. Ten KGs at least.' Charlie pointed towards the wave the fish was making where its back nearly cleared the water's surface. 'What a beast! Just saw its head – catfish, I reckon.' He thrust out a hand (the other kept the rod high, tense). 'Hi Jules. You must be Simon.' He quickly shook my hand then gripped the rod, flicking the reel to spin out more slack for a second then pulling the fish back again sharply.

'Guys, this is Bernardino. He says he can guide us. He's been all the way to the Serranias.' Bernardino leaped up from the log, beam-ing a gap-toothed grin and shook our hands enthusiastically. Then he sat down again and watched the fish as, over the next five minutes, Charlie sapped its energy and finally hauled it out of the water where it lay, gulping air through a wide shovel mouth. It was about 70 centimetres long, a 'cat' as Charlie had said, three kilos with a grey-brown mottled back that tapered to a sharply swept, pink-tinged tail. Around its mouth four long barbels flicked the air sporadically as the catfish lay still for a minute or two before resuming another bout of violent thrashing as it tried to get back to the Beni.

The Australian was overjoyed with his catch. Was it a *suribim* or a *jau*? His tones were almost reverential as he recited the names of South America's finest sport fish. Could it be a *pintado*? Or even a *bagre*? Bernardino settled the argument, nudging the gulping fish with his foot.

'Nice *tujuno* you've got there. You're going to eat it?' When Charlie said that he wasn't, Bernardino looked slightly disappointed, and on seeing the fish slid back into the water the guide made an excuse and left us.

'Quiet, isn't he?' I commented. 'Is he all right?'

'He's just a bit shy, that's all', Charlie said. 'He's a really good guy. A real *hombre de la selva* [man of the jungle] too', he added. 'He's been a logger, guided tourists. He says he's been to the tops of several of the Serranias – dropped by helicopter to put up radio masts – when he worked for the oil company. He'll be fine. Just wait till you get to know him.'

He dismantled his rod and we headed back into town to the Club Sociale. 'Sunset views across the river, Brazilian-sized portions of steak and the waitress is pretty "goshtosa" too.' Charlie 'sold it' to us, and, over steak, chips and a fair few beers, he talked his way onto our expedition.

He said he had come to the Amazon for the angling. 'Just one real monster – get my piccy in *Modern Fishing*. I reckon the Madidi is the sort of place to get it. Untouched. No pressure from fishermen.'

Charlie said time was no problem. Nor was money to a point. He would provide his own share for anything that was needed. He had just hit 40 and left his work as a carpenter. He planned to carry on for about a year until his money ran out. He said he could always pick up more work when he got home. Right now, Charlie planned to go to the Amazon and catch the biggest monster fish ever. Then he would go to the Brazilian coast, 'hit a beach and party'. He would find a 'Brazilian *chica* with buttocks like drumskins and samba his rocks off'. With turns of phrase like that, it was impossible not to find Charlie endearing.

But part of me still rankled with the total change of plan, the way our search for the *Mono Rey* – my search for the *Mono Rey* – was transforming into some alternative idea now that the folding canoe hadn't arrived. Julian and Charlie said not to worry. This was Bolivia; things had to be flexible and, for the moment, I let it go. Maybe I was being over-anxious. I just wished I could have more confidence in our guide who, for all his recommendations, had scarcely said a word to any of us concerning his supposedly great experience. His arrival at our hotel room later that night, accompanied by a toothless woman with her skirt pulled up far too far over her belly (we presumed she was his wife), did little to inspire me further. Bernardino smiled gingerly, shook our hands limply, but apart from a slightly embarrassed grin was far from forthcoming. We guessed his coyness must have something to do with money. It was Charlie who did most of the talking, arranging the negotiation of wages ($15 a day for up to three months) and where we wanted him to guide us. Occasionally the woman (who we found out was called Maria) would pull her husband away and there would be a flurry of insistent phrases in a language, possibly Aymara, which none of us could understand. Soon the reason for Bernardino's embarrassment surfaced.

'Amigo Charlie, you pay me now', he said. It was almost a question. 'I need money for rent and to put a down-payment on some land in San Buena …'

The sentence trailed off. There were more negotiations. Charlie held out a wad of dollars.

'Two weeks' advance', he said firmly. Maria snatched the notes out of his hand and stashed them beneath her waistband.

When she and Bernardino had gone, we all paid Negro a visit. 'Don't look so worried, Simon. He's a good man', Negro assured me. 'I trekked up to Apolo in the mountains with him last year, and from what he was telling me I think he knows some of the routes into the Serranias. He's not very used to foreigners and their ways, but he is one of the few people who have been anywhere near where you want to go. I think you'll like him.

'But there is one thing, and I mean this seriously.' Negro fixed each of us in his gaze in turn. 'When you ask him anything – anything important, make sure he has to give you a full answer. He's a bit of a "yes" man. He'll agree to everything. That isn't always good.'

CHAPTER THREE

The Undumo

BERNARDINO WAS CONSIDERABLY more forthcoming, once he was away from Rurrenabaque and his wife. After we had set off, his story needed no prompting.

'I never actually saw it, just the signs', he said, struggling to make himself heard over the engine and creaking noises coming from Chichito's truck. 'The oil company had put us down on the top of one of the ridges by helicopter. We used machetes and chainsaws to clear a space where they wanted to plant a radio aerial, and that's when we found the ripped up palm trees and the footprints.'

It was two days later. We were in the back of a red and yellow Landcruiser pick-up, hurtling along a mud road towards Ixiamas. While Julian and Charlie sat amongst the rucksacks, I stood at the front with Bernardino, leaning onto a tubular metal frame that had been welded across, gripping on white-knuckle tight each time that our driver, fat Chichito, king of the road in a baseball cap and shades, swerved to avoid the holes in the highway.

'There were marks on the trunks of some thin palm trees', Bernardino continued, straining his soft voice against the squealing of the metal frame and the buffeting of the wind. 'Other palms had been pulled up, broken and smashed. One of the men said that the

Mono Rey had done it.' He paused, gripped the cross bar in front of his face momentarily as we hit another pothole, and carried on. 'We found some footprints. They were the same size as a child's.' He held out a clenched fist to indicate the size. 'But they weren't very clear as it must have rained since they were made. Some of the others said they heard the *Mono Rey* that night, after we'd got back to our camp down by the river at the bottom of the mountain. They said it was a howling noise, not like a *tigre* or any other animal they had heard before.'

'But they might have been lying', he shrugged, 'You know how it is when you have lots of men together.'

۞

The road we were driving down roughly followed a contour with the Susi ridge to our left. We sped past farm plots of yucca and plantains, some still charred underneath from recent burning. There was a mass of felled trees and shiny new growth where weeds had already taken hold on those plots that had been cleared but not yet burned. Elsewhere fast-growing trees with multi-lobed parasol leaves for soaking up maximum sunlight had consumed any land left untended, and beyond this secondary growth the true rainforest started. The individual trunks of some of the largest emergent trees stood out, stark yellow-white against an otherwise muted backdrop. But the view was hazy, the outlines indistinct and the sky grey and flat. Bernadino informed us that the burning had caused the haze. It had been particularly bad this year as the dry season had been so long. I presumed that the deforestation along this road was recent – a preconception that all slash and burn farming was the result of new settlers who colonized as soon as roads were built through the jungle. Bernardino put me right on that.

'These people, the Tacana', he said, 'have been here for hundreds of years. They're Indians, but not fierce like the ones that Julian wants to find. They are *mansos* – tame. Christians. They stay in one place. They farm their *chacras*, then in two or three years when the soil has run out they cut and burn a new one where an old clearing grew over years before.' He answered my next question before I asked.

'Oh no, I'm not Tacana', he said dismissively, as if Tacana was something lower than him. 'I'm from Apolo in the mountains. I am Aymara.'

※

He probably had more in common with the Tacana than he liked to admit. His town, Apolo, like Tumupasa (which we passed on the way), Ixiamas and many of the settlements of the mountains and jungles north-east of La Paz, had been founded by Franciscan missionaries. From the seventeenth century onwards they had introduced settled agriculture, set up a network of trading routes (including the road we were using now) and had Christianized the native tribes. To an extent. At roughly midday, as we entered Ixiamas with its grid pattern of white adobe houses in an open area of grassland below the ridges, we were to see, and nearly drive right into, some of the legacy of Franciscan–Tacana culture.

Two columns of men wearing monster masks (plastic ones, probably bought in La Paz) were half-marching, half-shuffling along the main street. They all wore broad, wicker cowboy hats, voluminous white shirts and, over their regular trousers, rose pink pantaloons: an imitation of the work clothes their ancestors had worn for the missionaries 300 years before. Over these, feathers and strings of beads dangled from their masks, swinging in time with their movements. Some of the men carried short, wooden batons with ribbon streamers. They shuffled, rhythmically stamping, sometimes twisting, sometimes almost reeling over, always in a semi-slow motion to the reedy fluting of a piper at the head of the procession. Other people in the street, the storekeepers and a few children turned to watch occasionally, but mostly they went about their business. This was the fiesta of Ixiamas, when the Tacanas dressed up in their Franciscan clothes. Bernardino said this marching-out of the village streets would carry on for another two days.

We briefly stopped for a drink then carried on through the savannah to a line of green in the distance where the forest restarted. We passed a hut with a radio mast and solar panels, and arrived at a plank-built bridge crossing a muddy river. And that, Chichito stated, was as far as he would go.

'Look', he said, nodding at a thick chain that stretched across the bridge. This was the start of a timber concession and he knew better than to cross it. This was a not entirely unpredicted decision, since earlier that morning he had intimated to Charlie that there was 'bad feeling' between him and the logging manager. He reversed back to the hut and helped us unload. Then he drove off, leaving three bemused tourists and an embarrassed-looking Bernardino amongst a pile of backpacks and food sacks in a clearing in the forest in the heat of the day. For several minutes none of us spoke or moved out of the protective circle of our baggage. After the noise and bumping and breeze of the truck ride, it was the stillness and the sudden wave of sauna humidity that were more disconcerting than our driver's departure. There was something almost unreal about the huge trees that towered above the clearing. One dangled a fly curtain of creepers from an outstretched horizontal branch, and from there came the occasional squawking of a pair of macaws, which was just about the only sound that pierced the virtual silence.

At the hut Julian, who collected himself faster than the rest of us, persuaded a scruffy young man to call ahead on the radio to ask about the possibility of onward transport. For most of the afternoon Julian bombarded him with questions, while Charlie smiled and made faces at numerous children and a pregnant girl who gathered around us, and I guarded the sacks against the snuffling predations of two small, hairy pigs that emerged from the shade under the hut. The flustered radio operator said he would love to help us but he would have to check with the 'chief' at the logging camp to verify that things would be all right. It was only a formality, he said. There was no need to worry. Things would be fine.

'*Seguro* – sure, we could use the road. The logging manager would be along soon in his jeep to speak with us.'

But things weren't fine. Nothing was happening and, when it became clear that no decision would be made that day whether we could even pass or not, we decided to set off on foot.

The radio operator's estimate of three hours to get to the camp proved to be over-optimistic, especially considering the loads we had to carry. We hadn't arrived by sunset and consequently spent an uncomfortable night wrapped in our mosquito nets at the edge of the road, which was the only ground that wasn't too boggy or covered with thorny vines to lie out on. We were particularly anxious that a truck would run over us while we slept. But none came, and the noises that I insisted sounded like tractors revving their engines nearby, Bernardino shrugged off as 'just toads'. As soon as it was light we set off again. Within an hour we had arrived.

It was a scene of utter devastation: a two-acre square where the forest had been scraped off the slick red clay that lay underneath and dumped at the edges. Under a long corrugated roof in the centre of the compound the whining grind of circular saws sliced through the thick, humid air. Caterpillar-tracked diggers pushed sawn planks into piles and the off-cuts onto a huge pyre that billowed smoke over the ripped-out remnants of the jungle beyond. In two weeks the licence for the San Antonio logging concession would run out. In the meantime, the loggers would make sure they had got their money's worth.

A pair of orange-winged Amazon parrots squawked shrilly overhead, flapping rapidly with stiff wings and landing in a lone tall tree at the edge of the clearing. We headed for a long, wooden hut raised on stilts above the mud that was sign-posted 'office'.

'You realize, Señor, that you will of course have to pay for a permit if you intend to travel on to the Madidi', said the man in the leather jacket from behind his mahogany desk. He had the contemptuous look of someone who knows they've got you in their power.

'He can't do that – it's a state-owned highway', Julian said in English. The man cut him a reproving glance and continued.

'Unfortunately the only person who can give you that permit is the chief and he's in La Paz. But I am in the position to issue a temporary "clearance".'

'And how much is that?' I asked.

'How much would you like to pay?'

Charlie muttered, 'Oh great! Bribery now. It's not even his fucking road.' We drew back to the corner of the office to confer. 'He's really got us by the balls', said Charlie. 'We haven't got much of a choice.'

'What would he do if we just carried on?' I proposed.

'I wouldn't like to find out', Julian answered. 'There are at least 30 people here. They've got guns. There's no law around here. You can forget what's right. These people can do what they like.' The logging sub-manager loomed across the desk. 'Offer him a hundred dollars all in', Julian suggested. But the man wouldn't budge. One hundred each was his price.

On the pretext of going for a pee, I walked over to an empty hut on the edge of the compound and activated my Global Positioning System (GPS). When I was reasonably sure no one was watching I held the phone-sized receiver out like a little offering to the gods until its screen had filled with the black bars that showed it had signals from three satellites. Then, miraculously, our exact location (to within 100 metres) flashed up. I surreptitiously extracted my map and marked on the co-ordinates. The Madidi was 40 kilometres away, straight; half as much again if the road carried on its present line (which Bernardino said was the way with logging roads). Back in the office a quiet but heated discussion was going on between the others.

Bernardino wanted to wait a while, then sneak away into the forest. We could cut a trail to the river. Charlie disagreed. 'We couldn't possibly carry all the gear cross-country', he said. 'I know we could hide some and return for it once we found the river, but I wouldn't trust it all to still be there when we got back.'

'Forty Ks', I said, breaking into the conversation.

'Two days. More', Julian commented. 'Have you seen how swampy the forest is? Half of what we passed on the way was under water. I wouldn't like to do that laden down if there wasn't a trail to follow. And walking along the road would be out, wouldn't it?'

'I say we go back to the bridge where the logging concession started', Charlie said. 'I noticed there were dugouts. What do you say?'

'What about the *Mono Rey*?' I asked. 'If we go down that river, we'll be so far from the Serranias, we'll never have a chance of seeing it.' Charlie and Julian just looked at each other. Maybe things had been decided whilst I was out the hut. I turned to Bernardino. He shrugged.

'I'm your guide. I'll do what you all decide', he mumbled disinterestedly.

'Look', said Julian, 'the Undumo is a tributary of the Madidi. It doesn't get to the Serranias but it does get to the right river. Call it a compromise.'

'More of a sell-out', I replied. I raced through all the possibilities in my mind, other routes into the Serranias. Surely, I reasoned, searching for the *Mono Rey* was the whole point of the trip. Maybe the others didn't see it that way.

'We could go back to Tumupasa – get over the mountains there. I know it would be difficult without the folding canoe . . .' My voice trailed off. I knew my argument wasn't convincing.

'We have a good-looking jungle river, half a day's walk back that gets us halfway to our aim', Julian said firmly.

Reluctantly, I had to agree. Though I knew it would mean setting off down a river of which we had no prior knowledge, in our present situation it looked the best option.

※

We all felt thoroughly exhausted by the time we got back to the bridge at Undumo. Charlie's feet were blistered and he said that the only way he would be travelling in the next few days would be by truck or on the river. At least the people at the hut were friendlier than when Chichito had dumped us there the day before. According to the radio operator, relaying our messages to the San

Antonio camp had just been 'work'. If we wanted to go down this river, then he wasn't about to stop us.

Strangely, though, he didn't know what was downstream. 'I've only travelled down one day in my canoe and the river's good all the way, although it's a bit shallow this time of year. Beyond that I don't know. But there was a man who lived further down and he said there is a place where there are many branches blocking the way and another bit where the river splits into lots of little rivers. He said the Undumo becomes a *curiche.*'

I ignored that word. It was just one of many I didn't understand. After the stress of the past few days I was eager to set off, to finally get into the rainforest. I put '*curiche*' to the back of my mind and genuinely forgot about it.

⚜

That afternoon, while Charlie fished and Julian constructed a framework of bamboo poles to hang our blue plastic rain sheet over, Bernardino and I searched the driftwood along the riverside for balsa tree trunks to make a raft. The radio operator had agreed to sell us a dugout canoe for $35, but it was only 10 feet long – big enough for just two of us plus the luggage. The other two would have to ride the raft, at least until we had eaten our way through some of the supplies. Luckily for us, finding the logs we required was not a problem. Balsa trees are very common in this area of the Amazon. They are found among the fast-growing tree-weeds that spring up when land is cleared. They often grow alongside rivers and are washed away as the banks erode, ending up in the jams of driftwood that litter the edges after the water has receded.

It didn't take long before Bernardino had found five suitable non-waterlogged trunks. I helped him pull them from the wood stacks, after which he trimmed them to the same length with his machete and instructed me to pull off any bark that remained on them. He then bound the five logs with rope to bamboo cross pieces to make a float 15 feet long by 3 feet wide. The entire con-struction, from extracting the logs to finishing the raft, took no more than an hour. Charlie and Julian agreed to take first turn riding it (Charlie said that it would make an excellent platform for fishing). Bernardino and I would paddle the dugout canoe for the present.

※

When the sun went down we lit a fire by the river. Our spirits were the highest that they had been yet: a mixture of relief and satisfaction that, after all the troubles, we were about to start, and excitement about the journey ahead. We tucked into a catfish that Charlie had caught earlier. He fried it along with chips made from some plantains that the people at the hut had given us. We even opened one of the tomato ketchups for good measure, as this was to be our last meal in 'civilization' for a while. Afterwards we lay back on the sand and watched the stars, scanning our torches now and then at the other side of the river where some small animal was rustling its way through a bamboo thicket behind the mud beach.

'Well, tomorrow the Undumo', said Julian, throwing a fish bone into the water.

'The *famoso* Undumo', murmured Bernardino.

Charlie nudged me from my stargazing. 'Madidi in a week, eh, Simon?'

'Yes', I grunted back.

The Undumo would get us to the Madidi but nowhere near the Serranias – the wrong direction entirely for the *Mono Rey*. But both Charlie's and Julian's (far more restrained) enthusiasm were infectious.

'There could be anything down there', I said. 'The guy at the hut mentioned several channels.'

'Bernardino reckoned there might be Indians', Charlie chipped in.

'Pacaguaras', said Julian. 'Bowl haircuts, feathers stuck through their noses like huge moustaches.'

'Bloody big arrows', Charlie continued for him. 'Shtonk – yaaargh.' He flipped over, gripping an imaginary arrow in his belly.

His eyes rolled and his tongue lolled to one side as he died on the sand then gave one last convulsion.

'There was this old hunter in the village in Surinam', Julian continued, ignoring the interruption. 'He was a Mawayan – the genuine article; lap cloth, long hair cut into a fringe at the front. He lived in a hut slightly apart from the others. They were Tirio. He showed me his arrows – six feet long with hard palm-wood points for spearing fish, or flattened ends for knocking out birds. And he showed me the poison he coated the tips with: a mush of ground-up plants and berries. It was his own recipe and he said that though he made it for the Tirio, he wouldn't tell them what was in it.

'Amaruna, would have been my guide. He could have taught me everything', Julian sighed. 'But the headman forbade it. He said I had to stay within the confines of the village until another plane arrived that could take me away. A month of hanging around. It was so frustrating.'

'And that's what you want this time?' I said. 'Another chance like you nearly had then?'

'Go naked with the Pacaguaras', Charlie sniggered.

'Well, learn about how they live anyway', Julian answered quietly.

❦

We fell into a relaxed silence, each of us in thought – Julian about his Indians, Charlie (I presumed) about his monster fish, me in a mixture of worry and anticipation. I realized that I was actually quite scared, a feeling which when I tried to pinpoint it was the same as when I had gone garden creeping with two friends one summer night as a teenager. The idea had been to traverse the gardens of our village without being caught, just for the thrill of it. The hardest part had been overcoming the fear to set off into the darkness. But the elation when we realized we had got across and not been caught had us singing all the way home. We had dared the unknown and, in the retelling, our story took on the proportions of some heroic epic.

Unexplored. *Terra incognita.* The *famoso* Undumo; home of monster fish, Pacaguaras Indians with feathers through their noses and maybe even the *Mono Rey*. And we would get away with it.

'*Seguro*', Bernardino said. Sure.

❦

The air was still and there were traces of mist hanging over the water when we set off the next morning. The river wound between high, red mud banks that gave it such a closed-in atmosphere that even just a few meanders from the bridge, it felt like we were isolated from the rest of the world. Bernardino and I paddled in silence, constantly scanning the banks for any noise or movement in the vegetation that would betray the presence of a monkey or a tapir. But so far, since Julian and Charlie had left us behind when our canoe had grounded in shallows, nothing had disturbed the overall stillness. There was just a background ticking of insects, the vegetation-damped piping of unseen birds and a faint splash each time our paddles cut the water.

A pair of curved-billed birds – green ibis – detached themselves from the shade of a cascade of leaves that trailed in the current and launched themselves out of our way. They glided in a gentle arc across the water, landing with heavy wing-beats on a pile of driftwood just ahead. As we reached the wood stack they took off again and gained another 30 yards on us. A dagger-billed wader strutted away from us along the logs. When it jumped off the pile and parachuted onto the hardened mud of the river's edge, its wings shone for an instant like a double sunburst in russet and gold, and I realized what it was. A sunbittern: half-heron, half-wader – a bird so hard to classify that it had been put in a family all of its own.

Then we were past it, absorbed back into the dappled green-black stillness of the river, flicking our heads around at the slightest movement or rustle from the forest. 'You have to look past the leaves and look for the differences', Bernardino whispered. He pointed at the wall of forest to our left. In amongst the trunks and leaves a palm frond was waving from side to side.

'What is it?' I asked. Bernardino craned his neck and half-raised himself out of the canoe. He shrugged and continued paddling.

The forest opened out slightly as we reached a tight meander where the current had carved the outside bank into a high cliff. On the inside edge, where silt had been deposited, fast-growing vegetation sprouted up, its young broad leaves bright against the more sombre primary forest. The first part of the beach was mainly bare, striped in places with heart-leafed creepers that snaked out across the sand. Behind there were dense stands of a cane which Bernardino called *chuchillo* (this was what we used each night for the frames of our shelters). The woody stems were around 10 feet high, topped with a fan of blade-like leaves. On the forest side of the *chuchillo*, but before the mature trees, there was a layer of balsas and cecropias. Fast-growing opportunists of any gap of light, they had simple branching patterns; they looked a bit like upturned, skeletal hands. Their leaves were multi-lobed and dinner-plate-sized, evolved to capture as much light as possible, so that they would shoot up and spread their seeds before the slower-growing forest species behind grew up to take their place. Creepers, *chuchillo*, cecropias, mature trees; this was an order of succession that was repeated with monotonous regularity at every river bend.

We headed the canoe for the outside of the curve and scooted around the gentle surge that we knew we would find there. The mud on the inside, I noticed as we passed, was covered in tracks from capybaras, tapirs and a jaguar. I presumed that the jaguar tracks were from the same animal that had left a trail on the last two river beaches. Maybe it walked a regular patrolling route. The prints were old. The mud had long since dried up and the marks were cracked and worn down at the edges. Bernardino said it hadn't rained for weeks. The river was low and apparently still getting lower.

The canoe grounded. Bernardino hopped into the shallows and indicated that I should do the same. He steered the now lighter boat partway across the sand bar until it scraped the bottom again, and together we pulled the hull into a deep channel near to the opposite bank. It was a manoeuvre we repeated at every meander.

While the others floated past on their raft, our canoe with its deeper draught would grind to a halt. The boat had been cut with hand tools out of a tree trunk and it didn't seem to have been finished off properly. The hull was a full six inches thick in places and must have weighed half a ton. Bernardino apologized for not being as strong as usual. He had inhaled sawdust when he was working 'in the wood', he explained. A doctor had told him to quit the job before he ruined his lungs. Now it hurt to inhale really deeply and he found it hard to catch his breath. He was having doubts about this river. He said that he was unhappy about continuing downstream unless the canoe floated not just half, but all of the time.

By midday we had been settled into the paddle and drag routine for five hours, and my mind had some time ago wandered far from looking for every difference and scanning every swaying clump of leaves for a jaguar. Whilst my arms kept their rhythm of stroke-lift-stroke, my mind wandered in a free-form association game of irrelevant details of lessons I had taught in school, an exploration of the rooms of my house, and even into a fairly heated internal debate on whether I should insure my car 'Comprehensive' or 'Third party, fire and theft' when I got back. Meanwhile, part of my internal processing wondered why someone was whistling at me.

'Weet weeyoooo!' A long, drawn-out wolf whistle. I drifted back into reality when I realized it was not in my dream.

'*Seringuero*', murmured Bernardino, 'Rubber tapper.' The call was repeated across the river.

'Um de Um. Weet weeyooo!' The cry of the screaming piha has to be one of the most familiar of all jungle noises. It's used in the background for every rainforest film. The first notes sound as though they are made by an entirely different creature: three low, ascending notes, as if someone had blown across the top of milk bottles, each containing a little more liquid. After that comes the whistle. Then it starts again, and again. Continually. I couldn't see the piha. Bernardino said they were notoriously difficult to spot. When I did see one a few weeks later it was like a dumpy female blackbird, uniform drab brown, nothing special.

'It calls when there are rubber trees nearby', Bernardino explained. He swept an arm around the boat. 'That's how the rubber collectors used to find their trees. This was all rubber country. Some people here got very rich.

'But not any more', he added when he caught my eye.

❧

In 1911 the Bolivian government commissioned a report on what was then the country's most profitable export – rubber from its lowland provinces. Ixiamas district was listed as having four estates: Porvenir, Porvenir de Bolivia, La Union and Nuestra Senora de los Angeles. Between them, these *barracas* (estates) had over 2000 *estradas* – workers' 'rounds' of between 100 and 150 rubber trees. The rubber worker, or *seringuero,* milked the trees for their sap by scoring the bark on the trunk and tying on a cup to collect it. He would make two rounds of his trees a day, once to set the sap flowing, the second time to collect it. He would then 'cure' the balls of raw latex by smoking them over smouldering *uruci* nuts; in addition to the other tasks, the nuts and wood to burn them had to be collected during the day. The work was arduous and there was seldom any time left for the *seringuero* to do anything but work his patch. All food and supplies (matches, machete, rifle, bullets, etc.) had to be bought from the estate, invariably at a highly inflated cost. This created a situation of debt bondage so that, unless the rubber prices were soaring, the *seringuero* would be continually working just to service his debt. Anything owed would have to be paid off before he left his *estrada* and, if he chose to work at another estate, his debt would move with him. Nevertheless, despite conditions amounting almost to slavery, when prices were high, and they were in the early years of the twentieth century, good money could be earned. So thought the thousands who migrated to the Bolivian lowlands to work the estates. Most were *cholos* (mixed Indian-white ancestry) from the Andes, but there were also many fortune seekers from Europe and the USA. Demand for rubber had soared since the recent developments of the pneumatic tyre and the motor car, and until it was supplanted by the produce of Asian plantations, the entire world supply came from the Amazon, in particular from areas watered by silt laden rivers from the Andes. Quite suddenly rivers such as the Putumayo in Colombia and the Acre in Bolivia attained international importance. In the Acre the rubber barons felt no loyalty to the capital, La Paz, from which they were so far removed, and so in 1899 they declared the region an independent state. Four years later the Acre became part of Brazil. The Bolivian government sent soldiers and there was some fighting, but with such long and difficult lines of communication their action could not be sustained. Eventually it was agreed that as compensation Brazil would finish building a railway line around the cataracts on the Madeira River to the Mamore River on the Bolivian border. This would at least allow access for Bolivian rubber to the ports on the Amazon from where it could be exported.

In the meantime Bolivia had to demarcate its borders to prevent such a fiasco reoccurring. The Royal Geographical Society was sought as a neutral party to produce a survey that would be acceptable to the countries involved: Peru, Brazil and Bolivia. This was how Major Percy Harrison Fawcett of the Royal Artillery came to be involved in 1906. He was the man the RGS appointed for the task. In the four trips he made between then and 1914 he was to explore more of the forested interior than anyone before or since; the maps that he drew and the data he gathered still remain the only 'on the ground' sources of information for some of the more remote areas. The borders Fawcett surveyed are the ones we see on maps today.

❧

A low cough from across the river snapped me back into alertness. Bernardino pointed to a cluster of branches protruding from the flow. One had a cormorant sitting on top. Its wings were outstretched, drying in the sun. Below it two flat heads, with eyes and nostrils level with the water, slid slowly towards the shore:

capybaras — sheep-sized rodents that look somewhat like dumpy, oversized guinea pigs. They raised themselves onto a mud shelf below the opposite bank and stood draining water for a moment, their heads turning to watch us as we got out to manhandle the boat past the snags. The cormorant saw us and chose to leave, skittering across the water's surface with its feet while its wings beat furiously yet failing to get it into the air. It gave up and sank up to its neck when it realized it wasn't going to take off after all. The capybaras decided they would move too. One let out a 'tuk tuk' shout and then both bounded up the bank in front of them, sending clods of mud tumbling into the river as they scrabbled for the cover at the top.

⫸⫷

When we caught up with Julian and Charlie again, they were almost overflowing with excitement.

'Fuck! You should've seen it', Charlie yelled as soon as we came into view. 'A tapir. It must've been the size of a horse. It nearly sank the raft.'

'It came up right under us', Julian enthused. 'When it saw us it charged straight for the shore.' They continued to babble on as they pulled out a lunch of dried bread 'tostadas' and started smearing them with jam (which immediately started attracting insects).

'Did you see the size of it?' (Charlie unconsciously wafted a small swarm from his face.)

'Could've ridden it mate', laughed Julian. I noticed his accent had turned Australian in the excitement.

⫸⫷

We journeyed on for a couple more uneventful hours before we decided to pitch camp for the night on a sloping beach at a particularly scenic river bend. The first thing Julian did, I noticed, was to cut a piece of *chuchillo*, set it into the sand and strap his video camera to it.

'This is our campsite.' He stated the obvious self-consciously, heaving his rucksack into the camera's field of view.

'Gonna bag me a tapir', said Charlie. Bernardino gave a 'thumbs-up' sign.

'Act normally', said Julian switching the camera off using the remote control, which was, of course, not the thing to say. After ten minutes of Bernardino grinning, me giving a commentary on how to set up camp and Charlie being David Attenborough, Julian gave up and slunk away to a quiet spot where he could show off our Brazilian shotgun to the viewing millions without interruption.

A little later he and Bernardino went into the thicket behind our beach to test it out. I heard no shots, but when they returned Bernardino was holding a lime-green, jackdaw-sized bird (an olive orependola) by its feet, its yellow tail fanning out as he swung its head hard against a tree trunk to finish it off. He wasn't impressed with the gun.

'Not much force', he sneered as he started plucking out feathers, ending up with a carcass so puny that its breast meat was only worth using for baiting our hooks. Dinner was catfish again. I caught it. I was so amazed at my success with just a hook and line that I held up my catch with my fingers under its gills for the others to see and was consequently spiked by one of its dorsal spines when it tried to wriggle free. I think the spines must have been poisonous. The pain was far out of proportion to such a tiny wound; it made me cry. The knuckles of my left hand swelled up overnight and stayed raised and tender for days afterwards.

❧

The next day the river got deeper and it seemed that Bernardino's worries about the Undumo being un-navigable were over. Though we still had to drag the canoe from time to time, we were starting to learn how to read the patterns of the flow and predict where the deep channels would be. Increasingly it was Charlie and Julian on the raft, limited to travelling at the speed of the current, who were left behind. At these times Bernardino and I would paddle forward two or three meanders, then stop and wait. I would watch the riverside swallows and flycatchers through my binoculars or sketch in my diary. We would move on either when the others caught up or when the *marahui* midges found us, whichever happened first. At around midday our progress was stopped by a tree that had fallen across the river. We slid the canoe up to the trunk and I clambered onto it to scout a way past. As I looked over the top, something growled. It was a short, rough snort, low enough pitched for me to realize that whatever made it had to be large. The noise had come from nearby but I couldn't see where from. I stopped dead still, cast my eyes each way down the trunk then out across the river. There were two shapes underwater, long, nearly as big as me and approaching rapidly. They broke the surface simultaneously about 15 feet from where I crouched, craning out sleek, brown heads with sharp white teeth. They were so close I could see every detail of the blotchy patterning on their throats and the water streaming off their walrus whiskers. The heads lurched towards me and in one fluid movement, the giant otters dived back under, looped around and resurfaced at the far end of the trunk. There they trod water, staring at me with light blue, goggle eyes. I held on perfectly still, not even daring to change the expression on my face. I had been told how fiercely territorial giant otters were, how they could see off or even kill a jaguar. For a moment we faced each other off. Then they were charging forward again, porpoising in and out of the water. Teeth bared, screeching and snorting, they arched their necks high one last time, then splashed back under. When I was certain they had gone, I realized I was shaking – though I wasn't sure if was out of fear or excitement.

Bernardino clambered up onto the trunk. He put his hand on my shoulder and apologized. Sounding genuinely sincere, he told me that the signs should have been obvious. He should have noticed the bare patch of mud slip-way down the riverbank and the fishy smell of the shit used to mark the territory. 'Now you will be famous', he said. 'Amigo Julian took your picture on his video.'

I hadn't noticed until then that the raft had arrived. Julian was messing with a tangle of wires that dangled from his solar panel charger. 'Sorry, Simon. Batteries not charged. I'm afraid I missed it all.'

'It's a shame too', said Charlie from the back of the raft. 'That expression you pulled could've shifted a jaguar in full charge. Pure terror, mate. Dingo ugly.'

CHAPTER FOUR

'Hombres de la Selva'

ATUG ON my arm jerked me into wakefulness and I felt the momentary disorientation that all roused sleepers feel, dis - turbed from cosy dreaming into sudden alertness. For a second I was aware of the air on my face, no longer warm as I remembered, but cold and clammy, biting into my lungs as I inhaled deeply. The noises had changed too. It was so quiet. There were no more bullfrogs croaking, just the rushing of water and the faintest ticking of insects. The pulling at my arm started again, more insistently – 'Simon! Wake up' – and I became aware of Bernardino, crouching by my mosquito net, pointing towards the water's edge. My eyes scanned in the direction of his outstretched hand. Everything looked grey and poorly defined in the mist that had settled over the stony beach. I could tell something was there, but more by where the water didn't glisten than by actually seeing it. An amorphous blob of shade that wallowed in the shallows, an outline of a broad back, something about the size of a donkey but lumpier like a pig or a small rhino. I caught a glimpse of a thick neck sprouting a bristly mane and a head with low-set eyes, almost prehistoric in appearance. I only got an indication of the animal's shape when it abruptly rose out of the water and stood to sniff at the air with a long, flexible snout that seemed to move independently of its body – a bit like a small periscope. Then, apparently satisfied that it was safe, the animal started slowly up the opposite bank and I realized what I was watching. A tapir.

It had nearly reached the thick vegetation at the top when Bernardino let out a piercing wolf whistle. The tapir stopped. Its ears pricked up and it turned to face us, the trunk nose testing the air for any whiff of our scent. Then, sniffling its way forward, the tapir started to amble towards us, across the stream, closer and closer. I slid out of my sleeping bag and crouched, transfixed by indecision: whether to stay perfectly still or risk the noise of extracting my camera from the rucksack. The tapir had not seen or smelled us yet and still it continued to approach, past my sandals, past where I had stuck the machete in the sand, past my rucksack. It walked right into Julian's mosquito net where he still lay sleeping. Then it snorted, leaped fully into the air and stampeded away with a remarkable turn of speed around the river bend. We could hear the pounding of its hooves against the sand, then a clattering as it sped over some shingle and finally a crashing and fading rustling of leaves as it found safety in the forest's edge. Bernardino and I were left shaking with elation. We had been so close. We could almost have touched it.

I was too awake now to consider going back under my net. Bernardino kicked the embers of the fire, used his machete to shave off the edge of a balsa wood stick that was lying on the ground and threw the pieces onto the smouldering charcoals. While he got the fire going I walked down to the river to fill a billy-can with water. It was a morning routine I was quickly getting used to; prepare kindling, light up the fire, get water boiling to make coffee and porridge.

Already the first rays of sun were slanting down through the gaps in the mist that rose from the Undumo, highlighting the treetops above the opposite bank. A pair of macaws flew over, bright crimson with blue wing tips. Halfway across the river they started shrieking and the whole peace of the dawn was shattered, their rasping 'rark rark rark rark' answered by other macaws in the distance and the high-pitched shrieking of smaller parrots as they

left their roosts and flew off in search of fruiting trees. I put the
pot on the fire and started packing up my sleeping bag. It was
damp, and sand from the beach stuck to it when I tried to roll it
up. Bernardino ambled over and shovelled out some coffee and
sugar into the pot. He scooped out a cupful and, slurping it with
his lips, he turned to me and announced, 'Today I will get you
lost.'

I thought little more of this statement until around midday. We
had made camp early, after only canoeing a few large meanders (the
GPS said we'd made two kilometres), so that Charlie could fish and
Julian could do some videoing and recharge the batteries with his
small, military-issue solar panels. After we had eaten a lunch of dry
biscuits and leftover fish, Bernardino said he was ready to take me
into the forest.

'Can't you hear the *marimonos* calling?' he said, cocking his head
slightly to one side and listening intently with a bemused, slightly
quizzical expression. I listened. In amongst the ticks and the whirrs,
the rippling of the river and the wind in the treetops, there was
something else: the squealing, trilling noise that I remembered as
the spider monkey food call.

'*Muchos* monkeys', said Bernardino. 'They find food. Then they
have a little fiesta. Come on. Let's go!' He got up, drummed his
fingers on his lips and screamed the same ululating call that Negro
had made on my first trip. The call was answered by other similar
cries from both sides of the river.

'Just to let them know we're coming.' Bernardino winked at me,
snatched up his machete and set off.

Away from the river everything was damp, shady and quiet. There
was just a ticking of insects and the slight rustle of a light wind in
the treetops to disturb the stillness. Bernardino led the way, swip-
ing occasionally with his machete and breaking twigs to mark our
trail, every now and then stopping to trill out the food call and
change our direction whenever the spider monkeys ahead called

back. Clutching binoculars, camera and sketchbook, I crashed through the undergrowth in pursuit, stopping now and then to extricate various equipment straps which became caught up on branches and vines. One time when he stopped to wait for me I could see annoyance across Bernardino's face.

'You make so much noise – like a tapir', he said pointedly, and pushed on.

The humidity was all enveloping. It sapped my energy and made me feel like I was gulping down as much water as air into my lungs each time I inhaled. There was as much moisture around me as there had been in the mists of the early morning, but enclosed beneath the protective envelope of the forest it had had no chance to condense out. Instead it just gave everything the vaguest sense of wetness, from the moss on the tree trunks that I steadied myself on to the reflective sheen on the ferns of the undergrowth. Soon I was drenched from the leaves I brushed past and the sweat that dribbled out of every pore on my body. I was aware of my own odour and of the mouldy, fungal stench of the forest itself, like that of an English wood in autumn but twenty times more concentrated. Bracket fungus stuck out from some of the trees and clusters of toadstools sprouted from rotting bits of branches on the forest floor. Fallen tree trunks crumbled into mush when I trod on them. Mould and lichen spread over leaves living and dead. In places huge yellowing palm fronds that had fallen from the canopy dangled from clusters of vines. What on first impression looked verdant and healthy was, in reality, spattered with the colours of decay: rust, brown and black. With conditions so perfect for fungal growth, decomposition happened so quickly here that nutrients were recycled in a closed system; the forest fed on itself.

I was so intent on keeping up with Bernardino and of at least making a show of walking quietly that I scarcely had time to snatch more than a glimpse up at the canopy. There was virtually nothing to see in any case: a sunlit clump of foliage, a gap of sky – rarely more. Up there was where growth would be concentrated, energy gathered through photosynthesis, then expended in encouraging pollination and spreading seeds. There would be the flowers and fruit, and their pollinators and dispersers: the bees and beetles, lizards, tree frogs, and the small birds whose twittering drifted down from time to time. There would be predators and their prey, parasitic animals, parasitic plants, symbiotic relationships between bees and flowers, ants and fungus; interactions of life with many species never once in their lives coming to ground. This is where there would be the monkeys, toucans and silky anteaters and, swooping at them from time to time from perches in the tallest emergent trees, hawk-eagles. Perhaps even the giant harpy eagle, so powerful and agile it could loop upside down under branches to pluck off a full-grown sloth. There would be vine snakes, praying mantids, small opossums with prehensile tails, kinkajous, katydids and a myriad more species. It was all happening thirty metres above us and, apart from occasional glimpses when something flitted across an opening in the leaves, Bernardino and I would miss nearly all of it.

We didn't find the spider monkeys. Bernardino reluctantly admitted they might have been scared off by his calling. But we did find howlers. We wouldn't have noticed them if there hadn't been an opening in the canopy, a small space with an uninterrupted view of the treetops. Howler monkeys are usually heard rather than seen. At dawn and dusk they bellow out ownership of their territories through cartilaginous voice boxes that amplify their roars. The sound carries for several miles. From a distance it sounds like wind in the trees. Close to, it's more like lions roaring. Seeing them can be harder though, as they tend to feed on the leaves of just one tree for most of the day, and prefer to sit still rather than move away and risk showing their presence.

Above us, copper-orange in the sunlight, a large male sat on an up-tilted branch of a huge emergent tree. It was a perfect position for bellowing out his claim. Further in towards the trunk there were three other smaller monkeys – females, Bernardino said. Their tails were wrapped around the branch on which they huddled. There were more monkeys in the canopy nearby. We only became aware of them because they moved, shaking the branches and alerting the big male to our presence. He shifted his weight and repositioned his body with arms spread out to hold himself, facing down towards us, his head nodding in a half-hearted threat display. When he failed to scare us away, he turned and nonchalantly sauntered along one of the branches until he got to its end which, under his weight, bent over just enough for him to reach into the next tree and pull himself out of our sight.

I turned to Bernardino to see if he wanted to follow. 'No', he said, 'Let's go back.' He swung around, slowly counting off trees. For an instant he looked thoughtful, then his jaw dropped. He slapped the palm of his hand to his forehead, looked at me with a worried expression and said, 'I can't remember the way back now. It's up to you.'

I knew he was lying but he had made his point. In my eagerness to watch the howlers, I had taken no notice of where we had been going and now I had no idea of the way back. I hadn't brought my compass or even made a mental note of which direction we had travelled in. Nor could I use the sun to guide me as the treetop canopy blocked it out. I was determined I wouldn't be put to shame. I remembered the last ten yards or so and retraced our route as far as I was confident then started looking for machete cuts. I remembered that Bernardino had a habit of marking the vegetation now and then. This was not so much trail cutting – that would create too much noise and scare away any wildlife. His cuts were always the merest flicks of the wrist, usually at soft, new growth and on the stalks of small trees that would slice easily and reasonably soundlessly. Using this train of thinking I quickly found the nearest mark, a diagonal slash across some upright green stems. The large, paddle leaves that they had held now lay on the ground in front of them and the cut stems oozed whitish sap that contrasted against the dark of the forest floor. Now all I had to do was extrapolate my line of travel and I would be sure to find the next cut. Simple.

It didn't work out like that. I followed on in a straight line from the two marks that I knew but found no others. It seemed logical that whichever way we had come, we would have battered down some of the vegetation or left footprints. Apparently not. There was no broken or trampled undergrowth and the ground here was covered in a dry leaf litter that left no mark when I trod down. I returned to the diagonal cuts. Bernardino leaned on a tree trunk watching intently and, at last, took pity on me. He whistled and pointed with his machete to a thicket three yards away. I had passed it at least twice already and failed to notice how the twigs at the edge had been snapped back. From there, I soon found another cut, then some more and set off along what looked like a trail.

'Amigo Simon!' Bernardino nodded 90 degrees left of my direction. I walked back to him, relocated the cuts and the lesson continued; me retracing our route with Bernardino waiting, then whistling at me whenever I missed his marks. Once or twice we came to patches where the undergrowth had been battered back into what looked like paths. Bernardino called me back whenever I tried to follow them. Those, he said, were the trails used by tapirs on their nightly journeys down to the river.

'Notice how the vegetation is broken', he pointed out. 'It's not cut. In places it's like a tunnel through the undergrowth. Follow it or wait around on it and you might find a tapir. It would make an easy route to use if we were lost, but as we're not, ignore it.'

Eventually we got back to somewhere I recognized: a tree with spreading roots and a knotted arrangement of lianas in front that I had briefly sketched in my diary when we had passed by earlier. I still had a very firm mental image of it and of our route immediately before. From then on I made fewer mistakes and we were soon back at the river. That tree, Bernardino said afterwards, was my 'landmark', but I needed to have more. The forest could all look the same, especially if you weren't used to it. I had to look out for features that were distinctive and could be remembered easily. These were 'way-points' I could use to divide any journey into sections. I could mentally 'tick them off' each time I passed one. Between them I obviously had to mark my route, but it wasn't necessary to cut that much, except where I changed direction. Each mark had to be in sight of the next. That way, I should always be in line of sight of at least two others. It was just a case then of knowing what to look out for, of being able to identify my marks once I had made them, especially several hours (or even days) later when I was tired, in a hurry or had forgotten where my trail was. If I was serious about going into the jungle, I had to know what did and didn't look right in the rainforest. Diagonal machete slashes through stems obviously stood out, as they couldn't have been made naturally. But so did broken vegetation if it was done in a certain way, for instance by twisting a branch over so that the lighter underside of the leaves showed. Cutting the bark on tree trunks could also be effective, particularly if the trees were of the sort that had bright white or even red sap. The trick was to make marks that would stand out enough for the trained eye to notice them, yet not take so long or make so much noise that I scared away any wildlife that I wanted to see.

'You have to look past the leaves', Bernardino told me. 'You have to feel how the forest grows and spot the little differences, the things that look out of place. Then you will have confidence. Then you will be a true "*hombre de la selva*".'

For the rest of the afternoon I set myself little practise tasks, looping around into the forest, always just about within sight of the camp, trying to reinforce Bernardino's training on making and following trails. It wasn't all that difficult, I decided, provided that I kept up my concentration, though how I would fare weeks into the jungle with no obvious landmarks would be a different matter entirely. I had the reassurance of a GPS that could pinpoint my exact position, and maps which, though largely blank, still had the rivers marked in and thus gave me some point of reference even if my satellite navigator failed. The likes of Fawcett and de Loys didn't have such niceties; they could travel for weeks without really knowing where they were, and that level of uncertainty must have been emotionally trying. By the time de Loys and his party had their encounter with the two apes, weeks of slogging through jungle had sapped them physically and mentally. They were tired and hungry. Some of the men had been ill with fever. They had been attacked several times by Motilones Indians and were jittery about the likelihood of further attacks. Several of their porters had already deserted.[1] They stopped to rest by a riverbank and suddenly the peace was shattered – not Indians attacking this time, but two giant apes. Little wonder that their reaction was to gun them down.

> I was exploring at the time the untrodden forests in the neighbour-hood of the Tarra river . . . and I came across two animals, the nature of which was new not only to myself, but also to the native woodsmen of my party. . . . These two animals broke out upon the exploring party, then at rest, and owing to the violence of their atti-tude had to be received at the point of the rifle.

The apes approached, screaming, breaking off branches and waving them in the air. They stood upright (though gripping onto bushes), shitting into their hands and throwing the excrement at the explor-ers. A volley of carbine fire saw to the smaller of the two apes – a female. The other escaped wounded into the forest. De Loys' men rushed forward and came across the body. They estimated it at five feet tall and weighing 180 pounds. Then they took it to the river, propped it up on an oil crate and took its photograph.

⚜

My line of thought broke abruptly as I found myself descending to where a muddy ravine, 10 feet or so deep, cut across my route. There were some thick lianas hanging strategically across. I must admit that daydreaming attacks by giant apes and my new-found confidence at jungle exploring had made me rather giddy. I was busy humming the theme tune to the Indiana Jones films as I launched myself at one of the vines and swung down to the stream at the bottom. I landed with a 'clump' on a large rock, with my feet astride a long twist of rotten vegetation 'rather like long squiggly

---

1 Out of a total of twenty in the party, including bearers, only four returned: the result of disease and Indian arrows. De Loys himself was wounded in the arm.

turd', I noted, as I spread my arms to steady myself. The squiggle uncoiled and hissed at me. I dived sideways into a bush.

I regained my composure from on top of the now-flattened bush and looked back. The snake had gone. I pulled myself out of the gully, and found a snake-free patch of undergrowth to sit down and compose myself.

I stayed there for some time, slowly calming down. Edged by some ferns and low bushes, I would have been invisible to anybody or anything that walked past. Shortly after I had sat down I noticed how the insect noises became louder, as if everything had shut up whilst I was crashing through and had come out again now the danger had passed. I could hear cicadas buzzing like metallic trumpets (several varieties) and the 'rustle rustle clap clap CLAP' as large leaves fell from the canopy. Something near to my feet was edging closer: an ant bird, robin-sized, slate-grey with black and white flecks on its wings. Slaty ant bird? It was as good a guess as any considering there were about twenty species to choose from in my bird book. They all looked the same, except for the number of white specks. In the canopy a 'rustle clap CLIP' caught my attention. Not a leaf. And not a monkey either; too quiet. A squirrel maybe? A squirrel cuckoo. Sandy-chestnut head and long, grey-black tail barred with white, it scurried along a branch above my head and disappeared into a clump of leaves.

I must have sat there for at least an hour sketching a palm sapling, quietly pencilling in the outline and colouring in the dark fronds with watercolour paint, concentrating on how the newer shoots in the centre were more verdant than the duller, algae-mottled fronds lower down. I was engrossed and only dimly aware of the ants and sweat bees that crawled down my collar and over my face as I tried to recreate the way the sunlight and shade were mottled through the foliage.

These on-the-spot painted sketches are something I've developed a knack for on my jungle trips. In about ten minutes I can knock up a passable picture of vines wrapped around buttress roots, a bird or some other jungle view; if it takes much longer, then I know I'm trying too hard. The result doesn't capture the life a

much quicker sketch would. The paintings I'm proudest of generally took the least time – no rubbing out, just a few pencil strokes
and a quick wash of colour – like my picture of a crocodile lying flat
out at a waterhole with a plover pecking around, unconcerned by its
mouth.

Watercolours are good like that. They dry quickly and are easy
to carry. I always carry a pocket set with me, along with a couple of
brushes and a film canister of water. When that runs out I use
whatever liquid is to hand: puddle water, sweat, spit. I draw the line
at using urine – I lick my brushes too often. I think it adds a certain touch when I can say that my pictures of the Amazon were
painted with real Amazon river water.

True, ten minutes for a picture is hardly quick, but I find I
observe my subject so closely that I notice far more than if I were
snapping a photo or even just staring at the scenery. For each
sketch, even the quick ones, revisiting them later brings back the
scene in its entirety. Not only the sights, but the sounds and smells
too. It can be unnerving how absorbed I can get. I can be concentrating so much on the curl of a new palm frond or on the pattern
of lichen down a tree trunk that I'll shut myself off to the ants that
are crawling up my trouser legs and, to an extent, to the mosquitoes. Once, when I got up after sketching some hoatzin birds across
a narrow creek, the small log that I had been resting my foot
against floated to the middle of the stream then sank in a distinctly crocodilian way. Another time I looked up to find myself
staring into the eyes of a tiny deer that had nuzzled between the
undergrowth and almost come within nibbling distance of my
sketch pad.

But there are certain things that can break even *my* concentration. Sweat bees: tiny, black and sting-less I have been told (at
least, one has never stung me). In a food web I think they would be
classed as 'decomposers'; they cluster around corpses where they
land to lap up any fluids that ooze out. But, maybe their true place
in the grand scheme of things is just to be annoying.

Failing a good corpse to lick, the sweat on my face was just as
good. The first one or two were tolerable. When I had a swarm

fifty or so strong I had to move. I could cope with them licking the salt – that just tickled. It was when they tried to walk across my eyes or crawl into my ears that they became too much. One went up my nostril and instead of blowing it out, I accidentally sniffed in. It came out my mouth the next morning when I coughed up some phlegm.

I gathered up my paint box and brushes, pulled the neck of my T-shirt over my mouth and nose to avoid breathing in any more bees, and headed back towards the river where I could hear Charlie shouting. 'Hey Jules, check this out! Simon! Come and paint this.'

With the fingers of one hand lodged under its gills, he was hoisting an enormous, flapping catfish above his head in triumph. As Julian reached him and I got down to the level of the beach, I could see him gently laying his catch along a patch of shingle where it wouldn't get sandy. He ran his fingers over its flat, spade-shaped snout and down one of its four whip-like whiskers. He stroked its grey and black tiger-striped back and lifted up a tall, pink dorsal fin so that it splayed out like a fan. With reverie he pronounced, 'It's a *pintado*. Reckon we'll eat well tonight.'

❖

By next afternoon it was clear that the character of the river was changing. The channel became deeper and more sluggish. It wound in tight meanders between low walls of cane-*chuchillo*, dotted with weedy secondary-growth trees. After several river bends there was no sign of forest behind. Turtles basked on deadwood branches that stuck out of the murky water. They vied with each other for prime position, stacking half on each other's backs like piled up dinner plates left to drain, tumbling in formation for cover as they sensed our approach. Fallen trees lined the river edges; bone-white piles of tangled driftwood, stripped of bark, leaves and smaller branches, eroded into sharpened spikes. Many stuck out from under the water and threatened to snag the canoe and the raft if ever we left the central stream. I remembered Fawcett having written that the most dangerous snags were 'submerged a few inches out of sight. . . . The twisted boughs are eaten away into wicked spikes, and, as the timber is often nearly as hard as iron, these snags can rip through a swiftly moving boat as if it were paper.'

In hindsight we should have realized what the change in the river meant, how it linked with the warning that the man at the bridge had given us. But we paddled on, mindful only that we would need an open area to camp. The cane thickets now totally enclosed the river and the usable channel was narrowing so that in places it was little wider than two or three times the width of the canoe. Then they almost totally blocked the way. Trunks and branches had piled up to make a dam with just one opening that funnelled the flow to a pool below. It was like a rapid but lined with a palisade of spikes that scraped down the sides of the canoe and threatened to impale us as we were sucked towards the gap. Bernardino and I back-paddled frantically, pulling at the water with desperate strokes that sent up whirlpools of sticks and debris but did not stop us. Eventually we gave up to the inevitable, crouched low and fended off branches. We were locked solid and I was over the side trying to pull away chunks of wood before the force of the water toppled the boat. I floundered in the strong current, fighting to keep from being wedged in the palisade. The shallow riverbed that I had expected turned out be a lattice of slippery roots and branches, which I slid off, lodging my legs in the gaps in between. Now I found myself grasping with one hand for a hold to stay above water whilst with the other I scrabbled at the logs that held the boat. Bernardino was at the stern, telling me to push, his voice scarcely audible above the hiss and bubbling of the water. I half-clambered up one of the trunks and launched myself at the front of the canoe. That was enough. It skewed sideways and plopped through the gap into the calm pool beyond.

At least our canoe had a streamlined front that slid between the snags. Behind, Charlie and Julian on the raft had become jammed. The full force of the flow channelled over the top, pushing off the stick of plantains that made up the only cargo they carried. Charlie and Julian fought against the surging water. Julian pulled at the branches of the dam, while Charlie wedged himself between the dam and the raft, pushing the front end away and down until it was clear of the snag that pinned it in place. Then he dived on the bound-up logs, his momentum forcing aside the parts of the dam already loosened by Julian, until at last the raft slid through.

We were soaked and the rucksacks had been splashed, but apart from the plantains nothing had been lost. The whole incident had been watched by two giant otters. As we turned the canoe and made ready to paddle on, we caught sight of their heads, peering through a gap between some floating branches at the edge of the pool.

⚜

The next logjam marked the end of the Rio Undumo. A mass of floating timber stretched fully across the river, and even from my position low down in the canoe I could see that the blockage stretched some way ahead. I edged the canoe up to the side and scrambled up a fallen tree. I was stunned by what I saw. Dead white trunks and branches of trees filled the river channel for as far as I could see. There was no more rainforest – just grass and reeds and dead trees. The Undumo had ended and I felt so desperate with the unfairness of it. How could a river just stop? I wanted to shout and hit things. I wanted to cry. As I stared ahead at the heaped-up piles of what must have been hundreds, thousands of trees, I knew for certain that we wouldn't get to the Madidi now. Not this way.

CHAPTER FIVE

The Swamp of Despair

FOR A WHILE we sat in stunned silence, Julian and Charlie on the raft, Bernardino and I on the dugout.

'*Curiche*', said Bernardino quietly. His face was expressionless.

'That's the word the man at the house used', I said.

'And you didn't tell us?' asked Julian.

'I didn't think anything of it at the time. We were so busy haggling over the price of the canoe. We finally seemed to be getting somewhere and everyone was so wrapped up in setting off.' Julian looked daggers. 'I really didn't think about it at the time', I tried to explain. 'To be honest, I didn't understand half of what he said.'

'I thought it might be like this', Bernardino said to nobody in particular. 'I didn't want to say anything – not when everything was going so well. Normally on a river this big, people would know what was down it but the people at the house did not. Not even three days down. I've heard about big *curiches* like this. There are anacondas so big they can eat a grown man. And caimans. Not like the little crocodile that bit you, Simon. Big black caimans – as big as this canoe.' He paused for a moment to let it sink in. 'And you can never get through', he added for good measure.

'You've never actually been to one yourself then', I said.

'No', Bernardino admitted.

We decided there was nothing we could do now except turn back and paddle upstream until we came across an open mud bank on which we could set up a camp. We all agreed that we would have to scout ahead on foot and see how far the logjam lasted. Then we'd be able to decide if we could drag or carry the canoe overland to where the river restarted, or possibly build another raft. None of us felt like carrying on today though; the end of the river had been too much of a blow to our morale for that.

The campsite we ended up at – a raised strip of damp mud between the main river channel and a small muddy pool – was by no means ideal. It was, however, the only piece of open land we could find. There was just enough room to set up a crude tent made from cut *chuchillo* poles, roofed with our blue plastic sheet. We cleared a little space to one side for our fire; the pile of driftwood on the downstream side of the camp would provide an ample source of fuel. We even found places to hang Julian's hammock, tying the ends to a driftwood trunk at one end and to a none-too-sturdy living tree at the other.

Once we had set up camp, we started our other jobs: fishing for the night's dinner and scrubbing our jungle-stained clothes. As a source of bait for fishing, the pool behind the camp was ideal. Cut off from the main flow, it was full of small, hungry catfish that caught on our unbaited hooks as soon as we threw them in. We cut them up and handed them to Bernardino to skewer onto a larger hook on a thicker line to pull out a big catfish from the main river. Charlie was sure it would be catfish that he caught.

'Big, deep pool like this. There'll be stacks of them, all feeling along the bottom with their barbies.' He held his hands to his chin and waggled his fingers, gulped down an imaginary hook. 'It's OK to swim, then?' 'No problem, eh, Bernie?' Bernardino looked up from baiting a hook and vaguely smiled. Charlie carried on. 'No piranhas here. Not caught a single one on this river. Some rivers are like that – big "cats" only. You might get a little turtle taking a fancy to you though.'

'Nibbling your *palanca*', said Julian.

'I'm going in fully clothed then', I said, and dived in holding onto my bar of soap.

It was good to wallow. I felt cool and free from the clouds of *marahuisas* that had descended on the camp. If I floated in one place long enough, they would find me, but I could confuse them easily enough by diving down and resurfacing a few feet away. Now and then things would brush against me; submerged branches probably, maybe the odd harmless catfish nibbling at my feet. This, I decided, was how it felt to a tapir. A good wallow once a day was all you needed. I rubbed the bar of soap all over my face, my hair and my shirt then thrashed around for a while to rinse it all off. Then I took off my trousers and washed them. I took little notice of Bernardino's complaints that he kept losing his hooks to something biting through the line. But when he pulled in the culprit, nothing could have got me out of the river quicker.

He held it up for us all to see: a frighteningly large piranha. Around a foot long, silver with a blotchy red belly, it flapped from side to side and gnashed its zigzag teeth against the hook. The lower jaw, jutting slightly further forward than the upper, gave it a menacing, brutish appearance, and the way it jumped on the line convinced me that if it didn't bite its way through the hook, it would leap to freedom soon enough. It wasn't that large for a piranha (Bernardino said the black ones grew to twice the size) but it was large enough. Where there was one there would be a shoal, and splashing around in an enclosed area of piranha-infested water during the dry season was something that I didn't intend to continue. Bernardino clubbed the fish over the head with the back of his machete, cut a section from its tail, used it to re-bait his hook and immediately caught another. Later he gutted both, wrapped them in large leaves and smoked them over the fire. We ate catfish that night, one that he caught later. We never tasted those two piranhas. They were eaten the next day by vultures that raided the camp while we were out.

Bernardino's mood deteriorated. It wasn't helped by the weather. Overnight it became cold and drizzly, leaving everything damp and us slightly miserable. Bernardino said this was a sure sign of the arrival of a cold 'snap' or *surazo*: a mass of frigid air blowing in from the Antarctic. *Surazos* were a common feature of the climate at this time of the year (June), each bringing several days of wintry weather. It was enough to convince our guide that he didn't really want to get out of his sleeping bag, let alone hack through bamboo thickets and wade through marshland. Added to that, Julian felt sick and said he wouldn't be coming with us to explore ahead, Charlie preferred to stay by the river and fish, and I had an insect bite on my lip that was busy swelling up to the size of a golf ball. I was the only one that felt we should go on that day. I broke open the cigarettes that were intended as gifts for people that we might meet, and gave a packet to Bernardino. I offered him chocolate pudding for tea that night and plied him with cups of hot coffee until at last by mid-morning he was ready to come with me to scout out the river ahead.

The hardest bit was just getting out of the camp. We were faced with a dense wall of *chuchillo* cane protruding out of sticky, water-logged mud. We hacked and threaded our way through, sinking up to our knees with each step. We frequently slipped, spiking our-selves on the poles we had cut. Eventually we hit dry land where the cane ended and an area of savannah began. The shoulder-high grass here was thick and matted having been flooded over and grown back since the wet season. The blades were tough and had serrated edges that cut our hands and arms. We had to push through as best we could, slashing wildly with machetes while whoever was behind trampled the grass down to make a usable path that we could get back on. Bernardino said to watch out for snakes and to really bash at the ground ahead before treading for-wards. That way any snake would be long gone by the time we arrived. Unfortunately, our thrashing around had the opposite effect on wasps. More than once we charged back the way we had come as swarms flew out at us to defend their territory. We soon learned to cut around the dead trees that dotted the *pampa*. Nearly all had nests in them.

Towards the line of the river the tree-skeletons started to become interspersed with newly grown cecropias, each no more than 10 or 15 feet high. Most had the usual multi-lobed parasol arrangement of leaves, but on one type they grew as long ovals that sprouted from offshoots forming sideways from the trunk. We soon learned to avoid these *palo diablos* – devil's poles – as Bernardino called them. Brushing against them would call out pla-toons of brown-skinned ants that stung like fire. I noticed that the leaves of the trees were untouched by caterpillars. There were no vines or lichen on the trunks. The ants provided a defence service, and in return the *palo diablos*[1] housed them in their hollow stems (which I found out somewhat painfully when I cut one down) and fed them sugar from nectaries at the base of their leaves. I had read about these 'Mullerian bodies', but I soon decided against being inquisitive and trying to find them. I was more concerned with squashing the ants that were busy surging up my sleeves; they were really quite vicious.

We carried on, our progress improving after we found a trail of sorts where some large animals, possibly capybaras, had done the hard work already and battered down a minor swathe of destruc-tion all the way to the line of the river. We had made a couple of hundred yards on this trail when we heard a rustling just ahead of us. Bernardino signalled me to stop just as a long nose poked through the grass in front, shortly followed by a pair of legs with huge, hooked claws bent inwards at the ends. Behind that was the bulk of the body – grey-brown, sheep-sized – then a huge down-turned brush tail, about the same size as the animal itself. There was no mistaking that this was a giant anteater. We stopped dead. So did the anteater. It short-sightedly raised its long nose to sniff

---

1   Fawcett wrote about these trees in his book. He called them *palo santos* – saints' poles – which made me wonder what had changed them from saint to devil over the last 90 years.

at the air, waving it from side to side, then, apparently satisfied there was no danger here, started forward again. It had virtually got to us when it caught our scent, turned, sweeping around its brush tail, and made off back down the track. We ran after it to get a closer look. Anteaters are not that fast. When it arrived at a patch of shorter grass we caught up with it easily. Bernardino grabbed its tail and pulled it to a stop. 'You draw it in your book, Simon.'

This was a situation the anteater had evidently never come across. It didn't know quite what to do. It arced its nose around to sniff first one side then the other. It knew where its assailant was but couldn't see it. Suddenly it was spurred into action, swinging round, slashing the air with its formidable-looking claws. These four-inch hooks have been known to kill jaguars. Bernardino pulled harder. He dragged the tail around and the anteater gave chase. Our guide, now in full retreat, hung on just in front as he and the anteater charged around in a full circle. I dived to the side. Bernardino let go and ran. The anteater stood still a moment, tensed. It swung its nose up and then sniffed to each side to check the air. Then it ambled away down the flattened grass trail.

'Did you see me?' said Bernardino triumphantly. 'Amigo Simon, did you draw it?' I held up my notebook on which I'd managed three or four very shaky pencil lines.

'I'll finish it off later', I promised.

❦

According to the GPS, the logjam continued for about a kilometre. Four separate river channels flowed out of the end. Each was only 10 feet or so wide. We clambered over the woodpiles and explored along the edge of the largest one for a short way until we had satisfied ourselves that it wouldn't block up again. Then we checked out the logjam. Surely in this mess there would be five or six balsa wood logs that we could build a new raft from.

When we arrived back Julian and Charlie were pig sick that they had missed the anteater. All they had done was sit around all day. Julian no longer felt as ill and had become first bored and then worried about us when Bernardino and I had been out for so long. He said he would not let the weather get him down again. We would go on tomorrow if that was what our guide thought best. He turned to Bernardino who just shrugged. 'I'm your guide. If you want to, I'll go along. I'm not bothered. I'll do whatever you say.'

'Offer him a pudding', whispered Charlie, 'It seemed to work yesterday.' Bernardino overheard.

'Pudim! Pudim!' he chirped, searching around quickly for a spoon. Julian reached deep into his rucksack to the secret place where he kept the sachets of 'instant whip' and with a flourish, pulled one out. 'Chocolate. My favourite!' Bernardino squealed with delight.

I reached over to Julian and gripped his arm before he could empty out the packet's contents. 'Tomorrow – the swamp', I said, staring Bernardino hard in the eyes.

'Tomorrow the swamp', he agreed.

⚜

Next morning we left the canoe behind and carried all of the gear to the end of the logjam. Then we set to, foraging for straight balsa logs in the piles of tree trunks that covered the river to build a new raft for the next stage of our journey. We found five suitable logs within an hour and spent the rest of the morning pulling and machete-hacking them free. We worked quickly with an obsessive sense of purpose, ignoring the clouds of *marahuisas* and the squadrons of *tabanos* (like an armoured horsefly with a bite like a stapler) which descended on us in the absence of tapir or something better to eat. Mosquito repellent didn't work as it sweated straight off. The only way we could prevent the flies from biting was by keeping fully covered up with long-sleeved shirts, long trousers and hats pulled down over our heads – all of this in the heat of the day. Worse were the wasps whose nests we kept disturbing as we manhandled the cumbersome logs through the riverside scrub. Several times we had to drop what we were carrying and sprint headlong back down our trail as angry black wasps issued out of the vegetation we'd just bashed. It was Charlie, always slowest, who bore the brunt of the stings, screaming suddenly then flailing his hands around madly as he tripped and slipped over the driftwood piles in his attempt to escape. Julian and I, hauling tree trunks between us, could do nothing more than stand and stare from up on the bank. By then we were too hot and tired to sympathize with anyone else.

When Bernardino had finished lashing together the balsas we launched off down the channel out of the logjam that we had scouted the day before. Although it looked placid, the current was surprisingly strong. It swept us along like a roller coaster ride as our stream divided again and again before finally dumping us at a dead stop in a maze of floating weeds and marshy islands. Many of these were dotted with white skeletons of trees that trailed beards of moss and luxuriant creepers. From these trees dinosaur-looking swamp birds – hoatzins – watched with red, reptilian eyes as we floated past, hissing down at us, squawking asthmatically and flapping off heavily whenever we came too close. On other trees sat 'screamers'. Grey, thickset, looking like some predatory turkey, they trumpeted out warning calls at our approach before taking off to soar high above the swamp, rather like vultures circling a kill. We punted the raft onwards, using our bamboo poles ineffectively as paddles whenever the winding channel opened up into a lagoon and the water became too deep to punt our way forward. We were still confident we would make it across this swamp. Surely all the small streams would join up again at the other side. It was just a case of following the channel with the strongest current.

The trouble was that there soon didn't seem to be any current left to follow. A mat of water hyacinth covered the surface, which even when pushed away tended to join up around the sides and back of the raft, enclosing us like a small island. More worrying were the crocodiles – black caimans, over 10 feet long – that would surface from time to time, always just ahead of us in the weeds, then ominously disappear again. Bernardino said he was confident these would cause us no problems as long as we stayed on the raft.

But what would happen though if one of us fell off or the raft sank? He declined to answer.

We made the decision fairly early on that we had to get right through this *curiche* or go back before nightfall. None of us wanted to spend the night afloat – not with the caimans. We were acutely aware of how few hours of daylight we had left. I was all for continuing, Julian wanted to go back and Charlie was still undecided. He was brooding over his numerous stings, lost in his daydreaming. Julian and I each tried to enlist him as an ally. As for Bernardino, he said it was our decision; he was just our guide.

'This is it', Charlie muttered distractedly, scooping up some water-weed on the end of his punt pole.

'Rio Undumo *finito*', said Julian, looking up at Bernardino for confirmation. 'So what's the decision?'

'I think we should go on a bit', I said. I felt that I had spent too much effort getting this far down the Undumo just to give up without really trying.

'Keep going – but there's nowhere to camp here', Julian spat angrily.

'This is choked', Charlie murmured, half to himself.

I was insistent. 'Yes', I said. 'This is choked but that's rainforest just a few hundred yards to the right.'

'Maybe we should try that other channel up there. Mm, maybe', mused Charlie, examining the weed. 'I think up here where it's just a carpet, man – it's not going anywhere. . . . What was that?'

He pointed at a patch of weed-covered water rippling where some animal, crocodile or fish had just sunk.

Julian and I tried to pole the raft backwards now, trying to get out of the grip of the hyacinth that surrounded us. The water was too deep for the poles to touch the bottom here; we had to use them as paddles and to fend off submerged branches that floated up against the balsa logs and held us in one place. Bernardino was clearly concerned. 'Give Simon the paddle!' he shouted at Julian. 'Push that thing under. No. Harder. Give it some force!'

Whilst Julian, Bernardino and I were all at one end of the raft, heaving it off a large branch that we had become stuck on, at the other end there was Charlie, still sitting down, fiddling with the weeds. He was lost in a world of his own, muttering to himself. I just caught the words, '. . . and the head of a fucking anaconda comes up here.'

We rocked the balsa logs off the snag and laboriously paddled back the way we had come to a narrow channel that we could see had a good flow of water. But even that proved useless as other streams split off it and its width narrowed to little more than that of the raft. We had to turn back again.

'This is useless', said Julian, 'I can't even remember the right way back now. Let's get out of here while it's still light.'

I was adamant. I would not be defeated. 'Look!' I pointed at the line of trees ahead. 'That's got to be rainforest – *tierra firme*. The trees there are big. It can only be a hundred yards, two hundred, no more. What do you think, Bernardino?' Bernardino was non-committal. He said it looked like rainforest for sure, but what if it was just an island and then there was more *curiche* beyond, more of the same – then what?

I was still determined to go on. One last attempt. If the others would wait there, I would try for the forest on foot. If it was dry land like I said, we could always ditch the raft and walk or wade there. I scrambled up onto one of the grassy islands and leaped across to the next and onwards until I was out of sight of the others. I made over 50 yards before I jumped short and landed in mud. I sank.

Suddenly I was up to my waist in water and mud. My legs wouldn't move. They were held solid up to my thighs. I reached out, grabbed for some roots that trailed from the island in front. Too far. As I shifted my weight, I sank deeper. Terrified, I screamed at the others to come and get me out. No one replied. I was out of their view and probably out of earshot too, held fast in sticky ooze that sucked me in further every time I moved. The mud was up to my waist now. The water was up to my chest. Panic welled up. My mind raced with thoughts of black caimans and giant anacondas, of never getting out, of dying. Here. Now.

CHAPTER SIX

Surazo

'CALM', THE VOICE inside said. 'Don't move. Lie forward. Spread your arms out.'

I let my body go limp, flopped into the water, arms stretched out in front. My chest submersed, grounding against the soft mud around my waist, my face just above the surface. Rapid breathing. I saw ripples, my reflection. My arms stretched further and, with imperceptible movement, my fingertips made contact with the dangling roots. They found purchase, applied tension, worked their way up. Soil tumbled into the water.

'Careful not to pull them away. Gently. Calm. Calm.' My legs tilted forward ever so slightly. I touched more roots, a cluster, and pulled. More soil fell. The roots slackened.

'Now!' Swinging my left arm in an arc above my head, I lurched at the islet and grasped at a clump of grass. I sank my fingers deep into the mud beneath and pulled. Seconds later I was on top, gulping air like a beached fish, shaking. For a moment I stared up at the sky watching the screamers circling, aware again of noise, a faint breeze and the sun on my face.

When I had calmed down I retraced my route back from island to island until I arrived at the raft. Julian and Charlie had scarcely noticed that I had been gone. If anything they were surprised to see me back so soon and so covered in mud. They had other things on their minds. Fish. In the middle of the raft lay a large carp, cut open diagonally across its middle, convulsing feebly.

'I got it with my machete as it swam past', Charlie enthused, re-enacting the scene. 'Dinner for tonight at least.'

'You look white', said Julian. 'What happened?' I explained. I said the swamp was impassable. I could see that now. We should get out and go back. 'That's not so easy', Julian replied. 'We don't know the way.'

'We've got the GPS. What's the problem?'

'It doesn't help us', Julian responded. 'We know the last camp's five Ks back that way.' He pointed at a line of dead trees on the horizon. It was the same view in all directions. 'But', he continued, 'we don't know which channel to take.' I followed his outstretched arm. The sun shone low over the reeds. The white trunks with their mossy beards caught the light. Three blue and yellow macaws screeched off to their night time roosts, their chests reflecting like gold in the rays.

'So, we're stuck for the night.'

Julian shrugged. 'Looks that way.'

🐚

By morning our groundsheet had sunk about an inch into the mud, and the water, squashed out of the ground, made a puddle around its edges. Charlie squatted by the lagoon with his shirt off, for once not being attacked by insects. His back was mottled with bites: blood blisters from the *marahuisas*, larger swellings where *tabanos* had pierced through his clothing.

Charlie sang under his breath. 'Feeling hot hot hot, feeling hot hot hot.

'This is the bug-free hour', he said when he noticed me. 'I timed it. Seven to eight – bug free. Then we get mosquitoes. They knock off around nine by which time the *marahuisas* are just warming up. Then there are the *tabanos* and the sweat bees. The tiny "blackies" start their shift around one, followed by the large black ones, the orange ones, then the black ones with orange legs. They all go home around six, then it's mosquito time all over again.' A flight of wood storks, white winged with leathery, pterodactyl heads glided over us and alighted in a nearby pool.

'It's amazing here', Charlie continued. 'Such fisho. Part of me wants to stay but I'm getting eaten. I reckon we have to go back. Bernie and Jules have gone to scout for the stream we came in on. Bernie reckons we could get back to Ixiamas in about four days walking. Then he wants to go back down the road to a village we passed on the way, called Tumupasa. He says there's a trail from there. So', he smiled, 'we'll be trying over the mountains like you originally planned.'

'It still doesn't help us if we haven't got the canoe though', I said, then walked back to the embers of last night's fire and tried to re-light it with some kindling shaved off one of the logs from the raft so I could cook up some porridge for breakfast.

When Julian and Bernardino arrived back a short while later, they were looking pleased with themselves. Apparently it hadn't taken long to find the way out. Wading through the long grass of the islands, they had soon found one of the blue plastic strips that we had left as markers on the way in. Then they had followed alongside the river channel until they had come to a spot that they recognized. Bernardino had dug up a nest of turtle eggs. They looked like ping-pong balls and fried up into a yolky omelette, which rose up so it had the same texture as crumpet. I put aside my principles about eating endangered species and tucked in eagerly with the others before we reloaded the raft and started the journey back. A flock of grey-headed parakeets zipped over our heads.

'Feeling hot hot hot', they screeched. 'Feeling hot hot hot.'

❦

It only took us three days to get back to Ixiamas, first on the river, then, for the last two days, pushing our way along a network of overgrown logging roads that criss-crossed the forest and open savannah closer to the town. We left much of the food back at the river, reckoning that we would walk faster with lighter loads and could always buy more later on. Still, the trek was tough and none of us voiced any objection to paying more than the odds to hire the one working jeep in town to take us to Tumupasa, where Bernardino said we would restart our expedition.

In Ixiamas (now a dead and partially boarded up place since the end of the fiesta), we received some excellent news. The canoe had arrived. 'Three gringos with rucksacks and a Bolivian?' said the keeper of the general store by the checkpoint barrier, who approached Charlie and Julian whilst they were waiting for the jeep. 'You must be them.'

He said he had been given a message from a driver from Rurrenabaque.

'Yellow and red Landcruiser – fat with sunglasses?'

'That was him', the man had answered. 'He said, if three gringos with a Bolivian arrived, I should tell them to go to Tumupasa because a canoe is waiting there for them.' The news was fantastic. I was overjoyed, though I couldn't quite believe it was true, not until I had actually seen the boat. Now we would be able to get on with the expedition as we had planned it. There would be no more of this skirting around the mountains and accessing the Madidi lower down. Now we could go right to its source.

❦

Tumupasa means 'white stone' in the Tacana language. *Tumu* is stone and *paza*, which means white, was hispanized into *pasa* at some point since Franciscan monks started a mission there at the end of the seventeenth century. The village, a line of low, adobe buildings – houses, some shops, a government office and an army post – clusters around a checkpoint on the Rurrenabaque–Ixiamas 'highway' on the north-east facing slope of the Susi ridge (which ends at Rurrenabaque). A line of jagged peaks rises up behind, cut here by a pass, through which there is a route to the Rio Tuichi and the high Andes beyond. In front,

> . . . the village looks over the forest of the central Amazonian plain,
> which at first sight, with its wide, uniform expanse and unbroken
> horizon, extending through half a circle at a distance of nearly forty
> miles, presents a startling resemblance to the open sea.

So wrote John William Evans, a British Geologist who passed
through Tumupasa in 1901 whilst leading an expedition to 'explore
the district of the Caupolican and the adjoining region to the
Northeast of the Andes of northern Bolivia'. Tumupasa was the
furthest part of his route from La Paz, a loop which took him
down the Cordillera and Rio Beni to Rurrenabaque, and then back
up the 'wide path' that led to San Jose on the Rio Tuichi, continuing up through the Serranias to Apolo. Evans was of the opinion
that this road had been in use since Inca times. In places it was
paved and there was even said to be a section where it passed
through an 'Inca' tunnel. Legend had it, amongst the villagers who
used the trail to take their cattle up to the mountains, that if a herd
was taken through, one animal always went missing here. The
tunnel was lost or grown-over now and the upper part of the track
between San Jose and Apolo had fallen out of use since new roads
had been built down to the lowlands and patterns of trade had
changed. But the section to the Tuichi was still open. It was this
route that Bernardino intended to take to get the packed-up canoe
and us into the Serranias.

⚜

Everyone was drunk in Tumupasa on the night that we arrived. At
least, the men were. Rip-roaringly, obnoxiously drunk, they clung
to each other, slobbering words of eternal friendship, and started
fights that they then forgot about the next moment. They sang
awfully, belched and farted, and made lewd suggestions to the
pretty girl of around ten who wove nimbly between the tables of
the restaurant to deposit more opened bottles of beer whenever a
hand was raised. Her mother, who ran the hostelry, stayed out of
the way at the back, frantically frying up grisly chunks of meat and
rice to feed the mob. I could see her wince each time another

empty hit the floor. For the most part her eyes stayed fixed on her cooking, though occasionally she shot reproving glances at the children from the street who popped their heads around the corner to giggle at the drunken men.

The cause for the celebration was simple. It was pay day. The men had stripped the area of its mahogany trees and had just received their cash.

I skulked low over my plate of chewy beef, reading a letter that Negro had put in with the canoe and praying that no one would come over and talk to me. There were two letters, in fact; the other was for Bernardino and was marked 'private'. He took it and went off down the street in search of 'a friend' who would read it for him while I tried to make some sense of Negro's half-Spanish, half-English scrawl, ignoring as best I could the attentions of a very drunk young man who had just sat beside me and was trying to read it too. Negro wrote that the canoe had arrived in Rurrenabaque the day after we had set off. When Chichito had returned and told him that we had started down the Undumo, he had known we would end up at Tumupasa. He suspected the Undumo became a *curiche* (he knew of other rivers in the *pampa* that did just that); this is why no one ever travelled it. And, he reasoned, Bernardino would go back to somewhere he knew. Bernardino's decision, the one he too would take, was obvious. He would take us along the old route into the Serranias, the 'Sendero Ancho' and that meant we would go to Tumupasa.

I handed the note over to Julian and started scribbling a reply.

'Where you from? You buy me a beer?' the drunken man next to me breathed in my face. 'What do you do for my country? Why are you here, my friend?' He slapped me hard on the shoulder. I lied something about not speaking Spanish and stared into my dinner plate. My new-found friend carried on for a while but eventually got bored and went away to bother a well dressed white man at a nearby table. They ended up fighting.

The situation was described to me by one of the loggers as a 'timber rush'. Demand for mahogany was surging and in places like Tumupasa, and even more so in Rurrenabaque where the main road crossed the big Rio Beni, you could earn a lot of money quickly. The sawmill at San Buenaventura was doing particularly well. Timber was floated to it down the Beni and brought by truck from the concessions around Ixiamas. This wood was then sawn into planks and shifted by lorry to La Paz. Much of it, the man supposed, would be exported.

Ironically, the rush had really started when logging had been declared illegal in the region. The large timber concessions, mainly working the forest past Ixiamas, were being forced to relocate since the area of the Tuichi and upper Madidi valleys had been inaugurated as the Madidi National Park. What had been happening since was that small, supposedly independent gangs had been going up the rivers to take out as much mahogany as possible before park guards were brought in to stop them. There was nothing new about loggers working up the Tuichi. Cutting down trees and selling the wood was the main source of cash income for many of the small-holders here. The problem was that now everyone was doing it, and to make matters worse on the forest ecosystem, the loggers were not only felling the trees but also killing a significant amount of wildlife in order to sell the meat for profit (spider monkey meat was particularly in demand). The current situation was clearly unsustainable. Some areas were already becoming 'logged' and 'hunted out' of commercially viable species, and now the loggers were moving further up the smaller, previously inaccessible tributaries, responding to an apparently insatiable demand for good quality timber. A government minister had visited the area. He had said that there would be severe penalties for anyone still cutting mahogany when he returned in five months' time. He had never returned. No one ever thought he would.

The direct implication this 'timber rush' had for us was that we could find no one willing to act as porters to carry our gear for the next stage of the journey. Everyone was either holding out for more logging work or too hungover to bother. Bernardino scoured the village. He said he knew lots of people here. Somebody was bound to help us out. His manner was strangely brusque with us. There was none of the 'Amigo Simon' familiarity that he had shown on the Undumo. I suspected it was something to do with the letter.

When he arrived back at the restaurant later that evening, looking dejected, we knew that the favours that he said he had been owed had not been paid back. It was only a day later, just as we were due to depart, that he finally found some porters. He beamed proudly as he presented the team that he had got together. I was less impressed. I'm sure this registered on my face. 'Rather young, aren't they?' I commented.

'Child labour', said Julian. It appeared we were to do the hike with little more than our cameras and the video in our 'day bags', while three youths of not more than fourteen had to carry the heavy rucksacks. I thought it smacked of exploitation. I told Bernardino, but he said not to worry; these boys were just 'young looking' – they were actually all very strong and used to this sort of thing. Besides, they were the best he could get, and with everyone being paid so well for cutting down trees they would have to do. At least, we convinced ourselves, they wouldn't have over-large loads. That job, the task of carrying the canoe skin, the poles and the paddles, went to an adult, a last-minute addition to our group called Maximo.

'Three children and the village idiot', was Charlie's reaction when Bernardino presented him to us. We stared at the chuckling apparition in baseball cap and voluminous shorts. He was probably in his thirties. It was hard to tell. He may have been younger but weathered by a life of hardship.

'Maximo and the Minimos; that's what he's brought us', Julian sniggered.

Bernardino said that Maximo had been unable to get work with the logging teams. His wife had left him for another man. Now he had no home and no belongings other than what he stood up in. He was willing, Bernardino said, to carry all of the canoe and the paddles as well.

'Carry the canoe and paddles', Maximo parroted Bernardino's words.

Bernardino carried on his by now impassioned speech, 'He

might not be very clever, or even look that powerful but he's strong like a *tigre*. You won't regret hiring him.'

Once we had re-divided the gear we set off. Without heavy packs to carry the path over the mountains was a pleasure to walk. We watched capuchin monkeys and razor-billed curassows in the trees. We talked to a villager we met coming in the opposite direction about a bushmaster snake that had made a strike at him not more than half an hour before. He held up a green plastic water bottle with venom-slimed fang marks to show us how close it had come. We met, swapped stories then continued, Julian and I taking turns to film the expedition while the boy porters nattered from under their loads and overtook us if we ever slowed down. Bernardino stayed at the back, chatting with Maximo who, with his over-sized load, was far slower than everyone else. Their conversations, I noticed, were rather one-sided. Bernardino did the talking. Maximo agreed and chuckled a lot.

By mid-afternoon we had crossed the ridge and come down to the near-dried riverbed of what in the wet season was presumably quite a wide river, but now was reduced in the dry to a puny trickle that snaked through an expanse of gravel and balsa saplings. This, Bernardino said, was the Rio Yariapo and we would be walking this way now in preference to the wide path. I knew of the Yariapo. Evans had said that it was where Tumupasa had first been founded – Santissima Trinidad de Yariapo – until it was moved over the mountains because of diseases that had struck. He had also written about a group of Christian Indians who, several years before his trip, had 'reverted to savagery' and set themselves up in the forest opposite the river's meeting with the Tuichi.

> They occasionally attacked and killed people travelling by balsa on the river, and took possession of their clothing. An expedition was sent from San Jose against them; two men were killed and the women and children were taken prisoners.

Evans rafted down the Tuichi from San Jose then tried to punt up the Yariapo. Unfortunately, he found it too shallow and so ended up walking the streambed until he reached the San Jose trail. His guides deserted him to hunt peccary in the forest. The thought struck me that if the Yariapo was downstream from San Jose, then it wouldn't be in our direction. Surely we had to go to the Tuichi's headwaters to get to the Madidi. I pointed this out to Bernardino but he brushed me off.

'It's quicker this way', he said tersely, then turned to relay new instructions to the surprised-looking boy porters, who by now seemed to be more intent on taking a rest than carrying on. 'We make three more hours before we stop to make camp', he ordered. Reluctantly (almost resentfully, it seemed), the boys finished their cigarettes, re-shouldered their packs and set off again.

৺

That night the weather turned on us. The wind got up and drove the rain sideways under our plastic tarpaulin, soaking the mosquito nets and our bedding. The temperature plummeted. Maximo and Bernardino huddled together, wrapped in Bernardino's sleeping bag. The boy porters miserably tried to share one blanket between them. By morning, they had gone. So had a bag of rice, a tin of sardines and one of our machetes.

'Well that's fucking brilliant', said Charlie when he heard the news. 'Stuck in the donga with eight loads and only five people to carry them. What are we going to do?'

'We can all carry more', I suggested. 'The loads will lighten once we've eaten some of the food.'

'There's still too much', Julian commented.

'Maximo can take what's left over. He can carry on with us', Bernardino said from the back of our shelter, putting his arm around our one remaining porter. Maximo grinned broadly and sniggered.

'Carry on', he said.

'What about him getting back?' I said. 'He has to understand he couldn't fit in the canoe. You have told him that the boat can only fit three? Four at a push, but certainly not five. It would break if we tried. As soon as the river is navigable, we will no longer need him.'

'It will not be a problem', Bernardino replied. He paused for breath and drew himself up as if to make an announcement, then faltered and mumbled something which I did not hear. Maximo gripped his arm and chuckled; a man who had come out with one set of clothes, with no mosquito net or blanket, agreeing, on the spur of the moment, to up to a week's work, at the end of which he would be left to find his own way back through the jungle. Perhaps Bernardino saw the concern on my face. 'Don't worry', he said. 'He's better with us. After all, he's got nothing to go back to.'

The weather stayed grim, as cold and dreary as Manchester in midwinter. Bernardino said it was another *surazo*. Rain fell continuously in a misty drizzle that covered everything with a layer of dampness, permeating our clothes then our bodies and sending our spirits crashing. We had nothing warm to wear and we froze, especially as we felt obliged to give whatever we could spare to Maximo. We saw no point in setting off, so we collected what dry firewood we could find, wind-proofed the shelter to an extent with cut palm fronds and sat it out. For three days. Three utterly miserable days. No sleep, no fish biting the hooks, no bush turkeys to hunt, nothing to do but sit around a fire under a plastic tarpaulin and eat our way through our rations. Julian acted as if he was ready to quit. He seemed withdrawn and hardly spoke except to construct long lists with Charlie of all the food they would eat when they got back to Rurrenabaque. Even that wore thin after a couple of days. For some reason, I felt it was up to me to keep the morale of the party up, perhaps because the search for the *Mono Rey* had been my idea.

'Fawcett had all this, you know', I said in a feeble attempt at conversation. 'Four days of cold and wet, then four more of cold and dry.' Neither Charlie nor Julian looked up from staring at the fire. 'He said there was ice on the puddles in the streets of Riberalta', I persisted. 'Some people even died of hypothermia.'

'Then you should have known it's this time of year that the *sur* comes', Bernardino snapped. 'First one on the Undumo and now another. We should never have set off.'

'I didn't notice him objecting to us paying him the money to guide us', Julian commented under his breath. Bernardino glared at him. Though Julian had spoken in English, it was clear he had understood.

𝕏

The river slowly rose. We sat and watched it. No one felt like moving. When the muddy water had reached so high that it was nearly lapping against the poles of our lean-to, I decided I had had enough. We had to do something to get our morale up, even if it just meant getting out of the jungle. We had to get moving again. The river looked deep enough now to use the canoe if it was lightly loaded. Two of us could paddle it and take a couple of the food sacks; that at least would lighten the packs of those who were left to walk. Anything, I reasoned, had to be better than just sitting around, killing time and feeling miserable.

Having inspired myself with a renewed sense of purpose, I stripped off my fire-crisped outer layers and stepped out of the snug shelter to immerse myself in the swirling drizzle. Not allowing myself to falter with the sudden cold shock, I unrolled the green, 16-foot skin out onto the sand. I left it there for a moment, watching it darken as wetness soaked in while I considered what to do next; how I would slide the elasticated aluminium poles into their slots and snap in the U-shaped cross pieces that lay spilled out along the river's edge. It was a tricky business. The poles, slimy-wet and bashed about through previous mishandling, needed an unexpected degree of force to wedge them in place. Their tension pinged them out at one end each time I set to work at the other. The structure only felt rigid when every last one had been pushed home and clicked under the line of puny, black plastic retaining clips that were riveted onto the bottom two poles. Then I stood back and admired it. The 'Mad River Canoe: 16·5', an upside down tent of green and black neoprene. It was a remarkable feat of engineering, I decided. But would it hold? I dragged it into the lapping water, held it as the frame twisted in the current. I felt it sag as Julian loaded on two rubberized sacks of food and crawled down the spars to take up the front paddling position. I pulled the boat fully into the flow and vaulted on.

Ten yards later we grounded. We got out, pulled the canoe through the shallows then set off again. Fifty yards afloat this time. Perhaps I had been over-optimistic in my assessment of the river. It was still so shallow that for much of that morning Julian and I were dragging the boat rather than paddling it. In the drizzle, we stayed cold and continually wet while the others pushed on ahead of us at a steady speed. But as the Yariapo swelled with the arrival of several feeder streams, eventually it became our turn to take the lead. We carried on for two or three river bends, then, worried that we might leave the others behind entirely, pulled up at a sand bar that looked suitable for a campsite and waited for them to catch up.

Bernardino arrived first. He bore down the beach towards us shaking the shotgun in the air. He was fuming.

'This gun is shit!' he shouted before he got to us. 'I've just had the perfect shot at a peccary. A whole herd ran out in front of me – at least ten of them. They stopped to have a look at me. I took aim and fired, and "pfzzzz". Nothing happened.' He shook the gun again and pulled out a cartridge from the breech. 'So I put in another shell and shot again and it was just the same. "Pfzzz"! No force. Like I told you when I shot that *tojo* on the Undumo – wrong sized shells. You bought the wrong size shells!'

'It's not our fault', Julian stuttered from his place in the canoe. 'We were in such a hurry at the last moment, you know. The woman in the shop said they were all right. How were we to know? We've never bought a gun before.'

'They seemed to fit in all right', I added.

'Well they're not', Bernardino snorted back. He pushed the cartridge back into the breech and wobbled it from side to side. 'Look, it's all loose. It shouldn't do that. That's why my shooting has been so crap.'

'We're cold. How about we camp here?' I suggested, trying to change the subject.

'Ugly!' spat Bernardino and stomped off down the sand.

We made camp two river bends later on a high bank above a narrow, cut-back meander. The site had been used before, presumably by loggers. The undergrowth had been cleared but the canopy trees left standing, so at least we had some shelter from the rain. Whilst Julian and I tied our tarpaulin roof between four trunks, Charlie helped Bernardino with the fire and put on some water to boil. We thought a helping of 'pudim' might go some way to get him out his mood. It felt the right time to break out the chocolate blancmange. Even Maximo had stopped smiling.

'Pudim!' announced Charlie, stirring the brown powder into the pot and smacking his lips together.

'Pudim pudim', Bernardino repeated distractedly and downed his mug of coffee.

I noticed he had collected several empty shotgun cartridges from around the camp. He was using my penknife to slice off the percussion caps. He pushed the plastic tubes that were left over from several of our undersized shells, and tied them round with a sliver of palm leaf.

'I won't be coming to the Madidi', he said quietly without looking up. Julian and I stared. Charlie, who hadn't quite heard or realized the implications of what our guide had just said, asked,

'What?'

Bernardino stood to face all three of us now. 'You've said yourself that your boat won't take four people, so I won't come', he said. 'I'll take you as far as the Tuichi, then Maximo and I will take some food and walk back. You three can walk to the Rio Hondo and get into the Serrania from there by yourselves.'

'But the Hondo is nowhere near the Madidi', I pointed out. 'It comes from a different Serrania entirely. You've been bringing us the wrong way. You had no intention . . .'

Bernardino cut me off. He spoke slowly as if drained of emotion. 'There are *Mono Reys* in the Serrania Chepite at the headwaters of the Hondo. That's why I was taking you there. The

Madidi is too far. We couldn't get there. We haven't got the porters or enough food.'

'He's right', said Julian, who was checking the map. 'With our present lack of progress, we're getting nowhere.'

I turned to Bernardino. 'But you're our guide.'

'That's why I'll take you as far as the Tuichi', Bernardino answered. 'Please, Amigo Simon', he added, 'there is something else I have to do.'

'Let him go', said Charlie, looking to me then Julian. 'We don't need him.' I shook my head.

'Not the Tuichi. No way.' I was adamant. 'That's not far enough. We can't get into any Serrania from there. The Hondo – or else you don't get the rest of your money.'

Bernardino glared. 'But that's another week.'

'And we hired you for ten', I snapped back. The guide looked to Charlie then Julian for support. But there was no eye contact, just embarrassed silence.

'The Hondo then', Bernardino agreed. 'Then I go home.'

CHAPTER SEVEN

The King Monkey

THE UPPER Rio Hondo. Slanting rays of late-afternoon sunlight play over the rippling water and catch on the
butterflies and clouds of gnats that hang over its surface. I
stand knee deep, poised with my machete ready to strike at a shoal
of trout-sized fish – *sabalo* – that are slowly pushing their way up
against the current. Even though they are close, not much more
than an arm's length away, I know that hitting one is more difficult
than it looks. You have to judge the refraction of the light from the
fish as it travels from the water to the air and aim above where the
fish appears to be. When you strike you have to hit straight. Any
angle between the blade and the water can make the blade veer off
its line. It's all too easy to hit your own leg. Until the shoal comes
closer for a clear swing, I know I have to stay perfectly still and
ignore the *marahuisas* that land on my body and legs, each leaving
a tiny speck of blood on the skin before it flies away.

I was only fishing, I reflected, because I felt guilty about not
doing my fair share of work. I was worried the others might be
annoyed at the amount of time I spent sketching and painting
whilst they were trying to catch fish for us to eat. To show willing
I should really have gone a couple of hundred yards downstream to
the deep pool where Charlie and Julian were trying to hook catfish,

but I couldn't be bothered to get dressed and smear myself with insect repellent again. My clothes were lying over some rocks nearby. I didn't want to get them wet now they were nearly dry. I thought I'd just slip out in my boxer shorts to the shallows close to camp and machete a *sabalo* as it swam past. There were so many in the river that it didn't look difficult.

A rustle of leaves and heavy footfalls by the opposite bank switched me into alertness. At the edge of my vision a large, brown shape waded tentatively through the shallows: a tapir, not more than 50 feet away, closing. I turned my head slightly, ever so slowly, to get a better look. It was small – about the size of a Shetland pony, maybe a young one. Its coat was a blonde-cinnamon, greyish underneath. It lifted its head and turned to cross some shingle in the middle of the river. I whistled 'fyeet', the catcall that I had heard Bernardino make when tapirs had come close before. The animal stopped, pricked up its ears and turned to face me. It snorkelled up its nose to sniff the air, baring its front teeth.

'Fyeet', the tapir whistled back, the note starting low, rising high then cutting off suddenly. I imitated. It came closer, its short trunk wiggling frantically as it tried to catch my scent. I called again. The tapir moved a step or two nearer, less certain now. It moved its head from side to side as if looking for ways of escape. Perhaps I didn't sound enough like a tapir to induce it to approach any further, but it still wasn't sure. It held its ground. I briefly toyed with the idea of making a dash back to the camp for my camera. The light was perfect. If I was quiet enough, I might be able to make it there and back before the tapir lost interest. I rejected the idea.

'Some things are not meant to be photographed, just experienced', I told myself.

I tried whistling a couple more times but my calls just weren't alluring enough. The tapir turned and ambled off back into the forest where it had come from.

Two days without Bernardino and we were on a high. We had paddled the canoe up the Rio Hondo, dragging it up numerous rapids, until we were now at a point where our goal, the green-grey ridge of the Serrania Chepite, stretched right across our horizon. It appeared to stick out from above the treetops ahead of us as if it were some cut-out backdrop, and in the crisp, clear air, left in the wake of the *surazo*, the sunlight picked out details on the ridge face – rain-worn gullies, trees with purple blossom, sheer faces of orange-streaked rock – where there had just been haze before. Within a day we would be there, be at a point where we could start exploring those ridges, where, of anywhere we had been so far, we might find the *Mono Rey*. A sense of expectation infected all three of us. We felt liberated from the bad weather and our bad guide. We felt we were on the verge of some great discovery.

By the time Bernardino had guided us to the Hondo we were glad to be rid of him. Guided! He had taken us for four arduous days, cross-country, up and over a series of vine-tangled hills that separated the Hondo from the Tuichi. He had said the forest here was so *feio* – ugly – because of storms that had blown down many trees ten or so years before. There were no trails to follow and so we had had to machete-cut the whole way. Lugging the canoe and the food sacks, our progress had been dispiritingly slow – four or five miles in a whole day. Bernardino had rejected our suggestions of following the ridge tops where the covering of small, wiry palm trees made the going marginally easier. He was our guide; he knew best, he had said. He had made us travel in a straight line. Our rucksacks had tangled in nearly every thicket. We had nearly sliced each other a number of times with the machetes as we had tried to cut ourselves free. And all Bernardino could do was to sit down.

'*Feio*. We can't carry on', he had said at every obstruction. Julian or I would point out the compass direction we had to go and push and hack on ahead until Bernardino had been shamed into following. He hadn't even taken us to the right river. He would have left us at some unmarked stream until I took its co-ordinates with the GPS and pointed out that it wasn't the Hondo.

'I have got you to a river. What more do you want?' he had shouted back at me.

When we had finally arrived the next day we were glad that he was quitting and surprised when he whined that he wanted to carry on with us now. We had given him and Maximo the money we owed them, plus some food and fishing gear for their return journey. We had even broken out one of the precious 'pudims' for our last night together.

Since then we had made two days upstream, rowing the deeper pools and just as often pulling the canoe up the water-slides of pebbles that accompanied each rise in the terrain. Rather, Julian and I had paddled and pulled. Charlie had spent his time walking alongside, casting a shiny lure out at the salmon-sized *mamore* that shoaled at every rapid. So far, he hadn't been lucky.

The paddle and drag routine had been going fine until the second afternoon when we had misjudged the current at a rise in level where the river cut a deep 'V' notch down an abrupt gradient. Charlie and Julian had been pulling from the front and I had been guiding the canoe from the back. I had slipped and the boat had swamped. The force of the water had been so strong that it had momentarily bent the frame like a banana until we had managed to unclip and pull out all the luggage. Several bags of oats and rice had become soaked. We emptied them out on some rocks to dry, but all that had happened was that they had attracted swarms of sweat bees. Now the food, about three weeks' worth, according to Julian, was ruined.

However, the loss of the oats and rice didn't demoralize us. We agreed it wouldn't affect our plans, at least not if Charlie could actually catch a fish once in a while. 'I had four hook-ups today', Charlie argued back, fending off my jibes over his bowl of soggy rice (with bees taken out) that night.

'Why don't you use a thicker line?'

'It wouldn't be fair', he explained. 'The trick is you have to catch the biggest fish on the lightest line. That's true sport fishing.'

'Sod sport. Just catch the fish. We need to eat', said Julian.

'No worries', Charlie grinned back. 'I'll shoot a fish if we get that desperate. One of those shoals of *mamore*. I couldn't miss.' But he did. With eight of our shotgun shells. It was the one thing that worried me, a doubt that gnawed at the edge of my excitement; how our supplies were going down.

⚜

The fact that we were no longer going to the Madidi had not upset me as much as I thought it would. With the toughness of the trek over to the Rio Hondo, I hadn't had time to consider it. Not that there really was a choice about the change of route anyway. We could either go to the Hondo with Bernardino (what promised to be a narrow and, according to the map, mountain-enclosed river with the possibility of seeing a *Mono Rey* in the Serranias at the head-waters) or we could go back and find another guide to take us to the Madidi. We all acknowledged that this could take weeks, and Negro's brother Irgen, the only other person we knew of with expe-rience of the Serranias, had 'gone jungle' (to quote Charlie). Consequently, any more time spent in Rurrenabaque would most likely be fruitless. We did not consider continuing up to the water-shed of the Madidi without a guide. That looked altogether more difficult (and potentially dangerous) than trying the Hondo. On the Hondo, it would merely be a straight there-and-back journey. We would take the canoe as far as we could into the Serrania Chepite, make a base camp, explore round for signs of the *Mono Rey* and then canoe back. Our map showed that the river ran into the Beni, and once we were there we could just float with the current to Rurrenabaque. The fact that we would be travelling without a guide for this next stage was a cause for some trepidation, but as it all looked fairly straightforward, we were more excited than worried.

It was too unknown for us to consider travelling the Madidi without a guide. The region on our map was much more vaguely marked than the Hondo, and we could see no obvious route back to civilization once we had tackled the headwaters. It was clear that it would involve a portage to get to the river and probably another to get back to a road at the end. We weren't prepared to make two lengthy treks through unmapped forest without someone who at least had more experience of the terrain than we did, even if it was unlikely that they had been to that actual area themselves. As Bernardino continually pointed out, our change in plan made little difference as far as looking for the *Mono Rey* was concerned. He said the apes were in all the Serranias; you just had to climb high enough and be very lucky – or unlucky – depending on how you looked at it. Most of the encounters he had heard about were when people had had their camps wrecked, and that, he said, was not a good time to go pointing a camera in the face of an angry, two-metre tall ape. Charlie said he doubted we would find one in any case.

'Even if it isn't just a myth – what's the likelihood?'

'Bernardino did say there were lots', I replied. 'So we might have a chance. But then again, he does often just say what we want to hear', I conceded, reacting in advance to the look of derision that was starting to spread across Charlie's face.

Julian was still imagining an attack by giant apes. 'Think of it. It would be unreal', he said distractedly. 'We should give it a go at least. We could leave some meat out or something.'

'We'd have to get some first', I said; I was thinking about our current lack of success with the gun or with the fishing.

'I'll bag us some fisho in no time.' Charlie winked at me, casting an imaginary lure far over Julian's head.

'I'll believe it when I see it', I mumbled *sotto voce* as he cast out again and started reeling back in.

❦

The next morning any question of Charlie's angling prowess was swept away completely.

'What a vicious capture!' he shouted out as his line pulled taut and a dark shape whizzed across the shallows, its arched back and dorsal fin fully out of the water, sending out a wake that was almost worthy of a small power boat.

For fifteen minutes he had been playing the line, bringing in the fish a little then letting the reel spin out some slack each time it tried to get away. His rod was nearly bent double with the strain at times. He always got this far and then the line broke or the 'almost-catch' slipped the hook. I had learned never to get that interested or involved. I continued sketching the scenery. Julian was playing with the controls of the video. It was only when the fish began to tire and Charlie looked as though he might actually pull it in that either of us took any notice.

I had to admit it looked big – 70 centimetres at least. But I was totally unprepared for how refraction of the light had disguised how deep its body really was. When Charlie reached in to haul it out by the gills I was almost as shocked as him to find that what had looked like a salmon was in fact deep and oval and shaped more like a great dinner platter.

'Check it out. A *pacu*!' I ran over to admire. The fish looked like a giant piranha. It had thumbnail sized scales that glistened like wet slates, yellow eyes and a battery of great, flat-edged teeth. 'For crunching nuts', Charlie explained gleefully. ' It must have thought the red lure was a fruit as it plopped into the water in front of it. I've heard these things will bite at anything coloured. Curiosity, I reckon. Food for four days maybe', he mused, as he laid the fish almost reverentially onto the sand. 'We'll not be going hungry now, boys.' Then he was off again, an explosion of utter joy at having caught the fish of his life.

'Holy Root!

'Shit!

'Shit. Shit. Shit!

'What a beast! Look at it! It's huge!

'This one is going to get into *MODERN FISHING*!'

After he had calmed down, Charlie did as he always did whenever he was particularly pleased with himself, or particularly sad or tired – in fact, any excuse would do. He pulled out his little bag of marijuana and rolled himself a joint. For paper he used pages from the Uruguay section of the *South American Handbook*, because he said that Uruguay was dead boring – 'Just flat and full of cows'. So far he had smoked his way through most of the country and was well through the section on Montevideo. He said it was a form of subliminal learning. 'Discovering South America through inhalation', was how he put it.

About an hour later, just as we were coming right up to the first ridges of the Serrania in the canoe, Charlie announced that he had lost his fishing rod. He began rummaging around the stores in the boat and decided it must be back at '*Pacu* Pool'. He looked to Julian and me, perhaps hoping one or both of us would volunteer to come with him. Neither of us met his gaze.

'It's not worth taking the canoe back', I said. Julian nodded. The thought of dragging it all this way upstream again was just too much. Nor did either of us feel much like walking back with Charlie. It was his fishing rod, not ours.

'If he loses it because he's smoking too much, it's his own problem', Julian whispered to me.

'I know. I'll go back on my own', Charlie sighed, sliding his machete out of its place amongst the rucksacks. 'You two go on a bit. I'll catch up.' He edged a step away from the canoe, started turning for the river's edge.

'We'll get up a few more river bends and make a camp. See you later', said Julian. Charlie sloshed away through the shallows. 'Take care. Light a fire or something if for any reason you don't get back before dark. We'll find you in the morning.'

※

He turned up a couple of hours later. By that time we had made camp. Besides his rod, he had also found his camera. This time Julian and I laughed off his leaving things behind as simple forgetfulness. But it was to happen again. Several times. We would settle down for a rest, Charlie would smoke a joint and one or two hours later he would announce that he had lost something. Us going ahead and Charlie catching up later was to become something of a routine. 'We'll carry on two or three more bends', we would end up saying. 'Catch us up. Light a fire if it gets dark before you get to us.' We got to the point of shepherding him during rest stops in the canoe, treating him almost as if he were a child. 'Now, have you got your rod? You haven't left your camera, have you?'

Mornings would be particularly bad because of Charlie's habit of smoking a spliff before breakfast. On several occasions, he even got into the boat facing in the wrong direction. He would sit in his place in the middle facing Julian or me, whoever was at the back that day. 'There's something wrong here', he would mumble and slowly ease himself around to face forward.

Charlie didn't have very far to walk back to find us that day. Shortly after he had left we reached a series of rapids and small waterfalls where the river burst out between the two sides of the Serrania. Clearly this would be extremely difficult to drag the canoe over, so we floated back to a thin strip of sand (on the right-hand side of the river, heading upstream) where we made camp and considered how we could get further.

Ahead we could see that the valley narrowed more or less into a gorge. Great spurs of weather-blackened rock jutted out across the river. Boulders, some as big as cars and small houses, almost blocked it in places. The slopes above were thickly forested, this cover thinning out (on our side of the river) as the ridge reached a vaguely triangular summit. On the other side the terrain was much steeper and less vegetated. The trees and soil had slid away in places, leaving bare rock which, over the years, had become dusted with a fine stubble of light green epiphytes or possibly moss; from this distance there was no way of telling.

Up there was surely the stunted palm forest where the *Mono Rey* was said to live. But how would we go about finding one? As Julian and I sat around waiting for Charlie to turn up it struck me that we had been so preoccupied with getting here that we had never fully considered the actual hunt for the *Mono Rey*. We knew we could climb up into the Serrania, take several days' worth of food and search around for broken palms and claw marks. But it hardly seemed likely that we would find anything that way, even if we knew what to look out for. I suppose I had been holding out for some sort of encounter like de Loys had had – screaming apes bearing down on us, shaking branches, looking fierce. I had imagined myself transposed into de Loys's place. Julian would video it all. My daydreams had a grainy, unfocused quality about them, almost as if they were snatches of his film. I always knew it was highly unlikely that any of this would happen. For a start, *Mono Reys* might not even exist (I was by no means convinced they did), and secondly, even if they did and we got to the places where they lived, what were the chances of finding one? In over four weeks of travel how many tapirs had we seen so far? Three. Jaguars? None. And yet we knew they must be there. In the forest you could be within ten yards of any animal, but unless it chose to show itself you would never know.

'Stick with the river', we decided. 'At least it's open. Delay the decision to go into the ridges. Certainly until we know what lies ahead.'

❦

Charlie was limping when he returned. 'Guys, I can't carry on', he said. 'It's this constant in and out of the water. It's like I'm treading on knives.'

'Fungal infection?' Julian asked. Charlie nodded. 'Why don't you take your plimsolls off once in a while then?'

'And have the *marahuisas* bite my feet? Not a chance. They swell up, then I can't get my "volleys" back on.' He slumped onto the sand and started rolling himself a joint. 'You two go and look for the *Mono Rey*. Get its balls for a trophy. Nail 'em to the fridge door. But I'll not be coming.'

'Your feet', Julian suggested.

'Hell no!' Charlie retorted. 'I'm going fishing. Did you see the size of those *pacu* in that deep pool over there? And there are *mamore* too. At least a metre long. You go off and do the explorer stuff. Find yourselves a big fucking ape. I'm going to bag me some fisho.'

❦

Next morning, Julian and I left Charlie fishing and set off to explore into the gorge with the canoe and just a day-bag of equipment (cameras, the video, my sketching stuff) each. We paddled as far as we could upstream before the wash from the rapids prevented any further progress, then started shifting the boat between and over the boulders that piled up along the river's edges. We upturned the hull, taking turns to stand in the river and hold it up, while whoever was unencumbered would clamber onto the rocks and pull the boat over from there. Eventually we reached a calm and open stretch of water where we could launch off again.

Beyond the cliffs the gorge opened up into a steep-sided bowl, enclosed by jagged-topped mountains. At the far end an enormous boulder had plugged the apex of two interlocking spurs and the river spurted out each side of this, tumbling 20 feet or so into a deep plunge pool. A base rumbling resounded throughout the valley; at the lowest threshold of the hearing range, it was more of a feeling than a sound.

We beached the canoe on some fine white sand at the edge of a deep pool that teemed with *pacu* and *mamore*, and picked our way through the boulders towards the cascade, wading the river's edge where the rocks were too steep or slippery to climb. In places there were gaps which had obviously been used by animals getting to the river. There were the prints of paca and brocket deer and, in great abundance, tapir. Their 'runs' of broken vegetation extended back up the valley sides on gradients so steep it was difficult to credit that such an ungainly animal could ever use them. Predators had also been here. There were the claw-retracted pug-marks from cats of three distinct sizes. Some, little larger than a domestic cat's, were perhaps jaguarundi or oncilla. Larger prints were from pumas or ocelots, and the biggest were jaguar without a doubt. One set of paw marks were the size of my hand. Judging from the lack of weathering and the remains of dew in the shaded parts, they had been made that morning.

'*El Tigre*. He's the king of this valley', commented Julian. 'He might even be basking on one of those boulders now.'

We had to see what came next, we decided; find out if it would be possible to continue on the river above the twin waterspouts. When we got to the cliffs at the end of the basin we started to climb, shinning up a fallen tree trunk then scrambling over bare rock until we reached a patch of vegetation where at least there was something to grip onto. The trees here were straggly and poorly anchored into what soil had built up in the crevices; many of our handholds pulled away as we slithered on our bellies over to an edge which, through the leaves, provided a view of sorts to what lay ahead. Easier terrain possibly. The valley widened slightly and there appeared to be enough shore at the bottom to walk or drag the canoe along through the white water patches of the river. Both Julian and I were tempted to investigate further. We clambered over the edge and lowered ourselves down the rock face there until we agreed it would be foolhardy to continue. The thought of falling and sustaining an injury where there would be no way of getting back shook some sense into us. We decided to 'play safe', return to camp and tell Charlie about what we had found. We climbed back over the spur and set off through the forest, hoping to contour around until we could find an easy route down to the canoe.

Though the slope was steep and dropped away alarmingly at times, there were plenty of straight, thin trunks for handholds and we made rapid and quiet progress. We were so stealthy, in fact, that we were right in the midst of the monkeys by the time we noticed them or they us. Suddenly there was a 'crash' in the canopy and debris showered down as something swung through the leaves above. I scrambled up the slope to get a better view. There was more movement in the branches and a shower of bark flakes as long limbs flailed out and caught the trunk I was holding for support, causing it to flex slightly then spring back as the creature immediately jumped away, landing on a low horizontal branch and looping a prehensile tail around it. It was a spider monkey – a big male. Long-haired and muscular, it was one more powerful-looking than any I had seen previously.

'Just look at its muscles', whispered Julian.

The monkey swung around to face us, crouching low with its body tensed and its jaw held slightly open so we could just make out its teeth. It bobbed its head low and bellowed out a throaty cough call. 'Owk. Owk, owk.'

Julian imitated the way he had seen Bernardino do. The call was answered at once by five or six others, a sudden commotion as black shapes leaped and scrambled into the upper canopy, while others, just as big as the first, joined him in guard position in the low branches above and around us. I readied my camera, pulled the zoom into focus on one of the pink-black faces, narrowing the field of view until the monkey's body filled the frame. It was over three feet long (I judged) from head to rump. The coarse, black hair was long and shaggy; above its head, it stood up in a distinct coif.

'Simon!' Julian's shout startled me and I jerked back as something hit my arm hard, nearly knocking the camera out of my hand, and thudded into the ground beside me. I glimpsed a branch, which must have been nearly ten feet long, bounce and crash into a clump of ferns as more sticks showered down. One caught my face and drew blood. Above me the canopy shook with enraged monkeys. The air was filled with their barking. I saw Julian skid past me down the slope and I ran after him.

When we had descended to what we thought was a safe distance I inspected my bruised arm and wiped the blood from the small cut on my cheek. In some ways the actions of these angry spider monkeys had been just like those of the 'apes' that had attacked de Loys, 'screaming, gesticulating, breaking branches and waving them like weapons'.[1] At least, I reflected, these ones had

---

[1] '*criant, gesticulant, cassant des branches et les maniant commes des armes*' – from Georges Montandon's recounting of de Loys's experiences.

not thrown excrement at us; I knew this was also typical aggressive behaviour. Why, I wondered, had de Loys and his friend George Montandon, the French anthropologist who persuaded him to publish the story, been so convinced that the animals that attacked him were apes rather than some new tail-less form of spider monkey? Perhaps it was because Montandon wanted to use de Loys's discovery as evidence of the parallel evolution of great apes in the New World. The existence of a South American ape fitted in nicely with his 'Ologenic theory of evolution', which argued that the more advanced hominids, and ultimately *Homo sapiens*, had evolved over the whole of the Earth from a number of parallel ancestors. For that theory to work 'Loys' Ape' had to be an ape, not a spider monkey. Rather hopefully, Montandon even went as far as to give the animal an anthropoid classification when he named it *Ameranthropoides Loysi* in honour of his friend. He cited three pieces of evidence to support his claims; the lack of a tail, the 32 teeth (the same number found in Old World apes) and the large size, which de Loys had measured as 1.57 metres. According to Montandon, this could be corroborated by comparing the animal in the photograph with the 45-centimetre standard size oil crate on which it was sat. Consequently, *Ameranthropoides Loysi* was roughly the same size as a large chimpanzee or an orangutan.

Yet all the remaining evidence pointed to 'Loys' Ape' being a spider monkey, even down to the absence of thumbs and the elongated clitoris that dangled between its legs – details peculiar to the genus *ateles* or spider monkeys. Although Montandon and de Loys thought otherwise, the animal in the picture looked like a spider monkey and, as for its size, Montandon's detractors argued that the standard crate that the corpse was sitting on was missing a plank, thus making the monkey appear larger. If this were true, it would have put the 'ape's' height at little more than a metre, large for a monkey, but hardly orang-utan size. The tail? Maybe that was just missing or out of camera shot. Without any part of a specimen to examine, just a photograph, the critics remained unconvinced. Several years later in the 1930s a large subspecies of spider monkey with a light blaze on its forehead[2], similar to the markings of the ape in the picture, was discovered close to where de Loys had had his notorious encounter. With this new evidence it seemed that the 'ape' story was finally discredited.

Maybe that was why de Loys never published the photograph and the story of the ape attack at the time of the expedition (1917–20). It was 1928 when Montandon brought it to light, and even he commented at the end of his paper on the possibility of the 'ape' being a giant form of *ateles*. Maybe if he had stuck with that, rather than using it to further his own theories of human evolution, he might have been taken seriously. As it was, the critics said that all de Loys had found was a spider monkey, maybe a big one they conceded, but not an ape and certainly nothing new.

As the spider monkeys had retreated up rather than downhill, Julian and I were little inclined to follow them, especially if that involved having things thrown at us again. While I pulled out a bottle of water and a packet of biscuits, Julian rewound the video and reviewed his footage through the black and white monitor in the eye-piece.

'Did you see the shoulders on those males? Powerful', he remarked. 'Those *marimonos* were bigger than any we've seen before, weren't they?'

I nodded. 'It's a shame they had tails or we would have really been onto something', I said. 'Even so, I know it's probably just wishful thinking, but it might be worth checking out if they really are something different when we get back. Who knows? We might have found a new species', I added hopefully, daydreaming how my discovery could be called *Ateles Chapmani*, 'Chapman's Spider Monkey', or even *Ameranthropoides Chapmani*, if whoever adjudicated on the naming of animals decided it was ape-like enough.

2 *Ateles Belzebuth*, the white-bellied spider monkey.

Julian finished reviewing the film and handed me the camera. 'The video footage isn't much good', he shrugged. 'Too much contrast. No sense of scale.'

No evidence. I could sympathize with de Loys on that. We finished the biscuits and headed back down hill to where we had left the canoe. Close by was a large rock, from the top of which we could scan around the entire gorge. The afternoon was wearing on and I knew we had to be getting back soon before the light failed, but I couldn't resist another look. I climbed to the top and tried to take it all in. Above the roar of the falls and the hiss of the rapids, I could make out the metallic squealing of a pair of toucans across the valley. Several pairs of red and green macaws were flying high overhead, their squawking almost lost amongst the other sounds. I stared at the triangular peaks ahead, at the wall of rocks and the white water at either end of this section of the river, and wondered what animals would come down to drink tonight. They might be on their way already, the tapirs and pumas, probably '*El Tigre*' himself. Walled in against the outside world, this gorge was such a timeless place. It felt like it could have been like this for thousands, millions of years. Some great jaguar must have basked in the sunshine on this very rock. I imagined him casting his eyes over the forest and the boulders and the raging river, and I imagined down on the shingle, just in front of where the twin waterspouts burst into the valley, a group of shaggy, man-sized apes. If the *Mono Rey* existed, I decided, then it ought to be here.

CHAPTER EIGHT

Leaving Charlie Behind

'ALL QUITE WEARY and tempers are flagging', Julian said in his video diary. 'We're crammed in together and you have to spend that much time close to people.

'It gets a bit heated at moments', he added with typical understatement. 'Charlie's a great guy but he's really laid back and there are times when you just have to be on the ball. You say "Charlie – pull, push!" It can be a bit difficult.

'Simon, on the other hand, is very hyper and he'll throw tantrums. Quite often he might blame Charlie or me for something when it's just something that happens. The boat's going to tip over or water's getting in or something like that . . .

'But that's the thing. The heat, the flies – the *marahuisas* are biting the whole time. We're worried about food. Half the time we're running out of milk. We're worried if we've got enough sugar. Food becomes everything. It becomes so important that you just think about "what am I going to eat today? Are we going to have enough food for the rest of the trip?"

He paused momentarily and looked straight to the camera once more. 'Still, it's fantastic to be here. It's just that we get these highs and lows . . .'

The video cut.

On trips like ours, morale is *the* vital factor. When you are travelling through 'unknown' wilderness where there is no chance of a quick and easy return, your state of mind, your eagerness to go forward, to achieve, is probably the most important determinant to your success or failure. When things are going well and your spirits are high you feel you can achieve anything. You can drag the boat up the rapids. You can climb into the Serranias and find the *Mono Rey*. You can suffer the hundreds of insect bites and the lousy food. And it is all worth it. But if your morale wavers then you are sunk. The itching from the bites becomes insupportable. You no longer see why you should have to suffer constantly feeling dirty and not sleeping properly. You feel miserable and you lose the will to carry on. Your mood flips from one extreme to the other, triggered by insignificant incidents. The loss of your 'favourite' spoon or someone putting more than his fair share of sugar in his coffee (inevitably Charlie) becomes more important even than when the gun accidentally goes off beside your head. You argue over who is not paddling enough and who is paddling too much, then you argue over who started all of this bickering.

'Jungled out', was how Julian put it.

Charlie said we were '*Marahuised* to the Max'.

Things slid when we made the decision to go back. With Charlie's feet the way they were and much of the food soaked and ruined, it was logical to return now. But how I resented it. The idea of canoeing down to the Beni just when I felt we might be within reach of discovering the *Mono Rey* made me seethe. We were faced with a week, perhaps two, of paddling the river without any real point other than to finish the trip, and I think it was this lack of any clear aim that led to the breakdown of the three of us as a 'team', and us acting the way we did. Charlie had caught his monster fish and was content just to be going back. So was Julian, as far as I could tell. And me? I had to abide with the group decision.

This was one of those bits of the expedition we just had to do, one of those unglamorous parts that inevitably takes the bulk of the actual time, the travelling between stages and the eventual return home. Seemingly without purpose other than to get you some-where, these journeys and what happens during them are ultimately as significant to any trip as the quest that leads you there in the first place.

※

We only stayed at the gorge for three nights. On the fourth morn-ing we set off downriver. We rode the fast water out the Serrania in one thrilling day of rapids and roller coaster excitement. Then the Hondo flattened out and so did our mood.

In his video diary, which I sneakily watched one afternoon while he was off fishing with Charlie, Julian summed up the tension that was growing between us.

'It's like confinement', he said to the camera. 'Tensions are strained. Simon is manic. He keeps on shouting at us "Wah! Be careful with my canoe. Paddle. Do this. Do that'. Charlie, on the other hand, is so laid back he's almost horizontal. We have to shep-herd him to the canoe in the mornings, just in case he leaves something behind. I don't know which of them is worse.'

I switched the solar panels back onto 'charge' and carefully made sure the precious camcorder and all of its leads were exactly how Julian had left them. I was fairly sure he wouldn't mind me viewing what he had filmed but I still didn't want him finding out. Julian was so bloody even-tempered. He never showed his feelings, not like Charlie and me. We would bicker for hours like an ill-suited married couple. Julian would just take it in, say something sensible about the state of the river and laugh at Charlie's David Attenborough impressions. I knew the way I was acting was get-ting to both of them. I knew how unreasonable my pleas to conserve food sounded, and the way I'd over-react if either of them got into the canoe clumsily. I could see how they talked freely with each other when I wasn't around. It was like some chemical imbalance and I could do nothing about it. Julian was so perfect. I was almost glad when he really cocked things up.

It started with his over-enthusiastic attempts at hunting from the boat. We rounded a river bend to see five Alsatian-dog-sized animals swimming across ahead of us. Several others were already climbing the mud bank on the other side.

'Capybaras', said Charlie at the front.

'No. Tapirs', I guessed wildly. I revised my opinion. 'Peccaries.'

Seeing a herd of peccaries crossing a river was something I had dreamed about. Coming across a herd is said to be a real adrenaline experience, exciting and potentially dangerous. First you smell their stale sweat odour, then, as you get nearer, you hear the clacking of their tusks as they snuffle en masse through the leaf litter for fruit, edible roots, small animals – anything that takes their interest. Their herds can be a hundred strong and of all the large animals in the Amazon, white-lipped peccaries (the larger of the two species) are the ones most likely to be hostile. Being charged by a 40-kilogram boar is not such a rare experience. They can cut a person up badly with their tusks and often the only way of escape is to climb a tree. Even then, peccaries have been known to wait around at the bottom or even dig around the roots to cause the tree to topple.

As we floated closer, we made out the pale neck band that showed these to be the smaller 'collared' type; a small herd, only ten or so strong. Still, it was a herd of peccaries, something we hadn't seen before. Charlie and I were thrilled. We lifted our paddles, allowing the canoe to float with the current while we extracted our cameras from the 'dry bags' and lined up for some good photos. We didn't notice Julian behind us, aiming the gun – not until he let loose a shot that nearly blew my head off. At least, that's how it felt. The end of the barrel must have been alongside my ear as the gun went off. I felt a blast of pressure, so loud that my head reeled as if I had been hit. It left my ear ringing for hours afterwards. Charlie fared little better. He later said he felt something whooshing past his head, the pellets he presumed. He spun around in his place.

'What the fuck was that for? You idiot! You could have blown our heads off.' Julian was silent. We had never seen Charlie genuinely angry before. Julian mumbled some response. 'Any fool could see they were too far away!' Charlie yelled at him.

I clutched my ringing ear and pointed out that they'd gone now anyway.

Julian's second and more serious mistake was with his steering of the canoe. It happened at a short section of rough water as the level shelved down a sharp right-hand bend. Julian lined the boat up badly and wrapped us around a tree stump that was sticking out of the water. In his indecision about which way to go around, we hit side on. Water flooded in. The canoe folded. I screamed at the others to get out and jumped over the side, the current, waist deep, pulling away my legs as I tried to push the hull off the snag. I could see the 'dry bags' and one of the oars swept into the wave that was gushing over us. The bags caught as the straps they were tied on with pulled tight, while the paddle – my paddle – washed away. Julian plopped over the side, then Charlie, and, with its load suddenly lightened, the boat lurched forwards off the log. Charlie and Julian both caught hold of it. I set off after the paddle, splashing through the shallows, diving into the deeper water at the bend. My last step as I launched off was so very nearly disastrous. A stingray shot forward from beside my foot. Maybe it lashed out with its tail spike. By the time I fully realized what had happened, I had been swept around the bend and was clutching onto my lost paddle, swimming for the shore.

When I got back to the others they had beached the mangled canoe and were emptying the bags out to see what had got wet. The food, now down to one sack full, had survived. All of Julian's stuff was still dry. So was mine, apart from my rucksack and some clothes which had been in it. They would dry quickly in the sun. Charlie had not been so lucky, however. His camera, which had been at the bottom of my sealed 'dry bag', was soaked. The bag must have had a puncture. Everything at the top – my camera and sketching equipment – was fine. Only Charlie's beloved old Nikon was ruined. He was nearly in tears. He looked utterly distraught. He stared at Julian accusingly.

'It's your fault', his eyes said.

I started dismantling the bent canoe frame, trying to assess the damage. My precious canoe, the one I had spent all my money on, looked wrecked. The hull poles were all creased. Sure, they could be bent back, but what strength would they have then? What if they didn't fit together any more? I tried to shut out that possibility, telling myself that we would not have to leave the boat behind and trek out of the jungle. It wouldn't come to that. I couldn't let it. I should have been steering, not Julian. I reproached myself for ever letting him have control of the canoe, my canoe. I pulled the frame out from the plastic skin, laid the poles on the shingle. Then I went over to my sodden clothes and laid them out to dry. This mess was Julian's fault. He could mend the bloody boat.

By nightfall, we had made another four kilometres and Julian's 'shame' had nearly been forgotten, by me at least. He had made a remarkably good job of straightening the poles and the hull seemed as strong as ever. But Charlie still harboured a grudge.

'Simon's at the back, steering from now on', he said firmly when we took up our positions to continue paddling.

After that, he remained quiet. Not even the sight of an enormous catfish in the clear water stirred him from brooding over his ruined camera. We carried on downriver in sullen silence.

※

The river ended. It turned to the right and dried out. Ahead, where it should have been was just a barren track of shingle and boulders that stretched grey and bare into the distance, like a newly scraped road. For a while we stared in disbelief, until Charlie realized what must have happened.

'All that rain during the *surazo* must have made it change course', he said.

We back-paddled a short way to where a narrow channel veered off to the left. Charlie was correct. This was the new route of the Hondo. The tug of the current pulled at the canoe, the full force of the entire river funnelling into one narrow gap. The stream was blocked by a fallen tree and we dug our oars in hard to make it to the shore before we were slammed against the trunk. From there we could see that the channel continued clear for at least 200 yards. The banks had been scoured clean by the floodwater into high cliffs of bare mud that overhung the river in places. Exposed roots dangled underneath. We unloaded the canoe, dragged it over the fallen trunk, put everything back in and pushed off again. The current was unexpectedly strong. All we could do was fend off the side walls and a palisade of driftwood spikes that closed in on us as we were sucked straight into a log jam. Fallen trees had piled up on each side. Between them a mass of floating debris had built up amongst the branches. A cloud of *marahuisas* billowed into the air and immediately started landing on our exposed hands and faces. The current was too strong to row back against and, within seconds, our bare skin was a mass of itching bloodspots. It was like the Undumo swamp all over again. Perhaps that's why we all reacted the way we did. We reached into the branches and pulled the canoe in until it was firmly locked. Then, with ruthless efficiency, we started unloading the gear. Julian climbed onto one of the fallen trunks and I passed up the rucksacks, paddles and our one remaining food bag. We did not speak. Charlie grabbed a machete, clambered along one of the branches and started hacking at it. His face was red with rage. It was more as if he was venting his anger than any realistic belief that he could actually cut through.

By the time Julian and I had manhandled the canoe past the jam, Charlie had lost his machete. I had to dive down under the logs and scrabble in the mud at the bottom to find it. I broke the surface holding the blade up as if it were Excalibur, and nagged self-righteously about how it was a survival item that we could not afford to leave behind.

We made all of a hundred yards until we hit another logjam. This one was much bigger. Every tree along the edges had been pulled down. Others had floated with the current and jammed up against the blockage. The entire river had been dammed. There was a deep pool on the upstream side and spurting torrents where water forced its way through. The debris continued for hundreds of yards. I felt the same despair I had experienced at the Undumo *curiche* and I struggled to suppress tears. I climbed onto the logs and made a position fix with the GPS to console myself. But when I drew our co-ordinates on the map it showed that we were five kilometres from where the river was marked. Julian said we should scout ahead to see if there was a way through. Charlie wouldn't come. He sat back in the boat, ignoring the new wave of *marahuisas* that had just found us, and started rolling himself another joint. His sweaty face looked lined and old.

'I'm in the swamp of despair, all over again.'

'I don't want to walk', Charlie let out quietly, sometime after Julian and I had returned. 'I don't think my feet are up to it.'

Neither of us paid him much attention. Having decided that there was no point staying with the river as we could find no end to the logjam, we had decided the best thing to do would be to cut across overland to the Beni and canoe from there. We had rolled up the boat and were busy dividing everything into loads to be carried.

'The thing is', said Charlie, wafting several small flies from his face, 'that fungus on my feet still hasn't healed.' He peeled off his plimsolls, revealing a mass of soggy blisters and flaps of skin, filled with muck. Some places on the soles of his feet were blotchy white, pitted with tiny holes.

'Yuck', said Julian, peering over them briefly before resuming his packing. 'I thought you were going to let them dry off?'

'I didn't think it'd be a problem', Charlie replied. 'I thought we'd be canoeing, not hoofing it back to Rurre.'

'It won't be far', I said, trying to sound reassuring. 'Twenty Ks max. It's just a case of cutting the corner to the river. Julian and I noticed a stream leading back from the jam that goes in roughly the right direction. This close to the Beni, we're bound to come across some logging tracks sooner or later that we can follow.'

No reaction.

'It makes more sense to pack and walk', said Julian. 'Better than messing around here.' Charlie didn't look sold on the idea, but at least he was putting his plimsolls back on.

'Ready?' Julian and I hauled Charlie to his feet and helped him on with his load.

🏵

We soon regretted the decision to walk. Following the bed of a small creek that led away from the logjam, we zigzagged between the beaches of sand and mud on the inside edge of each meander, continually crossing so that we could keep as straight a line as possible. We had banked on this being less demanding than cutting a trail overland, but I wasn't convinced. The mud on the stream's bed sucked us down so that each crossing sapped our energy and, in the open, the sun's heat felt magnified by the fact that we had covered up totally to keep out the biting flies. We were soon dizzy from dehydration, lapping up handfuls of murky water each time we crossed. And as we tired, we lost our edge, forgot to check that handholds weren't covered with fire ants or to watch where we trod in case of stingrays. More than once they jetted out from near our feet, but luckily none flicked their tails up; the wounds caused would have prevented any hope of walking out of the forest.

We became spread out; Julian in the lead, then me, and Charlie always last – at least a river bend behind. Occasionally we could hear his curses and once I caught a cry for help. I rushed back but by the time I was in sight of him he was apparently out of difficulty, stumbling forward with his head down, mumbling and swatting at the flies around his face.

'He keeps on slowing us down', Julian said when I caught him up. 'He should realize he's getting too old for this. If he took more care of his feet, we could be there by now.'

We continued on through the afternoon until we came to a

place where the bank on one side of the river had been cleared and pushed or dug into a ramp, perhaps to launch a boat or to get a vehicle down to the water. The slope had now grown back with dense, waist-high grass and, on the level ground at the top, we found a track, also grown-over, luckily leading off in the direction we wanted to go. There was also a partly disintegrated wooden pontoon and, virtually entirely covered in a bright, heart-leafed creeper, a plank-built hut. I pushed the door, but as the inside stank of rot and was full of bats, we didn't go in, though we did decide to use the flat decking of its veranda, with its overhanging roof, as our campsite for the night.

Charlie took two hours to turn up. He looked worn out and slightly in pain. He sank down to the ground and lay still for a while until Julian came over with a mug of tea and said he would have to fish as we had nothing to eat and the light would soon fail. But without bait he caught nothing. All we had for food that night was rice flavoured with a chicken stock cube. I was silently furious. We could have been at the Beni today if it hadn't been for Charlie's rotten feet. We could have still been in the Serranias looking for the *Mono Rey*. As far as I was concerned, there had been no reason for us to come back – retreat more like – in the first place. We had failed because of something as trivial as personal hygiene. Because Charlie wouldn't dry out his feet, I had given up everything I had planned. It wasn't even as if he had been in on the trip in the first place. He had just come as a passenger at the last minute because the canoe hadn't arrived. I was sure Julian was as sick of the delays as me. Perhaps he might still want to carry on. We could dump Charlie back at Rurrenabaque and have another go. I couldn't be this close, just to give up over someone else's bad case of athlete's foot.

I felt so angry that even the sight of a troop of howler monkeys taking up position in one of the trees across the river to bellow out their evening chorus didn't give me the usual buzz. Instead of showing my annoyance, however, I acted cheerful, tried to make Charlie feel that he was still part of the 'team'.

'After we get back to Rurre, rest a bit, what's anyone doing next?' I said.

Julian grunted. Charlie picked an insect out his rice, studied it for a moment, then squashed it between his fingers.

'I think the *Mono Rey* . . .'

Julian cut in. 'Forget that, Simon. I'm done with the giant monkey thing. Floripa, Brazil – party, that'll be me for the next month. How about it, Charlie?'

'Huh? Yeah, cool, man.' Charlie stared at a small tarantula that had just dropped from the rafters, then flicked it away, disinterestedly, with his spoon.

'We'll take that track tomorrow', Julian said decisively. 'We'll be at the Beni by afternoon. We've walked this far – it can't be much further.'

We were ready to walk out of the jungle early the next day. Charlie was slow packing. Then his rucksack split. We wasted more time.

The track must once have been a logging road, but now it was a tangle of low trees and vines, enclosed by high primary forest on either side. We threaded our way forwards, slashing with our machetes at the twin-hooked 'cat's claw' vines that sprouted where the vegetation had previously been cut back. My left trouser leg had been ripped open by one the day before and now the outline of the tear was marked on my knee by a red area of swelling where ticks had got in. I had removed a cluster of them the day before; they had looked like maroon berries with legs down the sides. One had burst when I pulled at it, leaving a slick of blood between my finger and thumb. Its mouth spike had been left embedded. I had stained the whole area yellow with iodine, but I could still feel the itching where the bite had started to infect.

For a while we left the path, tiring from the exertion of constantly cutting, but our progress was even more disheartening in the tall forest, our way continually blocked by swampy thickets, oxbows left where the river had changed its course. They were choked with vegetation and full of biting insects.

Two hours later there was no sign of Charlie. We waited ages until we heard the noise of his machete cutting. When he burst into view, he disturbed a wasps' nest and was stung on both eyelids.

He was going to go back to the river, he sobbed between staccato breaths. At least he knew it would be the right way. He would go alone if necessary. This route was no good; we had to listen. With his face puffing up, his nose and eyes streaming, and his barely coherent ranting, he seemed deranged. I should have been more understanding. I should have at least done something about the stings. But Julian was making ready to go and I did not want to be left behind. I shouted at Charlie to shut up. I told him off as though he was one of my back-chatting school pupils. I was unnecessarily vicious, but it quietened him down.

When I turned to set off again Charlie followed submissively. I gave him the map and the GPS to assuage my guilt, then I lost him virtually immediately. The only concession I made was to machete mark some of the trees I passed to show the way I had come and to lay out an arrow of sticks for him to follow when we reached a crossroads in the trail.

The path became narrower but more open. It appeared to be recently cut. It wound between the larger trees and, when it reached streams, there were trunks felled across and long poles sunk in the mud at either end to provide balance as we traversed. In places we found footprints. Although these did not appear to be that new, we felt sure the path was in regular use and that it had to be leading somewhere.

'South-east. The Beni.' I'm sure Julian thought the same. When we saw a light gap ahead, we put on an extra rush and pushed out into the open.

But it wasn't the Beni. It was just a clearing. On one side an enormous tree stump with wide, flanged roots stuck ten feet or so into the air. It had been cut straight across. On the other side of the clearing there were smashed branches and battered down vegetation. The space in between was also flattened but there was no trunk. It had been taken away. There were just a few discarded planks, tapered ones, rejects and piles of orange sawdust amongst the bright green new growth that had sprung up since the tree had been felled. For a short while Julian scouted around for a continuation of the track, but his lack of success confirmed what I had already decided. This mahogany was the reason for the path. Here was where it ended.

I glanced at my watch: ten minutes past five – nearly an hour and a half from the crossroads. We could get back there (just) before sunset. We would be bound to meet up with Charlie on the way. But we didn't. We arrived back at our marker just as the daylight was giving out. It was eight hours since we had last seen our companion. My arrow of sticks had not been touched.

❈

Yoporobobo is the name given in northern Bolivia to the Fer de Lance snake. It is about a metre long, tan and dark brown diamond-backed with a distinctive, triangular shaped head. A pit viper, it senses heat from its warm-blooded prey – rats, small birds – using special sensory depressions between the eyes and the nostrils. *Yoporobobos* live on the forest floor where their diamond patterning gives them excellent camouflage and makes them very easy to tread on. And they are 'bravo': they strike out if they are molested. Sometimes they 'dry bite', and if one *does* bite you, that's what you hope for. *Yoporobobo*s are very poisonous.

> '[The] Venom is fast acting and very painful. It rapidly destroys blood cells and tissues and produces extensive necrosis (decomposition) of tissue around the bite site'.[1]

A person who is bitten must receive antivenin quickly. The bite is often lethal.

None of us carried antivenin. It wasn't available in Rurrenabaque. But we had seen a *yoporobobo*, a dead one that Bernardino had found by one of the streams on the way to the Rio Hondo. If Charlie had been bitten by a snake, at least he might have known which type it was, taken some consolation if it wasn't a Fer de Lance. But what else could he do? Apply a tourniquet and

---

1   *A Neotropical Companion*, John C. Kricher.

hope he could slow the effect of any poison until somebody walked along the track? Some hope.

My line of thought drifted on. Anyone with experience of rainforests knew that if you were to do a risk assessment of the dangers, snakebite didn't figure highly. Traumatic injury and its aftermath were far more likely to kill you. When Yossi Ghinsberg had become lost in the upper Tuichi – only 50 or so miles away from here, I reminded myself – he had fallen backwards down a bank in his delirium and spiked himself up the anus with a branch. With the blood loss, his exhausted state and repeated bouts of fever, he had been lucky to be picked up when he was. He had been lying in a rough shelter on a river beach, already in a state of partial collapse when they found him. How much longer could he have lasted?

And now Charlie. It was a sickening feeling to wake up with, as I stirred in my sleeping bag and took stock of where I was: the crossing of two tracks, where I had placed an arrow of sticks the afternoon before. It was way past dawn. The frame of poles that I had cut to hang my net from had partly collapsed when it had rained sometime during the night, and now the damp gauze lay crumpled across my upper body. Where it had rested on my cheek was itchy with mosquito bites. I also could feel irritation on the skin under the waistband of my boxer shorts. I had felt a burning sensation there some hours before, but when I had investigated with my head torch, the battery had been weak and I had seen nothing that might have caused the pain. Now the prickly-heat feeling had returned – and it had moved. I slid my hands down my shorts. My fingers touched fur and I drew them back more out of surprise than from the stinging which I felt across their tips. Without moving any part of my body, I carefully lifted up the waistband and scooped out the caterpillar I found nestling there. Three inches long, covered in black fuzz, it had left a line of raised red welts between my hips. I flicked the caterpillar out of my net and dug into my medical kit (which I had been using as a pillow) for the antihistamine cream.

Julian was crouching by the embers of last night's fire. He was 'kitted-up', ready to go. 'No Charlie.' I stated the obvious. He shook his head. 'Which way? Left or right?'

1. The 'Ape' shot by De Loys' party. Venezuela, ?1920.

2. Percy Harrison Fawcett, Pelechuco, 1911.

3. Fawcett with fish at the Rio Madidi, 1913.

4. Fawcett with two Guarayo braves, Rio Heath, 1908.

5. Rurrenabaque (the waterfront) 1907 – a view little different today, except that the buildings are now more permanent.

6. Fawcett surveying a line of rapids on the Rio Colorado (Peruvian border), 1913.

7. A rest stop on the journey up the Rio Tuichi: Alejandrina, Leoncio (walking along the *lancha)*, Justino fishing.

8. Angry anteater.

9. Bernardino with shotgun and plucked bush-turkey 'handbag'.

10. Julian showing off his trousers which have been eaten by Sepe Ants.

11. A *curiche* swamp by the Rio Madidi.

12. Lost in the Madidi swamps. 'The last resting place of Coronel Jose,' according to Irgen.

13. Irgen and the author arriving at the Madidi 'Highway'.

14. Charlie and his 'monster' Pacu.

'Take your pick.'

'We could go back and look for him', I suggested.

'No point. He'll have gone some other way.'

'He'll manage', I said. It was meant to be a question, but it came out like a statement. Julian nodded.

I downed several handfuls of uncooked porridge oats and washed them down with the last of yesterday's river water. Then we set off. We took the left – east – path. It was as good a direction as any. But not the right one, we decided after two hours. By then the track was so closed it looked virtually no different from the surrounding forest. By the time we had backtracked to the crossroads, half the day had been wasted, my feet had started to blister and I felt wretchedly tired. Julian set a furious pace. He seemed determined to get to the Beni, even if it meant leaving me behind, which, as the afternoon wore on, was happening more and more. I sang marching songs in my head to keep up my pace and to ignore the blisters. This worked when the track was flat and wide but if I stumbled on a root or had to stop to concentrate on one of the log bridge crossings, my rhythm would be gone and I would be shuffling, cursing like Charlie with the discomfort, until I could shut my mind again. At one point, when Julian was in the lead and I had stopped to retie my laces, I saw a jaguarundi: a black cat with a flat face, long body and short legs. 'A sausage cat', I giggled to myself. It crossed the trail in front of me, stopping to stare disdainfully before slinking off into the undergrowth.

By nightfall, the situation was getting worrying. We had headed south-east as much as the trails would let us but we still hadn't arrived at the Beni. I reproached myself for having left the map and GPS with Charlie, not that there was anything I could do about that now. Julian didn't seem as bothered. He just kept going. When the light dimmed, he switched on his head lamp and carried on. He had found footprints, he said. A logging camp had to be near. Not long after, we came to a small river and saw the glow of a fire on a high bank on the other side.

The camp was a collection of mosquito net tents, hung above raised, log platforms under the forest canopy. A tree that had fallen (or been felled) across the water acted as a makeshift bridge. While Julian and I clambered across, the inhabitants of the camp gathered at the other side. There were two men standing and a woman tending a blackened pot and some charred plantains at a thatch-sheltered fireplace. Julian held out his hand to greet them but no one accepted it. When I made it across, I could see his attempts at starting a conversation weren't doing well. I scanned my eyes around the camp. There were sleeping places for at least seven people. The ground was strewn with litter; empty oil cans, food tins and plastic bags, spent cartridges and animal bones from monkeys and from tapirs, most probably, judging from their sizes. On the fire was a spider monkey carcass. Its fur had been singed off and its limbs twisted back on themselves at an impossible angle. The heat had caused the lips to stretch back, so that now its face was contorted into a grisly rictus grin like some medieval demon.

The two men looked uneasy at our presence. They didn't speak. The woman turned her plantains over and stared at us. The men flicked their eyes around furtively, first at each other, then at something at one side of the camp, a pile of things, animal skins possibly. Eventually the older of the two (I later heard the woman call him Renaldo) came over and squatted next to where we had dumped the rucksacks. He ran an appraising eye over the waterproof fabric and the aluminium poles that protruded from the top.

'So, what are you doing here?' he said at last.

'We're tourists. We're trying to get to the Rio Beni', Julian answered.

Renaldo looked at our torn clothes and at the scratches on our hands. His eyes came to rest on the shotgun, which was lying alongside Julian's leg. 'Why the gun then?'

Julian's glance caught my eye. 'To hunt *mutum*', he smiled.

'Can I have a look?'

'No', said Julian, his expression fixed. He reached over to touch its wooden stock.

I broke the strained silence.

'Do you have any food you can sell us? Have you seen another gringo – also with a backpack?'

Renaldo shook his head, then asked, 'Does he have a gun?'
Julian answered instantly. 'A rifle', he lied.

Renaldo spoke some words quickly to the woman by the fire
who then dished out some cold rice onto a metal plate. On top she
laid a roasted monkey forearm. It looked like it could have come
from a baby, except that where the thumb should have been just
ended in a stump. Renaldo passed us the plate and withdrew to the
fire. Soon the younger man joined him. They spoke to each other
in hushed voices. The young man sounded urgent, insistent about
something. In contrast, Renaldo's tone was calming, almost concil-
iatory. Julian and I tucked into the meal, ripping off shreds of the
fibrous meat with our teeth and cramming in handfuls of rice until
we had eaten every grain. Julian, I noticed (despite his feeding
frenzy), surreptitiously passed several shotgun shells from his rucksack into his trouser pocket.

With rest and food inside me, I had the luxury of feeling guilty
about Charlie again. I had hardly thought about him during the
day, I had been so focused on getting to the Beni. Now that I was
safe, I was flooded with remorse. Our second night without him.
Oh God – what had we done to him? He could be anywhere now,
undoubtedly lost, maybe even injured. My mind ran through the
possibilities: arterial wound, open fracture, animal attack, snakebite.
He might be dead or dying right now, and it was our fault. We had
left him. We had been so keen to get out ourselves that we had let
him lag behind. We had known what we were doing. We could
have stayed as a group but Julian and I had chosen not to. I turned
to Julian.

'We should go and look for him', I grunted through a mouthful
of rice.

Julian said nothing. He stared ahead and reached out again for
the monkey arm. 'Maybe these people would help us. We could pay
them.' Again, no answer. I desperately wanted him to take up the
suggestion, for him to do something. All I wanted now was sleep,
more desperately even than helping Charlie. I had found safety. I
couldn't face the idea of losing that and going back into the forest
again. I tried to rationalize my guilt. I wouldn't know where to

look, I told myself. There's no point going in the dark. It would make no difference.

'After all, you invited him along in the first place', I carried on.

I tried to pass the responsibility. Julian finished chewing and swallowed.

'He's just too slow. It's his own problem', he said. And although I knew it was wrong, I agreed. We had been walking for fifteen hours that day and two whole days before that. We were done in. Our feet were masses of blisters and insect bites that were going septic. Our clothes and our skin were ripped by thorns and hooked vines. When we got to the Beni, when we got to somewhere where we knew we'd be able to get 'home' from, then we'd worry about our lost companion. I leaned back against one of the wooden platforms, shut my eyes and soon drifted into an uneasy half-sleep. When I woke up – I don't know how much later – I noticed that both rucksacks had been moved closer to the fire. The top of mine was open. One of the poles had been taken out and was being passed between the men, who were snapping the elasticated sections together. I eased myself up, walked over to Renaldo and gently took the half-extended pole out of his hand. 'It's for my canoe', I said as I dismantled the rods and slid them back into my pack. I pulled the rucksack over to Julian and gently kicked him awake.

Not a word was spoken until Renaldo pointed out a trail that led out of the camp and said, 'Two hours.'

Julian and I slackened our pace when we could no longer see the glow from the fire. The light from our head torches made the shadows spin alarmingly as we followed the loggers' line of machete cuts. I was so tired that, after our initial getaway, I half dozed off while I stumbled onwards, only dimly aware of the path, the reflected green points of spiders' eyes that caught in my torch beam, and the leaves that occasionally slapped against my face. Perhaps Julian had slowed. At least I was able to keep up. I focused on his turquoise rucksack and followed (for hours, it seemed) until he stopped and there was Charlie, lying on the track by our feet.

He was looking up at us, blinking in the glare of our head lights. I heard him murmur something about being given directions by a logger and walking until he had had to rest. We started crying. We hugged each other. It was the release of some dreadful oppression, a wash of emotion. In my exhausted state, I don't know if it was over Charlie being alive or just out of a sense of liberation from the responsibility of having left him. I was still weeping when I heard Julian urging us to go on as the Beni had to be near, and I heard myself promise Charlie that I would not leave him again. But I did. I couldn't walk that slowly, not without the pain of my blisters jarring at every step. I had let him lag far behind again by the time Julian and I stepped out onto the breezy expanse of gravel that was the shore of the great river. I threw down my rucksack, lay down beside it and slept.

❦

Surprisingly, Charlie wasn't angry with us. Next morning, while I built up the canoe and Julian cooked porridge (just about all the food we had left) over a huge driftwood fire, Charlie said,

'What's the point? We all did what we had to in order to get out.' His voice was subdued. 'I just walked and walked. I went down so many trails that just ended, or started heading the wrong way. When I found some fresh machete cuts, I figured they had to be yours. So I sat down and waited but you didn't come back. I stayed all night. I couldn't get any wood to light – it was too wet.' Charlie stared for a moment at his cigarette burning down and continued.

'In the morning I chose another direction and carried on. I knew I'd get here in the end. Especially after I met a logger who told me the way. He walked past me on the trail, lugging a great, big mahogany plank on his back. He only stopped for a moment. He didn't even ask me who I was.' Charlie's voice trailed off.

'You would have come to look for me?' I said 'yes', but I wasn't so sure. Luckily before I was drawn further, Julian produced three chocolate bars from his rucksack.

'I carried these for you miserable people, all the time since Tumupasa', he announced.

'And you ate the other fifteen yourself', Charlie cut in straight away. 'Disco in Rurre tonight. I know it', he said, his face cracking into a broad grin. 'Chuckster's decided. He needs a beer. Badly. A few other things as well – like female company. Julian's all right, but he's ugly as sin. Dingo ugly, mate. So ugly, the dogs turn and run when he comes in the house.'

'Go out and get me a *chica*', Julian chipped in with an Australian accent.

'Ah', Charlie sighed. 'Disco, a restaurant, beers, women – a Brazilian *chica* with buttocks like drum-skins.'

'Goshtosa', he mouthed. Then, gyrating his shoulders to some unheard rhythm, he sang to the jungle his true desires.

'DISCO-MOTION!'

Charlie was back.

CHAPTER NINE

The Devil's Bite Mark

THE RIO BENI felt like the sea. It was half a mile wide with expanses of shingle at the edges. The jungle was just the merest smudge in the distance. The wind blew up waves with white caps. The white, gull-billed terns that wheeled over us with their skipping, buoyant flight made me think of days spent by the coast.

We drifted with the current. There was little point in paddling. There were no reference points on the distant shore, no way of judging our progress, just the ever so slight enlargement of a line of mountains ahead. These peaks, an offshoot of the Susi ridge that ended at Rurrenabaque, had a distinctive semi-circular chunk missing along the top edge which, I remembered from my first trip into the forest with Negro, was close to where the river cut through the Serrania. The notch was a familiar landmark to all the boatmen on the Beni. They had given it a variety of names over the years; Espejo, or peephole, and Bala, which signified where some celestial cannon ball (a *bala*) had been shot through the mountain range. The name I liked best was the 'Devil's bite mark'; Negro had told me the legend that God and the Devil had both tried to cut through the ridge to let the Beni past. The Devil only managed to bite out the chunk which we could see now, and then God had shown him how to do the job properly by slicing right through with his machete. I knew we would soon be floating into that cut and the thought scared me rigid as I remembered the rapids at the entrance. Though they had not been a major hazard for Negro's motor *lancha* on my previous trip, I remembered the waves that rebounded off the rock walls of the canyon were easily big enough to capsize my small and badly dented canoe. Hopefully, though, our passage would not be as fraught as that of Fawcett's contemporary: the mining engineer A.V.L. Guise, who tackled the same cataracts on a balsa wood raft around 1913.

> Into the defile we rushed, the river churned into foam by the huge boulders with which its bed was strewn, seeking to obstruct our progress. Into this turmoil we were hurled, our boat bobbing about on the angry waves, escaping the disaster that threatened at every moment only by the herculean efforts of the Lecos,[1] straining madly at their paddles. Around a sharp bend we hurtled and again another bend, and into one more boiling cauldron, until at last the canyon ended and the river again expanded and continued placidly on its way.

Perhaps Guise had exaggerated in the retelling. I was worried about the rapids, but I didn't remember them being as bad as that.

⚅

For now, though, we sat and watched the clouds and the terns. Charlie tried fishing, casting a lure far out behind the boat, letting it trail in the hope that some *dorado* or *suribim* would mistake it for a little fish and snap it up. He soon gave up.

'Too murky', he sneered at the water and broke the rod back into its four component pieces. 'Disco in Rurre.'

His words sounded hollow now.

---

1   The Lecos were a tribe of Indians that lived in the region around Mapiri. They were particularly known for their prowess in piloting balsa rafts and were employed by many travellers, including Evans and Fawcett in their journeys from Mapiri down the Beni to Rurrenabaque.

❦

I sat staring at the sludgy water, dipping my hand in side-on to the flow like a little rudder, watching the effect that the bow wave I created had on the entrained suspension, the way the eddies swirled an inch or two below the surface which itself was glassy clear. For a while I experimented, stirring at the water, scooping up handfuls, watching how the drops splashed and rippled, and seeing how long it took for these disturbances to be absorbed back into the soup-like sub-layer. I was fully absorbed, as if in some self-induced trance; the spray of drops hissed like the pattering of light rain on leaves.

❦

Most of the direct force is stopped by the canopy, of course. The higher layers of foliage slow the drops' descent and collect them into rivulets that stream onto the undergrowth, hitting the leaf litter in great jolts that pound dents in the peaty earth so you can see through to the red clay underneath. In places a machine-gun spattering of mud and leaf litter coats the bases of the trunks and lowest leaves in a papier mâché sludge that will set hard in the heat that is sure to follow.

I can see five or six trains of drops pouring into a pool in a narrow cut that marks the occasional course of a stream. The pool's level has risen, and the twigs that built up at the end when the water was last here have been sluiced away, leaving a patch of slick moss that looks as if it has been combed through with the current. Under the slight overhang, where a trickle washes over some sticks, a pair of glossy-backed beetles have found refuge, along with a tiny black-brown frog with spatulate toes and a yellow-white throat which pulses with the same frequency as the drip-dripping of the water.

When the rain stops the stream continues running high for a while. The sun switches on, the forest steams and the trumpet cicadas immediately start their sawmill grind. The river over the ridge courses with mud washed in from the banks. A pair of capybaras that sheltered under the branches of a logjam during the downpour pull themselves out and stand for a second, streaming water. The coarse hair on their backs dries into tufty spikes in the sudden heat.

Around the next meander, three men peel back the tarpaulin they pulled over themselves when they beached their dugout. They push themselves back into the flow, hopping out as one to hold the wooden hull still when it becomes clear they cannot progress in the swollen channel. They brace themselves against the current and pull the boat upstream.

I can never quite see the faces of these men or really decide who they are. They aren't Indians. They wear long trousers and broad-brimmed hats but whether they are loggers or explorers, I can't decide. I like to think they are traveller-scientists, like Alfred Russell Wallace and Henry Bates who roamed the Amazon in the nineteenth century, collecting species, cataloguing their finds in pages of exquisite watercolours and meticulous notes. Working for years in conditions of hardship and often solitude, afflicted by bouts of fever, these men – these British men, my forebears (though maybe that is just self-flattery) – postulated theories of mimicry in butterflies, pollination of fig trees, and natural selection as the driving mechanism for evolution. Ideas that would eventually shape our notion of natural history. They and the geographer-adventurers like Fawcett who came later knew what the forest does to you. They felt the heat and humidity, suffered the ever tormenting buzzing and biting of insects. Enclosed, unable to see further than the next river bend or the trees in front of them, they must have known the self-doubt and apathy that can debilitate as much as any disease. Yet though they often received little credit for their work, even if their copious records and collections managed to get back to Europe with them (Wallace lost virtually his entire work of four years spent in the Amazon when the ship on which he was travelling back to England caught fire and sank), they continued with a passion that comes across in the artistry of their diary pictures and the vividness of their text. Wallace, Fawcett, Bates; they saw the green fire that hummingbirds reflect when they are hit by the light, the electric blue morpho butterflies and the impossible tangles of vines and passion flowers. They felt the power of the thundering waterfalls at the rivers' sources and the tropical storms in their full rain-pounding, lightning-flashing intensity. It affected them so deeply that, like Wallace, who then went to the jungles *of the Malay archipelago and Fawcett who lost himself in Brazil, they went back for more.*

🎇

We passed the mouth of the Tuichi, and the flow rushed slightly as the river spilled out over a ramp of rounded stones. In amongst the hissing and bubbling of the water another noise asserted itself, a mosquito whine that surged into full motorbike volume as its source appeared from behind an island. A motorboat *lancha*. Our minds filled with thoughts of rescue. We discounted any possibility that it might be travelling up the Rio Beni. Here was a boat that could take us through the Bala and, with any luck, all the way back to Rurrenabaque. If it were empty, we could load the canoe on whole. We could be back that day. We started waving with our paddles. The ends were bright, sky-blue plastic so it would be hard to miss them. I even stood up in the canoe for a moment but Charlie told me I was being silly; I would have us all over.

The *lancha* reached the white water ripples of the shoals where the rivers joined. There was just one occupant. We could make out a green shirt and a light-coloured baseball cap. The boatman had evidently see our signalling and was now steering towards us, the outboard's revving rising in pitch as the *lancha* picked up speed in the open water. When it was close enough for us to recognize the man's face, the realization of our amazing luck had us whooping and cheering and windmilling our oars like we had just come first in a race. That the *lancha* was piloted by someone we knew was not that unlikely; between the three of us, we had met many of the tourist guides and loggers in Rurrenabaque and Tumupasa. But meeting this particular guide, here and now as we drifted down the Rio Beni, seemed beyond coincidence. It was Irgen Janco – Negro's older brother. We realized it must be him as he pulled the hollowed-tree hull alongside our puny boat. Here was the Janco brother we had heard about but never met. The one who had prospected for gold up the Rio Mapiri and worked on ranches near Ixiamas. The brother, Negro had told us with admiration almost bordering on awe, who travelled solo in the forest right up to the Serranias themselves. Irgen's resemblance to Negro was obvious; dark-skinned and well muscled, he had a slightly Spanish look to his otherwise Indian features. A gold-edged front tooth glinted as he greeted us.

'Simon, Charlie, Juleen.' He leaned over to shake our hands. 'You're early. From what Bernardino told me when he got back, you should still be in the Serrania.'

Bernardino back! We hadn't given it a thought. But it was two weeks since we had seen him, ample time to return to Rurrenabaque. Our questions came all at once.

'When – how did he get back?'

'What are you doing here?'

'Can we have a ride?'

Irgen held up his hands to stop the tirade. 'Si, si, si. I will tell you everything on the way back to Rurre, if you want . . . but what will you do with the canoe?'

'That's easy', said Charlie, who had already started shifting the rucksacks onto the *lancha*, 'We will put it on your boat.' Then he noticed the seal-sized lump that took up most of the centre section of the dugout. 'Fuck, what a fish!'

'I caught that *bagre* earlier', Irgen said, with just a touch of pride.

✺

When we had transferred everything across (about two minutes), Irgen revved the engine and we sped off downstream. He said he was coming back empty after delivering supplies to Negro's tourist camp up the Tuichi. Luckily for us he had set off late, otherwise we would have had at least two more days on the Beni, and that was if we managed the Bala canyon. Looking at the state of our boat, he doubted that we could have got through. For this *lancha*, though, the waves would be no problem. Four hours would see us back at town.

'And Bernardino?' Julian asked, cutting off my rambling account of how we'd nearly sunk the boat then lost Charlie. 'What happened to him?'

'Ah, he had his problems, Juleen', Irgen said. 'He was so desperate to see his wife since he found out in Tumupasa that she had left him and gone to La Paz.' Julian's face was blank. 'You didn't know. I see. It's like him not to bother you with his problems. Anyway, when he and Maximo got back to the main river, first they lost their hooks so they couldn't fish for food, then there was no transport. It was two days before a *lancha* came past and that was going upstream. It took them eight days to do what should've taken three. Bernardino was beside himself with worry.'

'And had she left him?' I asked.

'Not really', said Irgen. 'She just wanted him to sweat. But', he added, 'I don't think he'll be allowed to go away on long trips like that for a while. A powerful woman – that Maria.'

'Dingo ugly', muttered Charlie. Irgen rolled his eyes. We knew what he meant.

❧

Speeding down the Beni was thrilling. It was exhilarating having a cool wind buffeting our faces and fantastic to be making genuine headway. When we reached the Bala Canyon where the river passed what we could now see was two ridges, Irgen revved the outboard up to full speed and aimed the boat straight at the waves that reflected off the sides. He took us through what Guise had described as a 'boiling cauldron' with minimal difficulty. The *lancha* veered to one side for a moment, swung around as Irgen eased back the throttle, fending off some rocks with a long pole, and we were through, riding the deep, calm channel between the ridges.

Julian gingerly tightrope-walked along the edge of the trembling hull and sat himself beside me. 'Irgen says he'll take us to the Madidi', he shouted into the wind.

'I thought you were going to Brazil.'

'I've reconsidered', said Julian. 'The way I see it is that we have this one chance. I keep on thinking of all those books I read before I came: Up-de-Graf with the Jivaros in Ecuador, Guerbraint who crossed half of Venezuela with a load of film equipment that hardly worked. And all those old explorers you're always on about. They spent years doing this. We can't just give up. We have to stick with it.'

I should have been pleased; my search for the *Mono Rey* might still be on. But all I could think was that I had only just escaped from the jungle, and I was about to go back to good food and proper beds and no insects biting me. I told him I needed time to consider.

'We have the chance now', Julian said, emphasizing the 'now'. 'Tomorrow, he'll be off into the jungle again. He reckons we could do it', he added softly. 'We could still get to the Madidi, find the *Mono Rey*, (nail its balls to the fridge) – *hombres de la selva* and all that. Ask him.'

Half-reluctantly, half-intrigued, I followed Julian to the stern where Irgen was steering the outboard.

⚜

'The plan you had was good', Irgen said, once I had clambered over the pile of rucksacks and empty oil cans that lay between him and the *bagre*. 'You just didn't give it time. If you had waited two more days, your canoe would have arrived and you would be at the Madidi now. In the *selva*', Irgen said deliberately, as if giving a lesson, 'you have to have patience.' He paused to consider for a moment then gave us the terms of his employment.

'I'll guide you, but to keep to your plan in the time you've got, it'll cost. You'll need this *lancha* and lots of gasoline, three big tanks. And porters – at least three. You can't go wearing yourselves out again lugging everything over the Serrania like you did getting to the Hondo. You have to be fresh when you arrive at the river. I want my brother Ignacio to come as motorman. He can carry some stuff too. It would also be doing him a favour to get away for a while.'

'And I think you should meet Lars', Irgen said. 'He's a Norwegian who works at San Jose for the national park. He's been to the Madidi. He went wandering off into the forest alone a few months ago and turned up weeks later at the bottom end of the river. The trip nearly killed him. Lars is the only person I know of who's been to the area you want to go to. We should find him, if he's not gone off wandering again. He might be able to tell us what the river is like.'

Irgen carried on with his plans. He recommended amendments to our route and suggested what food we would need. He told us that we would have to trade in our shotgun for a proper rifle and said I would have to show him how my little computer navigator worked and how I kept track of our position on the maps. When he was nearing the end of his 'list of demands', Julian nudged me and smiled. 'Remember, we were always told this guy was the one who could sort it,' he said to me in English.

I turned to the guide. 'You really think we could get to the Madidi, look for the *Mono Rey* and canoe the river back in four weeks? That's all I have.'

'It's possible', he replied. 'Realistically, I don't think we're going to see the *Mono Rey* – not in the time we have; that's even if it does exist, which I personally doubt. But the Madidi interests me. It's a challenge. I think with your boat, once we've straightened it out, we've got a good chance. One week to cross the mountains, two down the river, one to get back. Of course if the mountains are too hard, we have to make up time by paddling harder.'

'And what if there's a logjam and a *curiche*?' I asked – this being my biggest fear.

'That won't happen', Irgen replied firmly. 'The Madidi flows between two sets of mountains.'

'Or if there's a gorge with impassable rapids?' That was my other worry.

'Lars made it on a balsa raft, so we should be able to do it. Though', he added, 'I don't know how far down he was on the river when he started. It's a chance we'll have to take.'

'Let's do it', said Julian.

'Yes', I nodded. Then I looked back at Charlie. He was eyeing up Irgen's *bagre*, running his hands down its long, sleek back, counting hand-spans across its whale mouth.

'What do you think, Charlie?' I said. No apparent reaction. Charlie lifted the fish's dorsal fin and splayed it out like a fan.

'Na! Count me out, mate', he said without looking up. 'I've seen all the fisho I need for now. It's Floripa for me. A Brazilian *chica* with buttocks like drum-skins. Party and pumping.' I had known that would be the answer. I didn't try to persuade him. 'Just one thing, Simon. Do us a favour. Take a piccy of me with this fish.' He hauled the *bagre* up with his fingers under its gills until it was level with his shoulders. 'Try to get the rod in.'

'But you didn't catch it', I pointed out. 'Isn't that cheating?'

'So?' said Charlie, 'All fishermen are liars and when this beast gets into *Modern Fishing*, who's going to know?'

⁂

Within two days of arriving back at Rurrenabaque we were ready for the off again. The cold beers, good food and decent beds that we had dreamed about over the past eight weeks were good but didn't really live up to the fantasies. Charlie's 'disco-motion' never happened; we were too busy sleeping. Once we had told Negro, his friends and anyone who would listen the story of our trip and soaked up any glory there was to be had, there didn't seem to be any more to do and, with the prospect of actually getting to the Madidi, Julian and I involved ourselves fully in setting the expedition underway as soon as possible.

Under Irgen's direction, we restocked with food, put out the word that we were looking for porters and traded our Brazilian shotgun for a second-hand American rifle.

Irgen was clearly impressed by our acquisition. 'Remington Speedmaster', he read off the shiny hardwood stock, stroking his hand along the freshly-oiled barrel. '*Automatico*. This is like a machine gun. Press the trigger and you get three *mutums* in one go. "Pam-Pam-Pam".'

He shot three imaginary curassows across the hotel bedroom wall. Then he told of how he had sorted all the transport. We would be using his friend Alcide's *lancha*, the one he had brought us back to Rurre in. Ignacio would take it back when we set off over the mountains. As for getting back once we had canoed the Madidi, Alcide's brother Chichito, the driver who had taken us to the Undumo, would be waiting with his Landcruiser at the Arroyo San Antonio, the stream where the new Alto Madidi highway had been built up to so far. He was working at a logging camp there and would be waiting, ready to bring us back to Rurrenabaque in 25 days' time, when we appeared out of the jungle after trekking overland from the Madidi. Two days later I would fly back to La Paz for my flight to England. The lift had to be there. Irgen told me not to worry. All was '*seguro*'. Chichito would be at the Arroyo San Antonio on time. This, Irgen swore on his honour. Chichito would have instructions to wait for five days. If we didn't turn up by then, he would send word and people would be sent to look for us.

We had food, transport, a guide. Now we needed porters but there just weren't any to be had. Although we let it be known that we would pay above the going rate, the reckoning amongst several men that Irgen asked was that the trip would be too hard. They preferred not to work or to try their luck with a logging team instead. On the day before we were due to set off we had only hired one man, a friend of Negro's called Leoncio, who came from the village of San Jose which was on our route. Leoncio was in his early twenties and looked very fit. He wanted a ride back to his village but was willing to put in a few days for us. He said he knew some of the trails beyond San Jose over towards the Madidi (or at least he knew people who did – which could prove to be very useful).

That left us with the problem of one porter still to get. We only knew one other person who might be available – Bernardino.

Julian and I went to visit him at the single room house that he was building on a newly rented plot of land at San Buenaventura. He seemed genuinely pleased to see us. He quizzed us about our journey on the Rio Hondo (he was especially concerned at how 'Amigo Charlie' had nearly died) and he eagerly flicked through my sketchbook. But he said he wouldn't come.

'It's probably better', he said, casting his eyes past his plot of banana and papaya plants towards the half-finished house. He handed back my diary. It was open at the page where I had painted the large spider monkeys that had thrown the sticks at us.

'This is the *Mono Rey*, you know, Amigo Simon. Not the big one without a tail. This is his brother, the *marimono* of the mountains. You are very lucky. Not many people see it. When you go further into the Serrania, I am now sure you will find the *Mono Rey* himself.'

❧

It was on the morning of Thursday 10 July, my wedding anniversary (I remembered, with a twinge of guilt) that Julian, Leoncio, Irgen and I set off up the Rio Beni in Alcide's best *lancha*, a 40-foot wooden dugout, built up at the sides with sturdy planks and painted in zigzag patterns of light blue and green. The middle of the boat was piled up with sacks of food, rucksacks and the bags containing the canoe. Leoncio, Julian and myself sat at the front while Irgen perched at the stern behind an enormous black tank of petrol – enough to supply the powerful outboard for the two day journey up the Tuichi to its limits of navigability. Irgen's brother Ignacio hadn't turned up. Irgen told us not to worry. We would pick him up a few river-bends outside of town. It was just in case the army stopped us, he said ominously. It would be better that his brother wasn't with us. Ignacio was in a 'spot of bother' with them, Irgen smiled.

When the final packing and refilling of the petrol tank was done, there was just one person to see us off from the Rurrenabaque waterfront: Charlie. He said he had woken up 'especially early to make sure we actually did go'.

'Go get yourselves that big ape', he shouted as Irgen pulled the outboard into action. 'Nail its balls to the fridge', we heard as the propeller bit the water and, in a spurt of white froth, the *lancha* pushed forwards.

PART TWO

Ant River

CHAPTER TEN

Up the Rio Tuichi

A T THE TURN of the twentieth century a climate of fear existed amongst the Tacana-Quechua of the upper Tuichi. Outlying farmsteads of the Franciscan mission village of San Jose de Uchupiamonas had been raided and villagers killed. Any fertile land not in the immediate vicinity of the settlement had been abandoned. The *barbaros* were back. Faced with a choice of death or slavery at the hands of the men who ran the rubber estates, the nomadic tribes of the Madidi (notably the Guarayos-Guacanaguas, possibly also the Toromonas and the Pacaguaras) had moved over the mountainous watershed and into more conflict.

According to Evans, who visited San Jose in 1901:

> In the wet season they (the *barbaros*) keep to the hills and do not cross the Tuichi, but when the river is low, even the *chacras* on the other side are not safe. About a year previous to my visit, two San Jose Indians were killed on the Rio Pavi; the *barbaros* stripped them of their clothes, which they tore in their hurry and made off at once, and the Rio Pavi is now rarely passed by the Christians.

The troubles were short-lived. By the time Fawcett was in the area (1906–13), the 'savages' had been killed or moved on, according to those in Rurrenabaque, to the mountain jungles along the Peruvian border: the Rio Colorado. That was where Yossi Ghinsberg had been heading on his search for the Toromonas, an offshoot of the Tacana, when he had become lost.

And Lars Hafskjold too. He had been aiming for the Colorado when he had set off alone on foot from San Jose in March, two months before we arrived in Bolivia; his journey should have taken him into the Madidi watershed, over the cloud-forested slopes of Cerro Atalaya, and beyond towards the Peruvian border. Before he went, he sent word to the Americans working for Conservation International at Rurrenabaque and at the Lake Chalalan camp. He said his trip would help him in his work with the Quechua-Tacana villagers of San Jose where he had so far spent over a year investigating how to integrate their lifestyle within the management of the National Park. He justified his decision to go, saying the expedition would be useful for researching native uses for rain-forest plants, especially if he managed to make contact with the 'wild' Indians that reputedly lived at the Colorado. Later Lars said that he just wanted to get away for a while.

Lars did not get to the Colorado. After a month with no word back, there was no real concern. The terrain was difficult, and if he had reached the Indians, it was quite conceivable that he wouldn't be able to send a message back. After nearly two months, his colleagues were sufficiently worried to be on the point of organizing an air search. However, where to look in the ridges and gorges of the upper Madidi was anyone's guess.

Lars turned up on the day the search had been due to start. A group of doctors administering to the settlements around the confluence of the Madidi with the Beni picked him up in their motor boat. He was floating down the river on a raft made from balsa logs. According to our porter Leoncio, who climbed over the pile of food sacks to sit with me as we powered up the Beni on the *lancha*, Lars had been starving and feverish when he had been found. He could hardly walk. His feet had been mushy with fungus. His hair had grown long and his face sprouted a bushy ginger beard. 'He looked like a *maneche* – a howler monkey – when they found him', Leoncio said. 'A great skinny *maneche* with red whiskers and long, spindly arms.'

Leoncio had moved over from sitting at the stern with Irgen and the outboard, not long after we had stopped to pick up Ignacio. The pick-up, a hasty pull-in at a tree-overhung section of river-bank, had all the surreptitious atmosphere of a suitcase exchange in a spy movie. Ignacio, in a new-looking, black leather jacket, a pair of trainers dangling by their laces around his neck and no luggage, had scampered out of the cover and clambered aboard while his brother nervously scanned up and down river, and gently played the outboard's throttle to hold the boat stationary. There was little family resemblance. Ignacio was older and thinner than Irgen. He had a weasly moustache and several long bristles on his chin. His high cheek-boned face had more of a Mongoloid, Indian look.

'*Buenas Dias*, Simon, Juleen', he grinned at us toothlessly, tweak-ing the peak of his baseball cap. Then, with arms outstretched, he tightrope-walked along the gunwale and sat himself down by his brother, who by that time had opened the throttle fully, sending us full pelt towards the wall of mountains that appeared to block our way. The name 'Serrania', derived from *sierra* (saw) seemed partic-ularly apt that day. The zigzag peaks bit into the grey cloud blanket above, leaving an off-cut sinking down the ridge face that dissolved into swirling eddies as it caught the wind gusting out of the gorge.

'What's with him?' I asked Leoncio, nodding furtively towards Ignacio.

'Irgen didn't tell you?' Leoncio looked down. He whispered con-spiratorially, as much as he could whisper against the wind. 'He killed the army Colonel.' I didn't react. It seemed a little far-fetched. 'It wasn't murder proper', said Leoncio, feeling out for a pole that he could use to fend off when we reached the rapid ahead. 'He took the Colonel up the Agua Polo – it's one of the streams off the Tuichi. The Colonel fell down a ravine. He hit his head and drowned. The boatman and the porters said it was Ignacio's fault for not guiding him properly. The police said it was negligence.'

'So now he's on the run', I said. Leoncio nodded.

'But don't worry. In six months it will all be OK. Ignacio will pay the police and they won't look quite so hard – if you know what I mean.'

We navigated the rapids at the end of the Bala gorge with comparative ease, Ignacio showing his skills as a *motorista* as he lined us precisely at right angles to the ugly brown waves that rebounded off the rock walls and sloshed over the sides of the boat. Leoncio and Irgen grabbed poles and dug them into the river bed, holding us for the few seconds Ignacio needed to swing round and lower the propeller fully when he was sure we weren't about to ground. For a few seconds the *lancha* slid back and threatened to slew sideways in the flow. We tipped over alarmingly. Irgen had evidently anticipated this. He stood at the front and dug in his pole to check our spin. When he was sure we were lined up, Ignacio let rip with the throttle and we slowly climbed up the gushing slope of water.

For the rest of the day, the going was easier. We turned up the narrower river Tuichi that paralleled the Serrania (its banks on that side had eroded into high, red mud cliffs). I leaned on the plank sides of the *lancha*, scanning for wildlife but seeing little except the ubiquitous white-collared swallows and various species of yellow-breasted flycatchers flitting over the water for *marahuisas* and other insects. I studied every cecropia tree for sloths, having read that these were a prime habitat. I hoped that one of the crusty, grey termite nests that clasped the branches might extend out a hooked claw. None did.

Several times, we were passed by loggers riding downstream on rafts of mahogany planks. Each raft was manned by two men who steered with paddles lashed up into a crude tiller arrangement at either end. For all their effort, the men's paddling had little apparent effect on the direction of their massive craft. Julian tried to video them several times but the loggers invariably turned away or pulled their shirts up over their faces.

Later in the afternoon we stopped to pick up some passengers, who hailed us from the base of a high mud bluff with steps cut into it. On the flat ground at the top was a cluster of low buildings, which Irgen said was Santa Rosa, a vanilla station with cabins for rich tourists who occasionally came to stay. The hitchhikers were from San Jose, a squat, mixed-race man in his mid-thirties and two teenage sisters. The older girl carried an infant in one arm and a baby spider monkey in the other. The monkey wailed intermittently and refused the chunks of banana that the girl repeatedly tried to feed it. Irgen said it was sick – too young to be taken from its mother – and would soon die.

The man introduced himself very formally. He shook us each firmly by the hand and announced a convoluted name, of which I only caught the first part, 'Justino'. He said that he, his wife and her sister had walked over from Tumupasa in search of work, but as there was none at Santa Rosa, they had decided to try their luck at Lake Chalalan, two hours upriver, where there was an eco-tourism project. He said they couldn't afford to pay us for the ride.

'Offer him work', whispered Irgen. 'I bet he'll take it.' I did and the offer was instantly accepted. Justino committed to ten days as a '*cargador*' (literally, cargo carrier) with no more than five seconds to decide. We now had our third porter and a complete team for the expedition. The problem of who would carry the canoe had been solved.

We didn't make it all the way to San Jose that day, and made camp as night fell, on a long, open sweep of sand alongside the river. Irgen and Ignacio constructed two shelters from *chuchillo* poles, draped over with plastic sheeting. Julian and I had one of these 'tents'. All of the Bolivians shared the other. It felt very much a situation of 'them and us'. With the addition of Justino and his women, our group had divided and we felt left out. From our separate lodgings, I could see Ignacio framed in the firelight. Judging from his exaggerated expressions and the giggling of the girls, he was telling some comic story. Irgen was heckling from the shadows – 'Get to the point. It didn't happen like that' – and Ignacio feigned annoyance, shooting off quiet asides to the girls that made them shriek even more. Then he continued his story, shrinking into the part of some frightened animal threading its way through some tangled forest, his body tensed, his eyes wide for the *tigre* that pursued him. Suddenly he gasped, fell back and sprang up, flapping his hands ineffectually against his imaginary assailant in a fight scene that lasted only as long as he could hold off from laughing.

'Popular, isn't he?' I commented to Julian.

'It might be because he's been giving away all of our food', Julian said flatly.

'But, surely Irgen wouldn't let him.'

Julian shrugged. 'I don't feel like ruining the festivities, do you?'

I watched Justino get up from the sand. He probed a pole into the flames and hooked out the blackened shell of a large turtle. There was a muffled thudding as he hit it first with his machete, then with a rock. Then there was a loud yelp, followed by laughter, presumably as he had burnt himself. They were having a good time and we were sidelined from our own expedition. When I mentioned how I felt to Julian, he pointed out that perhaps I was being over-sensitive. 'When we get over to the Madidi, things might be more tense. Maybe they just have to blow off some steam now before we get going.'

'What about the food?' I was about to ask.

But Julian answered before the words had come out my mouth.

'We'll restock when we get to San Jose.'

The river became narrower and rougher as we approached the mountains we would be climbing over. The valley sides drew in increasingly on either side and the flood plain all but disappeared. The Tuichi now had a discernible gradient. Most river bends were now accompanied by rapids where the flow tumbled over from one level of riverbed down to the next stratum of resistant rock. The fast water was sometimes at a constriction where the flow gushed through in one sloping 'chute'. More often, however, it slid down a widening of the river, hissing over a broad ramp of pebbles and boulders. At these we would all be over the side, heaving the hollowed trunk hull up through the shallows, then holding it in the deeper water against the vicious tug of the current while Ignacio lowered the propeller and tried to make some headway before we were pulled back. Then it would be a race to scramble back in over the sides before we lost the hull or our footing. One time I fell and slid the full length of the *lancha* until Ignacio grabbed me by the arm and hoisted me back aboard.

'With your spirit, I was going to nickname you *Tigre*', he said as I sprawled over the petrol tank and spluttered for air. 'But, I don't think you're quite big or strong enough, so I think I'll call you *Tigrecillo* – little jaguar – instead.'

For some reason I had always expected San Jose de Uchupiamonas to lie on the river like a miniature version of Rurrenabaque, so I was surprised to find that the village was actually sited some distance inland. Leoncio led Julian and me on the half-hour climb up a jungle trail to get there. The start of the settlement was marked with two man-high wooden crosses, decorated with tissue paper flowers.

'They are to keep disease away', Leoncio said. 'In the time of my grandparents, the village was by the banks of the Tuichi. There was a lot of illness there. Many people died. The survivors decided they had to leave that place and start again here. Now we have the crosses to make sure the bad never comes back.'

I remembered how Evans had commented on the numerous re-sitings of San Jose.[1] Franciscan brothers had founded the village around the end of the seventeenth century, but since then it had been moved several times when the location had been judged to be 'unhealthy', or following attacks from the *barbaros*. When Evans visited the settlement it was at its present position: a clearing of open land with a small lake 'used for washing and bathing' and a 'magnificent view of the Eslabon mountains, in the intervals in which the still higher summit of Huaina Jatunari may be seen'.

---

1   The Chupiamonas is a river valley some way up the Rio Tuichi. It is one of the previous sites for the village.

Evans described a 'large church (with) a belfry with two or three bells and a convent of a single storey', but Julian and I found neither. We reached the lake with its view and continued up to a small plateau, which appeared to hold most of the wooden houses that made up the village. It was midday and the place was deserted. Apart from the rustle of the wind in the trees, the occasional screech of parakeets and crowing of cockerels, San Jose was silent, asleep. The people, I supposed, would be tending their *chacras*, cultivating manioc and plantains. Some might be in the forest hunting, or gathering plants for medicines or for construction, like the *jatata* palm, whose fronds were used for the roofs of all the houses. Some might be working for the new National Park, perhaps at the tourist camp at Lake Chalalan where Justino and his women had been going before we had picked them up. Justino's wife Alejandrina had told me that since the park had been inaugurated, she had at last been able to earn a living without travelling all the way to Rurrenabaque. She had presumed Julian and I must be scientists who had come to study the rainforest, and when we had told her we weren't, her eyes had lit up.

'You're journalists then', she had said to us. 'You have come to interview Señor Lars, now he is so famous!'

'If we could find him, we would', I thought, remembering the conversation of the night before. But right now, with the village so empty, it looked like we would never meet the Norwegian. Julian and I criss-crossed the grid of houses. We bought some toffees at a house with an open shop front (the only place with anyone there) as an excuse for asking where Lars lived, then we followed the shop owner's directions to a rough shack of vertical planks with a mould-blackened palm thatch roof. The windows were shuttered. We waited, each at opposite corners, between us covering every possible route in or out. It was midday and, as well as being uncomfortably hot, we were aware that we should return to the *lancha* if we intended to make it to the highest navigable part of the Tuichi that day. We made one more cursory sweep of the village and set off back. And then we saw him, a tall man in jeans and an old shirt, walking barefoot around the scrub at the edge of the buildings. It wasn't his height or the slight sun-bleaching of his brown hair that gave him away, but his stride, which was far too deliberate for a local.

'Lars?' we called out (it was a polite, 'Do you mind?' sort of enquiry). Lars turned around, stared for a second then walked towards us. He was in his late twenties, maybe thirty, sunburnt over an underlying initial tan. His hair looked like it hadn't been cut for some time. He thought we were zoologists, or maybe photo journalists.

'It's your hats and khaki clothes', he explained with some amusement. 'You look like you're trying to be David Attenborough.'

'We're going to the Madidi', I burst out. Lars carried on smirking. Maybe that was his natural expression. His light blue eyes stared at me in a way that was unnerving. I felt he could see right through the jungle explorer exterior that I had constructed to the tender parts underneath; my worries about the trip, my doubts about finding the *Mono Rey*, insecurities that it might not exist at all. His stare was not malicious, but I felt ridiculous, embarrassed.

'We thought you could help us', I said lamely.

Lars considered for some time before he said anything. I looked at his feet. They were tanned black and splayed out wide from not wearing shoes. He said he couldn't talk now as he was busy. He spoke deliberately, as if translating the phrases in his mind through Norwegian and then Spanish before finally vocalizing them. I had the impression that we had disturbed him. We were some uncomfortable reminder of his previous life and, though not impolite, it seemed he would have preferred us not to have been there. Why didn't we stay the night? Then he would tell us everything. Right now he had arranged a meeting with a local farmer to talk about his crops – it was part of his research study in the economics of agroforestry. He started to go but then turned.

'It's very hard, you know', he said. 'You really shouldn't do it unless you know what you are letting yourself in for. I was away for seven weeks – no food, bad feet. I could hardly walk.'

Did he really think he could put us off? I tried to tell him of all of our experiences on the Undumo and the Hondo, how we had got lost in the swamp and of how Charlie had been left behind. We were experienced at this sort of thing. He had to know that. But it just sounded like boasting, trying to impress him. Finally Julian cut in and saved Lars from my ranting.

'Are there big rapids?' he said. '*Curiches*? Any major obstacles that we need to know about?'

'Please. We need to know', I added. 'We won't keep you long.'

Lars fixed each of us in turn with his staring eyes and started talking, tentatively at first, then gaining momentum as he relived the experiences. It was if some internal barrier had been breached. Once he had started he seemed to have forgotten his appointment with the farmer entirely.

Lars said it had always been his intention to get to the Rio Colorado. He wanted to find out if that was where the 'wild' Indians had really gone. He knew some of the paths through the mountains and was sure that it would only take a few days to cover the 80 kilometres to get to the river. After a week or so of hiking, he was already low on provisions and it became clear to him that his idea had been over-ambitious. He decided to return to San Jose. He walked downhill until he reached a small river where he made a shelter and stayed for a few days.

'It was beautiful', he said. 'There were no biting flies at first and the forest was fantastic. There were three tapirs that hung around close to the camp. One night one came right up to my net where I was sleeping but it took fright and ran away when I reached out for my camera.' Unfortunately, with the tapirs came lots of *marahuisas*. 'I had to move on', Lars sighed, staring into space.

Here his story became harder to understand. It was unclear whether he actually decided from the outset to go down the river, or whether it was a decision forced upon him because he realized he was lost and had no idea of the route back to San Jose. He built a raft of balsa wood logs and half-hauled, half-floated it through alternating stretches of pools and rocky shallows until he came to a larger river – the Madidi, he presumed. There was enough water to float, but with only a pole to guide the raft, he had little control of it and kept getting stuck on the snags that filled the river.

When his food ran out and he lost his last fish hook, Lars hoped his botanical training would help him find edible plants. It did, to a point. Unfortunately, at that time of year (March) there were few trees fruiting, and finding the *papas de la selva* (jungle potatoes) that he expected to survive on was harder than he had anticipated. At one point he came across some loggers who gave him a bit of rice and told him that it would not be long now before he reached the Beni, at which point he would find more people. It was a false hope. On his raft, limited to drifting at the same sluggish speed as the current, the larger river was still weeks away. Lars started to lose track of time (his storytelling became vague then). He remembered he was constantly plagued by biting insects and that his feet were so infected with fungus that he could hardly walk, let alone gather food. Despite this, whenever he was at his hungriest and most desperate, he always found something to eat; he said it was as if someone was looking after him.

At this point Lars became quite insistent, looking hard at us as if to check we were fully taking it in. 'It was Francisco Navi', he said. 'He is the Tacana shaman here. He somehow psychically kept track of everything I did. He told the villagers not to worry. After I had got back, he told me exactly what I had been doing at certain times: "remember those fruit you found there, or those potatoes – I found them for you". It was incredible. You must believe me.'

Lars looked earnestly into my eyes. He spoke with almost religious fervour. He said he was convinced of Navi's powers. The old man lived in a house of *chonta* palm wood at the edge of the village. The house always felt cool in the day and warm at night. It had a palpable energy that you could feel. At night the women would sit in one room and the men would stay in another, drinking and talking quietly. People would go to the medicine man to be healed. Lars had done so himself. He didn't tell me what was wrong with him, only that he had been very ill. He said that Navi had worn a feathered headdress and used mystical stones. He had felt a tingle 'almost like an electric shock' when the shaman had touched him and within days he had been cured. When he fell ill again another time, the healing had only taken two hours.

Lars didn't think the arts of the Tacana mystics were dying out now that the people of San Jose had more access to modern medicine. He knew of another shaman at Tumupasa and said that Navi, who was now 87 years old, had passed on much of his knowledge to his son who in turn was teaching his own son. All three men were very calm and serene. All possessed an inner energy you could feel when you shook their hands. Lars had no doubt about this 'power'. His conviction was like that of a 'born again' convert. His eyes, which had so disconcerted me at the start of our conversation, now showed a desperate need for affirmation.

'You do believe me?' he implored, once he had unloaded his entire story.

I said I was unsure. How could I know unless I had seen for myself? I looked away, embarrassed by my lack of faith. He said we should stay. He could tell us more. He said he had to go – his appointment with the farmer was important. If we stayed, he could tell us everything we needed to know about the Madidi. It could save us time in the long run. Any aloofness in his manner had been stripped away. He was almost pleading. I looked to Julian, but I knew he felt the same as me. We knew what we had come to find out. Lars had mentioned no falls or swamps on the river. As for the headwaters themselves, it did not look like he had been there. He had descended a tributary. Our river remained unexplored. With our limited time we were anxious not to lose a day. We declined the offer and said we would let him know how we fared. Lars wished us luck. He shook our hands and then he was on his way.

'Just one thing', I said as he was leaving. 'What do you know of the *Mono Rey*?' Lars's face was blank. Once again I felt self-conscious as I had when we met him. I had blown all my credibility. 'A giant tail-less monkey that lives high in the Serranias. It eats palm hearts', I continued. Lars looked puzzled for a moment.

'The villagers here talk about something like that', he said. 'But I haven't seen it. I don't know any one who has. I think they call it the *Ucamari*.' He turned and walked purposefully towards the edge of the village without looking back.[1]

&

Back at the *lancha* Ignacio and Irgen had cooked up some fish that a passenger we had picked up on the way upriver had paid us in return for the ride. We wolfed it down with platefuls of sticky rice and some grapefruits that Justino had brought from Santa Rosa as we told them what we had found out about the Madidi. Irgen listened intently, nodding when the information confirmed what he already knew.

'Ignacio and I have been talking about the route', he said finally, unfolding the map that I had lent him. 'We'll set off walking from a stream called the Agua Capyvara – it's about four hours more. Ignacio's been there before.'

Ignacio added, serious for once, 'We can follow the stream up part of the way, then find a spur that takes us right to the top of the Serrania.' Irgen pointed out the route on the map, leading his finger up a stream to a place where the contours indicated a slight dip in the ridge top, then around on a level to another stream that flowed northwards to the Madidi.

'It's not the shortest way', he said, 'and it involves a fair bit of climbing, but it is direct and straightforward, something we have to think about when we'll be in such thick forest that we won't be able to really see where we're going – or even use your satellite navigator most of the time.' He passed the map over to me. 'What do you think?'

I was impressed. Irgen had obviously thought things through.

1 In October 1997, Lars Havskjold set off again in search of the 'wild' Indians at the Rio Colorado. This time he intended to access the river from the lowland, Peruvian side. He arrived at Cuzco, Peru and, shortly after, there were unconfirmed rumours of a tall, fair-skinned man with two Indians, poling a balsa upriver from the town of Puerto Maldonado on the Rio Tambopata. Lars has not been seen since.

He had gathered all the information that he could on the area in the time since Julian had first suggested the expedition to him, and worked through all the possibilities. He knew how to use the maps and link the information on them with his own knowledge of the forest, and he was not afraid of using our satellite technology for navigation. I felt sure Irgen wouldn't sit down and balk at going on as Bernardino had done. I was beginning to realize that in deciding to carry on and in hiring this guide, Julian and I had made the right choice.

By the time we arrived at the inlet where the Agua Capyvara fed into the main river, it was too late to divide out the loads for carrying. While we tied up the *lancha* in a lagoon between two ridges of hardened mud rocks, set up the mosquito nets and gathered wood for the fire, Irgen went off and shot an olive orependola. He chopped the breast meat off and handed around chunks of it to bait our hooks. But the fish weren't biting and food that night was tinned sardines and baked plantains, heavy stuff that nobody wanted to carry.

'We'll put the rest on top of Justino's pack', Ignacio joked. 'He has more of a penance to pay than the rest of us.'

'A what?'

Ignacio explained. 'You know the girls on the boat yesterday? The older one, Alejandrina – she is his wife. Well, he's been getting off with the other one too – her younger sister – behind her back.' All eyes went to Justino who was busy munching a blackened chunk of plantain.

'It's true. It's true', Justino spluttered.

'You crafty dog', muttered Leoncio. He was from the same village and he never knew. Justino smiled sheepishly. Ignacio was in his element.

'And that's not all', he continued gleefully. 'There's another one back home that he's got in trouble.' He ran his hands over an imaginary pregnant bulge. ' Ay Cuñada!' he laughed, 'Oh sister-in-law!'

Leoncio was still taking in the revelations. 'What a man!' he muttered. Justino smiled, embarrassed. There was nothing he could do or say while Ignacio was in full flow.

There was a palpable sense of excitement the next morning amongst all six of us as we readied ourselves for the trek over the mountains to the Madidi and the Janco brothers hid the outboard in the forest. Justino did indeed have the biggest pack. He carried the canoe skin, the poles and all the pieces of the frame. On top of that Ignacio placed the remainder of the plantains. The load was huge and stuck at least a foot above his head. He also had his own rifle to carry as well as the two paddles, taped together.

'This is your penance', Ignacio said after he had put the plantains on top. 'And if you slacken, I'll whip you with this mitu vine.' Ignacio whirled a short length of vine above his head then went over to his own considerably smaller pack and tied the home-made rope to the top.

When Julian tried to test the pack's weight, he warned Julian sharply. 'No *jodas*! Don't mess with that. It may look small, but it's really heavy.' Then his face was all smiles again. 'Juleen. We go off to find your Indians now.' He pinged an imaginary arrow at Leoncio who smiled briefly, then resumed his packing.

'And Simon. I'll protect you when the *Mono Rey* comes to get us', he shouted over his shoulder as he hoisted his pack and set off into the forest. 'You may be a mouse but don't worry. You are amongst jaguars.'

'That's where you've got it wrong', I yelled as he disappeared into the vegetation. 'Perhaps I am the jaguar and it's you who are the mice.' Then I pushed back the gateway of leaves and followed Ignacio up the slope into the warm, clammy shade.

CHAPTER ELEVEN

The *Marimonos* of the Mountains

THE TREK OVER the Tuichi-Madidi watershed felt like one of those old Tarzan movies; six of us in single file, winding up and along the jungle-covered, knife-edge ridges that led to the Serrania itself. Laden down with packs, paddles, ropes and rifles, we cut our way forward through the tangles and scrambled across the cliffs of mud and rocks where the ground had slid away.

'If the *Mono Rey* exists, this is where it will be.' I mulled the thought through my head as I – almost unconsciously – checked each handhold for thorns and snakes. 'No, higher still', I corrected myself. 'Where the forest thins – in the palm thickets and stunted bushes of the ridge tops. *Mono Rey*: the size of a man, strong enough to rip his arm out of its socket, shaggy black fur, throws sticks and shit when angry.'

Images of giant monkeys wound through my daydreams. I could visualize the scene, an age-worn black and white film with lines and scratches and a slightly jerky effect to the movement; this was the bit where the apes threw rocks down on the explorers and their train of bearers.

I became aware that the column ahead had stopped. Irgen was sending Justino and Leoncio downhill to look for water. I handed my two plastic bottles over and slumped back against my rucksack to snatch a few moments' rest before the order came to carry on up. I listened to my breathing as it slowed back to its normal rate, and vaguely contemplated whether I could be bothered to delve into my rucksack for some sweets I had bought in San Jose. I slid out of the straps and was pulling myself to my feet when I stopped. Someone, something was watching me. Not Irgen, Ignacio or Julian; this was something else. The feeling went right through me. I scanned the bushes around in front of where I was half-standing and locked on. A pair of amber eyes stared from a mottled patch of shade 15 feet ahead. They were fixed on me, motionless. Features started to materialize like an optical illusion revealing itself; a feline head, a long, striped neck, the curve of a back; three – no – four feet long. *Tigrecillo*, ocelot. The spots and stripes of its coat merged so perfectly with the shadows of the undergrowth, that even though the cat was so close, I dared not take my eyes off it for fear of losing its position. I slowly raised my arm to point, to attract the attention of my companions who were sitting on the ground nearby.

'Look! *Tigrecillo* – there on that log.' They couldn't see it. Julian peered along the line of my outstretched arm yet missed the cat. I still had eye contact.

'You're imagining it', said Ignacio.

'No, look, it's right there.' Perhaps the loudness of my reply startled the ocelot. Now it moved and the others saw it as it slunk along a fallen log, tensed itself in a half-crouching position then sprang silently up the hill, into the undergrowth and out of sight.

Ignacio snatched up the shotgun and started forward.

'I could get good money for that coat', he said. I glared at him. Earlier, he had told me how he thought that hunting for skins was wrong. I reached out to bar his way. He stopped. Suddenly there was a crash of leaves, a high pitched 'peyeeeep' above us. Ignacio pushed past me with the gun into the bushes where the ocelot had just gone. There was a shot, the clatter of something falling through leaves and branches, then a thud.

'*Mutum!*' Ignacio shouted from behind the thicket, emerging moments later with a black turkey dangling by its feet in one of his hands. The bird wasn't dead yet. Even though its neck looked broken, it was still flapping its wings feebly. Ignacio swung it around and smacked its head against a tree trunk.

'*Rico* – rich. We'll feast tonight', he said, handing me the upside-down bird.

It was a beautiful specimen: glossy green-black with a tail edged in white and a blunt, crimson beak that extended up its forehead like the casque of a hornbill – a razor-billed curassow. It hung limp in my hands, the anal opening at the base of its tail contracting and opening sickeningly. Ignacio grabbed the body and pulled out a handful of feathers.

'It's best to do this now while it's still warm', he said, pulling out more until, in just a couple of minutes, he had transformed the curassow into an oven-ready bird that wouldn't have looked out of place on the shelves of Sainsbury's. Except for the head with its red, razor beak. He then looped a short length of vine around the head and the feet, and slung it over his shoulder, rather like a handbag. Julian and I pulled on our packs, chatting noisily about the ocelot as we followed him up the slope. Not more than a minute after setting off, there was a rustle in a bush ahead of us and the merest glimpse of a long, brown tail disappearing.

'Idiots', said Ignacio testily. 'If you didn't spend so much time talking, you would have seen that puma that just crossed our path.' After that we continued the climb in silence. Of course, we did not see the puma.

The first peak we got to was both inspiring for its promise of a view and also vaguely discouraging as I could see there was so much more to climb. I scrambled up the steep slope, taking care to follow Julian's every move because I knew if I slackened my pace, I would just have Irgen's machete cuts to follow and these were so infrequent that I was sure to lose them. The patch of sky ahead became less obscured, brighter as I neared the top. I suppose I had been hoping that this would be the summit of the Serrania, though if I had considered that we had only been going for about five hours, I would have realized how improbable this was. Disappointment struck as I reached a clear edge where Julian and Irgen were waiting, peering down the other side. By then I could already see this wasn't the end, just a peak on a minor ridge which then sank precipitously before carrying on up and down like a saw blade until it joined the bulk of the main mountain ahead.

Ignacio was already cutting downwards, hacking at the tangle of vines that blanketed the edge and yelling at me to hurry up as this place was surely open enough to 'see' the satellites. I lowered myself down the near-vertical slope, taking care not to spike myself on the pointed stakes left by Ignacio's cutting. At the most open area I could find I heaved off my pack, held out the GPS and waited for the bar chart on the screen that represented transmitting satellites to fill up. Three good signals and I would have 'lock' and a position fix. But today it seemed to take an eternity and I watched the black rectangles flick on then disappear again. The only things getting a fix at that moment were sweat bees. They swarmed around my face, over my glasses and up my nose as I held up the navigator, determined to find our location before the others overtook me and left me behind.

'No *jodas* Simon. Stop fooling around', Ignacio chided as he clambered back to see what was taking so long. Then he turned on Julian, who was busy getting out the video. 'No *jodas* Juleen. No *jodas* with the video', he said and stomped off along the ridge.

I gave up with the GPS and scurried after him, walking in his footsteps as he edged across a gash of red earth and rocks, where the tree covering and topsoil had slid away. For a while I was tightrope-walking a lattice of roots that projected out from the edge, noting, but not stopping, to consider that there was open space beneath my feet. I ignored the sweat bees that were burrowing down my shirt. All my concentration was fixed on Ignacio, putting my feet where he put his, standing clear of his machete swipes, then reaching forward for the same cut branch and vaulting round it until my feet touched firm ground once more. The tangles and landslides continued into the afternoon. Most of the time we managed to cut a line along the top of our *cuchillo* (literally, knife) until it joined the main ridge. The terrain, though steep, was more open under foot, with vertical tree trunks for handholds and no cliff edges to fall off. Many of the trees here were decked with bromeliads and ferns, which took their moisture straight from the clouds that would well up around the summit every morning. The canopy was thick, and in the shade beneath, fleshy, broad-leafed herbs and tree ferns abounded. Some of the undergrowth had new shoots growing up from thicker woody stems. Leoncio said this was probably an old trail made by a hunter from San Jose. He doubted these old cuts would lead all the way to the Madidi though. He said there would be no reason for anyone to go there. There were enough animals to hunt for food near to the village; why go any further? Irgen told us we would make use of the trail tomorrow. Even if it didn't go far, we would make faster headway than with the machete hacking we'd been doing. But right now we should be looking for a place to camp, and that would mean descending to somewhere we could get some water. First we would try to find out where we were.

As there was no chance of getting a satellite fix in such thick vegetation, we followed the hunter's path a short way and cut across to a tree fall right on the ridge edge where there was an opening in the foliage large enough for us to get a view. There, stretched in front of us, hazy in the distance, was the next ridge – the Serrania Del Tigre, the 'jaguar ridge'. It was deep green-grey and misty, a vast area of unbroken forest with no gaps, no roads, no signs of humans. Immediately below was a flatter area, the saddle that marked the watershed of the Rio Hordon (a river which led back to the Tuichi) and the headwaters of the Madidi. The canopy of the forest down there was so dense that there was no way of telling where either river started. We could see it would be important that we descended from our Serrania sufficiently far north to prevent ourselves ending up at the wrong river's headwaters. We stood for a moment, lined up along the fallen trunk, lost in the view and in contemplation. It was Irgen who broke the spell. We had to go down now and make camp while there was still enough light.

We woke up engulfed in cloud. A pall of heavy mist hung on everything, causing us to drip as much as the moss on the tree trunks during the climb back up the ridge to find the hunter's path. My glasses steamed up and so, when we found ourselves in the middle of a group of spider monkeys virtually as soon as we had regained the summit, all I was aware of were dark shapes crashing through the leaves around me and barks of alarm which sounded strangely disjointed in the water-sodden air. I wiped my glasses on my T-shirt, dropped my pack and ran to an opening in the under-growth ferns where I could see that Irgen had a good view of the canopy. The monkeys swung around and past us, hurling them-selves across the gaps between the treetops, flailing out with hands, feet and gripping tails before disappearing into the leaves and fog. These *marimonos* had the same thickset look as the ones that had attacked us on the Hondo. Their faces were grey with a touch of pink. Their coarse hair was shaggy and black, except under the arms and between the legs where it appeared lighter, yellowish; in the sharp contrast with the whitened sky the exact colour was hard to tell for sure. The hair on their heads had a definite style. It swept in from both sides into a narrow ridge, which stuck upwards and forwards as if it had been gelled in place. Irgen said Bernardino had been right. Could I not see that these *marimonos* of the moun-tains were different from the smaller, black '*negritos*' of the flood plains? I replied that I would like to think so, but as far as I knew only one type of spider monkey had been listed for this area: the 'black' *Ateles Paniscus Chamek*. Leoncio chipped into the conversa-tion.

'It's something everybody at San Jose knows', he said. 'The *marimonos* in the Serranias are bigger – and a different colour too.'

I had to admit, the coloration was not unlike the descriptions I had read of *Ateles Belzebuth*, the long-haired, or white-bellied spider monkey, which was the species that the cynics of de Loys's story had said was the real ape in his photograph. In the '30s and '40s, after the picture had been discredited, several specimens were 'collected' (i.e. shot and preserved) in the region of the Tarra valley, close to where de Loys had his encounter. The males were large for spider monkeys, though not the one and a half metres that de Loys had claimed for his specimen. They had light brown fur on the underbelly and between the legs, and a light 'blaze' on the forehead, similar to the markings of the 'ape' in de Loys' picture. One geologist explorer, James Durlacher, even went as far as sitting up the monkey he shot on a tree stump and photographing it in much the same pose as Loys' Ape (though he positioned the tail in full view across the body). He published the picture in *Explorers' Tales* in 1936. It seemed to heap more ridicule on de Loys' story.

As for the monkeys that we had just seen, it seemed wishful thinking to believe these were some new species or even *Ateles Belzebuth*, a species which was recorded as ranging south only as far as Northern Peru and the eastern Amazon of Brazil. Of course, it crossed my mind that my opinion might change if we had a 'specimen'. I felt it could be that these *marimonos* were the root of the *Mono Rey* stories. But Julian and I had made a rule from the start that we would not shoot the wildlife (with the exception of bush turkeys and rat-like pacas, both of which were abundant and good to eat), and even though I desperately wanted to know more about the coloration and true size of these spider monkeys, it was a rule I swore I would not break.

Although we never re-found the hunter's path, we made good progress all the same in the relatively 'clean' cloud forest at the top of the Serrania, following that until around midday when the land tumbled downwards again and we were forced back into the thickets and vine-tangles of a sub-ridge that appeared to lead north. As far as we knew, this was the direction we wanted to go, but as the vegetation had been too thick for me to confirm our position with the GPS, there was still the awful possibility that we might be descending to the Hordon rather than the Madidi side of the watershed. We started looking for open places where satellite signals might get through. Wherever the forest thinned out slightly Irgen would give the order to rest. Everyone would sit back on their packs, wait for Justino with his heavy load, and gather their breath while I wandered around, holding up the GPS and shaking my head as only one or two of the signal bars on the display would ever fill up. Even when I occasionally had three, one of these would always cut out when a satellite moved out of 'line of sight' on its orbit, the radio waves blocked by a clump of thick trees or a mountain ridge. The attempts to fix our position were not only exasperating, they were also wasting our time. We aimed to get down to the flat that day.

'Show me how to work it. I'll climb up and find our position', Irgen said after I had failed for about the sixth time. He knew as well as me that the best option, one that I did not care to take, was to climb above the canopy and try from there. I looped the receiver's cord around his neck. 'The trees here are small with lots of branches. It shouldn't be too difficult', he continued as he started climbing, closely followed in the trees by Ignacio, Leoncio, Justino and finally Julian, who obviously saw this as a welcome diversion from the muscle-straining effort of carrying heavy packs. They made about 20 feet and shook the branches, whooping as if they were true *marimonos* whilst Irgen carried on higher until he was out of sight amongst the leaves. I was the only one who stayed on the ground. Irgen soon got the position fix, relaying his progress to me and asking instructions via Julian, who was perched precariously about halfway up. Whilst they clambered down, I plotted the co-ordinates on the map. Confirmation. We were on the Madidi – or at least a tributary of it – and we had made a surprisingly good distance. We could now come off the ridge and go down to the river.

❧

For the rest of the afternoon we were wading down a rocky streambed, hard work in that the ground was uneven and slippery, and especially demanding for Irgen at the front, as he had to cut the vegetation away. Otherwise it was easy, as there were no worries about getting lost. All I had to do, in my place third in the line, was follow in the sure knowledge that we would arrive at the Madidi.

As the hours passed and I tired, I mentally closed off from the sur-
roundings. So did the others, it seemed. We trudged on in silence
except for the sloshing of our feet through the water and the occasional grunt from Justino whenever his pack caught on an
overhanging branch. When Irgen suddenly flung his hand up to
signal 'stop', the whole 'train' concertinaed into him like a scene
from a slapstick comedy. Justino was last. His momentum, under
the weight of the canoe, passed through Leoncio, Ignacio, me and
then Julian, and nearly pushed our leader right over the edge.

'Wah! Bitch of shit!' he swore as he threw himself backwards
and staggered for a second with the stream gushing around his
legs and over the lip of the waterfall. It was a sheer drop, 50 or more
feet straight down to another pool, edged by vertical rock faces as
if someone had got our river valley and sliced it off midway. There
had been no warning, no roaring of falling water. Perhaps the noise
had been muffled by the mass of leaves pressing in on both sides.
There had just been the stream and then there was the drop.

'Well, it's obvious we can't get down that', said Irgen, his eyes
scanning the river's edge for possible routes out. 'And there's no way
I'm going back, so we'll have to find a way to cut around sideways
and find another knife ridge to go down.'

Ignacio went to check out a way across. He tiptoed across the lip
of the fall, then lunged for an overhanging branch on the other side
of the stream. The wood flexed but took his weight. Then he was
across, gripping into mud and tree roots with his fingers, grasping
at the undergrowth, slashing with his machete as he edged his way
across the near-vertical slope. Justino followed. The branch sagged
further under the weight of the canoe in his pack and propelled
him into the mud bank where he held still for a second then scrabbled for safety like a startled armadillo. When he had found a sure
foothold he took his huge rucksack off, wedged it against some
roots and waited with one foot in the water and one hand gripping
a narrow tree trunk for me to come next. I unclipped the belt of my
rucksack and inched my way onto the lip of rocks. I felt the current
tug at my feet. One slip, I knew, and I would be over the fall. I
looked only at Justino, fixed on his outstretched arm and the

branch that hung half in the way – it would be a swing of around five or six feet. I shifted my weight onto my front foot, ready to make the jump and, for one heart-stopping moment, it felt that the water would pull me over. My feet slid suddenly and I leaped. I grabbed at the branch and swung, my feet over nothing for an instant until they struck the bank, slid down and stopped. Justino grabbed my pack.

'Woo', he let out and hauled me roughly towards the line of cuts that marked the way Ignacio had gone. Here the plants were thin and straggly, growing over where the ground had slid away some time before. My boots skidded on the red mud under foot and I followed the rough trail Ignacio had made, kicking my feet in for better purchase. Soon I caught up with him. He was sweating profusely and panting heavily after the exertion of all the cutting. He said it was too steep to carry on along. It was just luck that none of us had not slipped down. It would be better to head up to where the forest looked thicker.

'More to hold onto when we start falling', he grinned at me and scrambled upwards.

⚜

By the time we camped that night, Ignacio and Irgen had seen a tapir ('A really big one with an enormous *palanca* – this is a good sign') and the stream had swelled and levelled off after having been met by another of about the same size. Now it had widened to five metres or so and flowed as a series of sandy-bottomed pools linked with miniature cascades as the water drained from one level to the next. Hand-sized electric-blue morpho butterflies lazily flitted about and shimmered in the patches of sunlight between the dappled, leaf shadows, and for once there were no biting flies. Perfection. We cleared an area of undergrowth on which to spread out our groundsheets and washed in the clear water while Irgen quickly pulled out two trout-sized fish with his hand line. They were fearsome-looking, with disproportionately large mouths bristling with spiky teeth.

'They must've been hungry', he said. 'Probably too big to get out of the pool. I'm surprised you didn't get a nibble yourself.' He pointed at the insect bites and scratches down my bare arms. Then he picked up his long knife, slit open the fish to remove their innards and passed them over to Leoncio who was preparing the fire.

'So', ventured Ignacio, 'we go on in the canoe tomorrow?'

'Not quite yet', I answered. 'We'd mostly be pulling the boat now. It's got to be at least three-quarters paddling before we lose all of you porters. It's still easier to carry as we're doing at the moment.'

'Besides', added Julian, 'we've hired you for ten days.' I noticed how he stressed the 'you'. 'Even allowing time for you to get back, we can go forward together for at least one more day. We'll leave some food here for your return. That'll make your packs lighter.'

'So we go on', said Ignacio, then he turned to Justino, slapping his knees. 'Ah, Justino. Your penance – it continues. Ay Cuñuda!'

❧

We weren't yet on the part of the Madidi that Lars had travelled. Julian and I were fairly certain from his descriptions that he had trekked further overland and probably arrived first at one of the tributaries flowing northwards that met up with the main river some way downstream. Irgen said that in some ways Lars had been travelling at a better time of year to survive by foraging from the forest. Then it had been March and the rains had just stopped. Many trees would have been fruiting, unlike now, in the middle of the dry season when the only fruit were *bibosi* – figs, and they were no good for humans, just animals. He pointed out a bare patch of mud, littered with the half-eaten remains of the plum-sized fruit and criss-crossed with the tracks of paca, tapir and deer. If we looked around, he said, we would be sure to find signs of predators too; footprints of ocelots and pumas, maybe a jaguar. '*Bibosi* are the only trees that produce fruit for most of the year. Animals will have come from all over the *selva* for the feast.' I picked up one of the fruit, dug my fingernails into it and broke it open. The inside contained lots of pinkish nodules. I licked it. It was sour.

The dry would continue until late October or November. The rivers would become shallower, harder to travel but easier to fish. Fruit would become impossible to find. When the rains came, any low-lying land would flood for a while, the forest would flower and the whole process would start again. It was worth remembering, Irgen said, that for all the apparent signs of the rainforest being a place of natural abundance, the life cycle of this part of the Amazon was seasonal. The difficulty or ease of surviving here for animals and people would depend on what time of year it happened to be.

❀

The next day, the Madidi changed abruptly. After a morning of slogging through knee-deep mud and sinking sand where any chance of cutting through the forest was denied, as the riverbanks were too steep and the vegetation too thick, we crossed a dam of boulders and the flow suddenly fanned out. The river spread across a bed of rounded pebbles and the bushes peeled back revealing a wide-bottomed valley with steep, forested ridges that came right down to the level of the river on both sides. In places, swathes of bare, red mud showed where land had slipped, and I remembered the descriptions of the 'falling cliffs of the upper Madidi' that Fawcett had written. On one of these landslide scars we saw a tapir munching on the grass that had grown up on a ledge. Julian and I were able to get really close before it raised its head, sniffed the air and bolted off. We were elated. Julian said he had shot some good close-ups with the video. I had managed a quick sketch. Ignacio snatched the pad out of my hand to have a look at what I had drawn. He studied the picture intently, at first apparently pleased and then a look of (mock?) consternation crossed his face.

'Where's its *palanca*?' he demanded. 'You haven't drawn its *palanca*.' Turning to the others he asked, 'That tapir; did you see the size of its *palanca*?'

'It was a big one', Leoncio agreed.

'*Muy macho*', Justino added.

'I was looking at other things. I was trying to draw its shape', I protested.

'But you missed the most important bit! How would you like it if I drew you and missed that?'

'OK. Understood.'

Ignacio carried on. 'And that spider monkey you drew yesterday. Its knob was too small too. From now on, I'll make sure we all look really well and make sure you draw things right. "*Mira-palanca*" [willy-watchers]. That'll be the name of this expedition. The Expedition "*Mira-Palanca*"!'

⁂

By midday I was getting left behind, as I kept stopping to map our progress with the GPS. With the flood plain giving so wide an angle of open sky, I should have been able to obtain position fixes easily. For some reason, however, the receiver was playing up and none of the co-ordinates it gave me would match up. Successive readings would put us in positions several kilometres apart in the mountains on either side of the river. It was very confusing.

When I caught up with the others resting on some rocks by the river, I could see a furry black shape lying on the shingle by their feet. Ignacio and Justino were holding their rifles. As Ignacio knew of our rule that we wouldn't shoot monkeys, I looked at Justino who, having joined the expedition late, wouldn't have known this.

'Who shot it?' I reached down to the spider monkey carcass, touched it. It was a *negrito*, small and black, male. The body was warm. The sparse hair on the side of its head glistened with still-wet blood. Some had dripped onto the gravel. Its eyes were open. They looked like the glass eyes on a cuddly toy. I was angry at its death. We had enough food to survive without hunting monkeys. I was also annoyed, though I wouldn't have admitted it at the time, that this monkey wasn't one of the big *marimonos*; if it had been, we could have shown we had found something new. I suppose I would have sat it up on something like de Loys had done, but I would have stood in the photograph so there could be no argument about its size.

'It was me. I shot the monkey', Ignacio said.

'There were so many of them and they were so close and this . . .' He held out the gun. 'What a rifle! It shoots so fast. Pam! Pam! Pam!'

'It's true', Justino added softly.

'I don't know why I shot it', Ignacio continued. He sounded quite apologetic. 'I was just playing with the rifle. But I'm sorry. I truly am . . . What shall we do with it now?'

'Do you want to eat it? It would be a waste otherwise', I said. Ignacio cast his eyes down.

'No. I don't want it any more. I'll leave it.'

'It's my turn with the rifle now anyway', said Julian cheerily, snatching up the Remington from the shingle just before Ignacio could grab hold of it. 'You've got some bullets spare?' The question sounded more like a statement. Julian held out his hand and Ignacio sheepishly retrieved eight or nine rounds from a top pocket. 'Watch me bag a *jochi*.' Julian spun around and walked back to where he had left his rucksack, sending up a cloud of yellow butterflies that had landed to lick the sweat.

Sometime later, while we were crossing the shallows at a bend in the river, he slowed down to let me catch up and said, 'I wouldn't trust that Ignacio further than I could kick him. He didn't give me all the bullets he had and he's still got the monkey. I saw him stash it in a black bin bag inside his rucksack. It's amazing how his pack doesn't look any fuller – makes me wonder if he had much in it to begin with.' We sloshed out of the water and onto a firm patch of sand, streaked with creepers, where the heat radiating from it hit us as if an oven door had just been opened. Julian caught his breath and continued. 'There was something he said to me earlier on. It's like he thinks he's carrying on with us – after we make up the boat.'

'Irgen. What's he got to say about this?'

'Not sure. I didn't ask him. It was just the way Ignacio said, "when *we* go down the river" not "when *you* go down". He's a dodgy character. I wouldn't put it past him to do a deal with Irgen and come in his place.'

'You're thinking so he can get away from this trouble with the Colonel?' I said.

We reached the end of the beach. Julian skidded down the sandy bank into the water and looked furtively around at Ignacio who had just crossed the previous river bend.

'We've got a canoe, a rifle and lots of food. What more could he want?' Julian asked rhetorically. 'I know I'm probably being paranoid, but keep a watch on your stuff. At least it can't do any harm to.'

⚜

Dinner that night virtually jumped out of the forest and into our laps. Just as we were making camp, setting up the plastic sheet tent on a framework of *chuchillo* poles on the sandy river beach, a paca burst out of the foliage on the opposite bank and plopped into the river just in front of us. It was an easy meal, too good to miss. As it scrabbled against the current, Justino snatched up his rifle and leaped up in pursuit, loosing off two shots then ripping off his shirt and shorts and diving after the animal before it was washed over the rapid at the end of the river bend. Simultaneously, Ignacio started pointing at the spot where the paca had appeared.

'*Tigrecillo*! Simon, Juleen, look. It's just sitting there. That's what chased the *jochi* out.'

'No *jodas*, Ignacio', I said, 'I can't see anything.'

'No. Seriously – look!' But I couldn't see an ocelot. No matter how much Ignacio pointed out which leaf it was under or got me to look along the line of his outstretched arm, it did not appear. Perhaps its camouflage was that good, or my eyesight that bad. Perhaps it wasn't there at all. I suspect Ignacio was getting me back for shaming him with the monkey. By the time I gave up looking, Justino was back holding his paca up proudly by the hind legs for all of us to admire; a fine specimen, hare-sized, russet brown with white spots like a fallow deer. There was food enough for that night and hopefully there would be some leftovers for lunch the next day. Julian said that was just as well. He had just done a 'stock take' on the supplies. They were lower than he had estimated. 'Someone's been "making free" with the provisions', he privately confided to me.

'Our friend again?'

Julian nodded. 'We're down on porridge, sugar and one of the jars of jam has gone. I suppose it was something we had to expect, but you'd think Irgen would show some concern. After all, what's left has got to last him, as well as us, for the next three weeks or so.'

The solution was obvious. Send the porters back. The Madidi was now navigable. This would be our last night as a large group. Tomorrow we would set off downriver. We told Irgen of our decision and he agreed it was for the best given the way the food was going down. 'One last night with the others', he said. 'Eat as much as you can of Justino's *jochi*. It may be the last meat we have for some time.'

In the remaining hour or two of daylight, Julian and I would have to be busy, he advised. 'When you've sorted out the food we will be taking and what you will leave for Ignacio and the others, wrap lots of Simon's canoe tape around the top of the sacks to keep the rain and the insects out.' He winked at Julian. I noticed how he over-emphasized 'insects'.

'And Simon', he turned to me. 'Make the canoe now. I want everything to be ready for an early start tomorrow.'

Julian and I set to work. Julian left out a small amount of food for the porters' return and divided the rest into two sacks, one for immediate use and the other, a waterproof rubber bag, taped up for later on; there was enough to last for a week or two. I built up the canoe, unrolling the 16-foot skin on the beach, then sliding – wrestling – the poles and cross pieces into position. It was harder work than I remembered. The poles, bent from the collisions on the Rio Hondo, wouldn't line up and the skin was less supple after all the patching that I had done. What should have taken fifteen minutes stretched to nearly an hour and this wasn't aided by the 'help' given by Justino and Leoncio. Seeing my struggle with poles that kept 'pinging' out of place, they were eager to rush to my rescue. They pushed poles into position, often in places they should never have gone into. They tugged at the skin and cross pieces until the framework of a boat built up, though not with the shape I remembered. Finally, I became exasperated. I yelled at them both to go away. I said I would figure it out for myself.

❦

We broke camp early. Everyone was in a state of high excitement, Ignacio, Justino and Leoncio about going back; Julian, Irgen and myself about the journey ahead. We took some final photos of the 'Expedition *Mira-Palanca*' against a view of mist where the mountains should have been and then the porters set off. Justino was fastest as they forded the river and started along the opposite river beach.

'Look at him now', Irgen commented. 'Without that pack, he's like a tapir into the bush.' Ignacio was last to get his stuff together. As we launched the canoe into the clear water, he yelled one last parting phrase.

'Ay Cuñada! Good luck! And remember, no *jodas!*' Then he too was on his way.

We were glad he didn't turn to look back. Before we had even made it around the river bend, the canoe had grounded in shallows. Irgen looked around at the receding figure of his brother. His expression said it all. There was not enough water in the river. We had sent the porters away too soon.

CHAPTER TWELVE

The *Ucamari*

THE MADIDI close to its source was sensational. Edged on both sides by tall trees and impossibly tangled masses of vines and leaves that dangled into the flow, the river wound in tight meanders around jagged spurs that shut off the view ahead and built up our anticipation of what would lie around each new bend. Frothing, white rapids sped us into deep, clear pools where catfish skulked along the bottom. Bamboo-lined narrows opened up into shallow lakes where capped herons with cobalt-blue faces and bobbing white crests fished amongst the boulders at the out-flow end. The herons seemed little bothered by the three men manhandling a heavily laden boat over the rocks to where the channel restarted. They carried on with their nonchalant pacing-out of the shallows while we launched off, paddling furiously against the suck-back of the current until we had regained the main flow. For a while the Madidi would run deep as it cut through a stratum of mud. On these closed-off river bends the wildlife had no fear of showing itself; here we saw spider monkeys hanging over the water to drink, tapirs snorkelling across the centre flow and giant otters, four at a time.

We came upon them quite suddenly at a narrow cut-back mean-der, four slick seals stretched out on the sand of the inside edge. It took me a moment to realize what they were as they lolloped into the river, disappeared for a second or two and then emerged no more than ten feet from us, necks stretched high, peering with blue, goggle eyes into the boat. The otters stood their ground, treading water and snorting like horses from under their glistening moustaches while Julian videoed them and I snapped off several pictures with my camera. As the current took us around the river bend, they kept their relative position, slightly ahead of us, four in a line, each taking turns to stretch high, inquisitive but apparently not hostile as the canoe travelled their patch of the river. Then they submerged, swimming under the canoe and away as we rounded the next meander and floated out of their territory.

The meander ended in shallows, just like so many before. We poled the boat between and over the stones that stuck out of the river until we ground to a halt. Again. Then, without bothering to take out the heavy rucksacks, we hauled until we reached a deeper channel. It should have been obvious what this was doing to the hull, but it was only when we found ourselves sitting in three inches of water in the early afternoon of the third day on the river that we actually decided to do something about repairing the leaks. In fact, we probably wouldn't have stopped so early even then if it hadn't been for Julian losing his 'jungle explorer hat' and the subsequent mood it produced.

'How can you be a proper explorer without the hat', I teased when I noticed it floating past us some time after we had beached the canoe. I waded into the water, grabbed the trilby and ran around with the soggy felt dripping over my head until Julian snatched it off me testily. He glared at me and I thought he was going to say something. Instead, he stomped away to where he had left his rucksack and tenderly stretched the hat out over a head-sized rock so that it did not lose its shape as it dried. His mood was, I reflected later, probably linked to the tension we were all experiencing at suddenly feeling very alone on the river now that the porters had been sent back. It also didn't help that since Justino's paca stew, Julian had been feeling rather delicate. Irgen boiled him up some bark to make a resinous tea which he called '*Sausa*', but all that did was to make Julian retch even more.

The place where we stopped was a triangular expanse of shingle, around a hundred feet on each side. A deep stream fed into the main Madidi on the downstream edge. A steep ridge rose straight up behind. Irgen had heard spider monkeys calling there; he said we would check those out in the morning. First, he instructed, I was to repair the leaking hull while he and Julian would fish in the pool where the stream met the river. I emptied the boat and laid out everything to dry, weighted down with stones as a measure against the stiff breeze that had sprung up. I turned the canoe turtle and started gluing patches over the holes. Although I had stuck on an extra strengthening strip along the centreline while we had been in Rurrenabaque, I had not reckoned on so much wear so soon. Where the poles ran lengthways against it, the neoprene hull had become thin and pliable. There were lines punctured right through in places where small pebbles, brought into the boat on our shoes, had found their way between the poles and the skin, and pressed in as a result of our combined weight above and the action from below of the rocks we had been hitting. I held out little hope that the patches I was putting on would last. I was finding it impossible to keep the ripped areas free from wind-blown sand, and when the patches scraped off I would be unable to replace them, as I had all but run out of extra material. I just hoped that the river would get deeper in the days ahead.

On the other side of the beach a pair of yellow-headed vultures were riding the air currents, swooping at little more than head height over the collection of stranded catfish that Irgen was amassing. I could see he was busy re-baiting his hook with a bit of the left-over paca meat for another cast into the pool. He looked to be in a state of sheer delight. Virtually every cast of his hand line would bring in a two- to three-feet-long *bagre*. Reeling them in involved, first yanking hard on the line as soon as the bait had been taken to ensure that the hook dug fully into the hard tissue around the mouth, then giving the fish a lot of slack as it raced away. At one point Irgen had cut his hand nastily when he inadvertently left the line wrapped around it. Now he held on more gingerly, letting the nylon trail far out before pulling it sharply and reeling steadily in whenever the fish headed back towards him, releasing the tension ever so slightly if it made a serious attempt for freedom. A *bagre* at full force would snap the line, so each had to be 'played' to tire it sufficiently before it could be hauled to shore. Irgen didn't kill the fish he caught. He left them up on the gravel beach where they would lie, flicking their feelers and making low grunting sounds. He said *bagre* was a 'fine fish', but what he was really after was a firm-fleshed *mamore* to eat that night.

By the time I had finished with the canoe and walked over, he was pulling in his fourth catfish. As he heaved it out of the river onto the shingle, I noticed a golden sliver plop out of one of its gills and start wriggling its way over the stones back towards the water. I reached out to grab the tiny fish before it got away, but when my fingers made contact, it disgorged a gush of blood from an oval sack beneath its body, escaping momentarily into the red puddle it had just created. Then I had my hands around it again and could feel the pinpricks of its spines sticking into my skin.

'Watch yourself', Irgen chuckled, hauling his catch fully onto dry land. 'That's a candiru. That's the fish that goes up your *palanca*.'

I'd heard about them before – everybody that visits the Amazon has – but I'd never actually seen one, or really believed the stories. For the most frightening fish in all of the jungle, you can forget the piranha which just bites you, the stingray that whips its poison-tipped tail into your leg and the electric eel. Here was a fish that was truly horrifying, one that would swim right up your penis and once up there would set its spines so it couldn't come out. There would only be one option then. Amputation.

I stared down at the squirming candiru in my hand. Roughly ten centimetres long, eel-like, greenish gold; it was busy burrowing itself in the gap between two of my fingers. As I opened them apart and prized off the shovel head, I caught a glimpse of the tiny white spines, two on each side, half concealed under its gill slits, digging into my skin. They pointed backwards. Pulling the fish by the tail would be useless. That would set the spines further in. I had to push it to get it off.

'They'll slip into any nice little hole.' Irgen laughed at my attempts to prise off the candiru. 'They like the gills of catfish particularly; they suck the blood. But they will enter wounds. They go inside veins.' He paused to consider. 'Arseholes they like. Vaginas. Particularly if a woman is having her period. Penises. They scent out the body fluids. That's why I wear tight pants', he added, pinging the elastic around his upper thigh.

I smiled weakly. I had only brought boxer shorts. I vowed not to go in above the knee next time I washed in the river. I finally succeeded in pulling the fish off and held it between my thumb and forefinger. The candiru waggled limply. I think I had half squashed it. It was half a centimetre in diameter. 'That couldn't. Surely', I said.

'Listen', Irgen whispered, conspiratorially. 'If the big ones – 18 centimetres long in the Beni – can manage it', he waggled his hand then shot it straight up, 'then a tiddler like that? No problem. They can make themselves very thin. They don't go up all the way of course.' I sensed he was enjoying teasing me. 'The tail's usually left hanging out.'

Somehow that made it even worse. The thought of finding a fish's tail flapping at the end of my penis flashed into my mind and wouldn't leave. I was so busy imagining the sheer horror of the situation that I almost missed Irgen's explanation of the treatment for this affliction.

'Set light to the tail with a cigarette lighter', he said, miming the actions, 'then pull for all its worth. Sometimes you catch them off their guard and they retract their spines back in, otherwise . . .' His voice tailed off as he pulled a face of exquisite pain and gripped his crotch. 'Don't worry, Simon!' he laughed, slapping me on the shoulder. 'It probably won't happen. And if it does', he added, clicking his finger and thumb as if holding a lighter, 'you'll be in very good hands!'

It's amazing how hypochondria can hit you. I could see my candiru, lying there where I had left it on top of a rock. It was probably dead by now, but still I had to check. I slipped away, unzipped my flies and went for a pee, just to make sure I still could.

Just getting into the forest the next morning to look for the spider monkeys proved more difficult than we had anticipated. To get onto the ridge, we first had to cross the deep channel on the edge of our shingle bank, then climb a vertical mud cliff 15 to 20 feet high. There was very little space between the bottom of the bank and the channel, so if we fell we would either hit hardened mud, fallen branches and stones, or land in the water. We placed one of the branches across the channel and used that as a bridge, then clambered up where a stream had cut a deep 'V' into the bank, gripping onto trailing roots for support whilst a trickle of water washed over us. Irgen and I managed this without too much difficulty as we were unencumbered, but Julian, cradling his precious video as if it was a baby, slipped. He fell a full ten feet and, trying to avoid falling into the water channel and soaking the camera, took the full force of the fall on his left arm and his back. When he made it up several minutes later, he looked flustered and it was clear he was in pain. He told us not to worry so long as he could get some good footage of the monkeys, which he hoped would be the 'new sort' that I was so excited about.

They were. Though we caught a glimpse of one of the *mari-monos* virtually straight away and heard their hiccuping food calls, Irgen said we had to be 'tactical'. He led us up the slope, through a mass of dew-soaked palms and undergrowth until we had out-flanked the spider monkeys. Now we were above them on the ridge, they were effectively trapped on its lower slopes. They would have to come past us to escape. We started to descend, and in the morning sunlight the views we obtained were fantastic.

The monkeys were feeding on the creamy-white flowers of a canopy tree. From our position on the high ground we were able to look at them on the same level, as they reached far out towards the narrowest twigs, gripping with just their tails and feet as they pulled at the petals then clambered back to the junctions of the branches to carefully feed on the edible parts before foraying out again. In the sunlight I could see the coloration of their fur; black on top, fading to lighter brown under the legs and arms. Their faces were greyish, speckled with pink on what I presumed were the older animals. The monkeys saw us and eventually swung out of our way, past us as Irgen had predicted. But there was no head-bobbing or throwing of branches. These *marimonos* had never seen people and had no reason to be aggressive. I made numerous sketches and was thoroughly satisfied. The only disappointment was the video. Maybe the fall had caused a loose connection. Julian had filmed the monkeys, he said, but the contrast was 'all funny'. The spider monkeys just looked black.

Irgen said it was a shame about the film but, interesting though the *marimonos* were, they were not the *Mono Rey*. He thought the *Mono Rey* was the same as the *Ucamari* that the villagers in San Jose talked about. *Ucamari*, I said, was the name Lars had suggested too.

'But did he tell you about the gringo scientists whose camp was attacked by one a couple of years ago?' Irgen asked me. I shook my head. Irgen continued. 'They were conducting a biological survey for the new National Park, somewhere on the Sendero Ancho up towards Apolo. They had a lot of porters from San Jose with them. The story is that a big animal came into their camp during the night. It went for some meat that had been left lying by the fire, then ripped through their food bags. Somebody shot a gun and scared it off, but it caused quite a bit of damage. A man who had seen it said the animal was an *Ucamari* – a *tigre* would never be that fearless. The porters were so scared, they wouldn't go into the jungle after that.' Irgen paused for a moment. 'You could've asked Justino. He probably knew more about this. Even if he wasn't one of the porters himself, he would have known them.'

I replied to Irgen that I had asked both Justino and Leoncio, but that his brother had ended my hopes of finding out any answers by saying that 'that giant monkey stuff' was just legend. I remembered how he had shot a glance at the two porters and how they had stayed quiet until the subject had been changed.

'There are *Ucamari* in the Serrania Chepite where you were two weeks ago', Irgen said. 'I was told about them by an old man, a

friend of my father's called Renato Lens, who used to collect cinchona bark there. One of his camps was raided by several *Ucamari*.
They wrecked the lean-tos and ate much of the food – the dried
meat "*charque*" and some of the rice. The old man tracked three into
the forest and shot two large brown ones. He told me that one
jumped six metres into a tree, ripping off branches to throw down
at him. The third one, which was smaller, escaped. Renato cooked
and ate the two he had shot. He had said they tasted like pork.'

Lens had come across *Ucamari* on several occasions. He said
they lived in large groups and, though active in the day, 'walked
more' at night. When the adults were foraging, they left the babies
in a cleared area, 50 metres square. Lens had described the *Ucamari*
as about one-and-a-half metres tall, covered in shaggy fur that was
about seven centimetres long. Some were larger – about chest
height when on all fours – and brown. Others were smaller with
black fur. He wasn't sure if these were different types, or males
and females of the same species. They often walked upright like a
man but had much longer arms and very powerful shoulders.

So far, it sounded just like the descriptions I had already been
given of the *Mono Rey*; added confirmation as far as I was concerned. The 'swinging six metres into a tree' and 'throwing
branches' made it sound like the *Ucamari* could be a spider monkey,
like Loys' Ape in fact. But there was something that Irgen added
later that made me question my assumptions.

'They also call it *Mono Oso* – monkey bear', he said. 'Its face is
small and sometimes marked with white; it's quite like that of a
fox.'

A spectacled bear. I sagged with the disappointment.

'Large, black and shaggy, lives in the high montane forests, has
an omnivorous diet; the hearts of palms could be included in that.'
I ran through what I knew about the species: its propensity for
climbing trees (more than most other types of bear), its small
stature (man-size), the variations of colour (black to dark brown).
It was the facial markings that clinched it – white patches, sometimes in rings around the eyes that gave the bear its name. I
mentally processed all the information I knew about spectacled

bears and reproached myself for being so easily fooled into believing the *Ucamari* was really a giant monkey.

'So it's a bear then', I said to Irgen at last.

'No. It swings in trees.'

I let the matter rest for the present, preferring to retain some vestige of hope that the *Mono Rey/Ucamari* really did exist, and that the whole trip hadn't been ultimately pointless. It was two nights later that the question of animal classification came up again – just what was a monkey?

We had camped under some trees that overhung a long strip of sand bordering the river. One of the reasons for this was that Julian was able to use his hammock rather than sleeping on a plastic sheet with a mosquito net hung over the top, which is what Irgen and I usually did. Irgen had shot a piping guan – a small black turkey with a white crest and blue facial skin and throat wattles; it was beautiful and very 'good eating'. Now it was roasting above our fire. There was an animal in one of the trees above. We could hear the leaves rustle and occasionally bits of twigs would drop on us as it jumped from branch to branch. I scanned up with my head lamp looking for eye-shine, but only once did I catch any reflection; two orange points, no real indication of what the animal looked like.

'*Wiche*', Irgen said. 'Listen to its call. Wichee. Wichee. It's a *Mono Wiche*.'

Mono – a monkey. 'Is it like the night monkeys that we have seen before?' I asked.

'No', Irgen replied. This was different. It had a pointed face, like a *tejon* – a coati. A kinkajou? I described what I knew about these. They look something like a pine marten, live in trees, a carnivore that eats fruit. Irgen nodded, 'Si si. A *Mono Wiche*.'

'But it's not a monkey.'

'It lives in trees', Irgen responded.

'That doesn't necessarily make it a monkey', I said. Irgen looked confused. I thought through his logic, how he had classified a kinkajou as a monkey.

'So the *Mono Rey*, the *Ucamari*, is also called the *Mono Oso*', I continued. 'Is that just a bear that climbs trees?'

'That's silly. Everyone knows bears don't climb trees', Irgen said. 'They eat ants. They have big claws and long noses.' I remembered *Oso Bandera* – literally, banded bear – was the name for a giant anteater. 'If it eats ants, then it's a bear?' Irgen nodded. 'And if it climbs trees, it's a monkey'. He nodded again.

So that was it. The *Ucamari* was just a bear. If the *Mono Rey* was the *Ucamari*, and I suspected it was, then all that stuff about Loys' Ape had just been wishful thinking. I had listened to the information and fitted it in with the ape story. I had heard what I wanted to hear then set off halfway across the world after an animal that ultimately I knew was probably just a myth. Of course, I had realized that the chance of such an animal's existence was tiny, and that even if it *did* exist I would hardly be likely to find one. But that glimmer of hope that something might be there had been the excuse for the whole trip, and as the jungle and the intensity of our expedition had sucked me in, I had let the hope grow to the point where I was now genuinely disappointed over what I should have realized was only confirmation of the truth. After all, it wasn't hard to see why such mystery had grown around the *Ucamari* – monkey bear – monkey king. Few people would ever have seen a spectacled bear. Living in the high cloud forests where conditions had always been too harsh for people to live, increasingly endangered as the lower altitude *selva* that linked their islands of habitat had been stripped away, the *Ucamari* would only ever have been seen by men like Renato Lens who scoured the ridges for cinchona trees to make quinine. And how many men still did that now that medicines were manufactured from synthetic ingredients? Their stories of attacks by man-sized beasts – giant monkeys (they climbed trees, didn't they?) – would have transformed in the retelling into the legend of the *Mono Rey*, a shaggy black ape that could pull a man's arm from its socket and (conveniently) only lived in the forests far too remote for people to ever get to.

There was, of course, another possibility. That the *Mono Rey* and the *Ucamari* were separate species. The behaviour of throwing sticks at aggressors was so monkey-like, after all. Swinging six metres into a tree was something not even an agile spectacled bear could do. But I felt I had to admit the weight of evidence was behind the *Mono Rey* being just a bear. Of course, there was the lesser 'prize' of the large *marimonos* we could claim to have found. Even then we could not be certain this was anything new. We had no evidence and, unless we brought back a dead one, who would believe *us*? A builder and a schoolteacher.

❧

The pool in my tree frog dream is nearly dried up. Several scum lines on the rocks around the edges show successive drops in the level. There is no dribble of water overflowing the dam of piled up twigs and leaves at the end. The moss there looks flaky and yellowed. A scum of dust, bark flakes and bits of leaves peppers the surface, rising and falling with the occasional ripple when a tadpole comes up to gulp the air or to snatch at one of the see-through, tube-like mosquito larvae that hangs from under the surface skin by a snorkel spiracle; hairy papillae around dark spots where the eyes will be waft micro-detritus into transparent mouth parts. One of the tadpoles is particularly bloated. Maybe it is of a different species. It already has a pair of hind legs which flex out behind it as it punts itself into the soggy leaves at the edge of the pool, nosing out larvae and smaller tadpoles to feed itself.

It is midday. The clouds over the far ridges have burned away in the sun so that the full cordillera can be seen, the mountains stacked up, fading away blue into the dry season haze.

I can see myself traversing one of the ridge sides, machete-cutting a trail in the shade beneath the canopy. Tree trunks rise up into a cathedral of great vaulted arches. Shafts of sunlight pierce gaps in the canopy, illuminating parts of the leaf litter in a dappled pattern which dances as the wind blows the leaves above. The undergrowth is sparse and I pick my way through easily. It's always so in my imagination. The backpack never weighs down as much. The heat is never as intense. The slopes are never that steep and the jungle is always open enough to afford a view all around. Maybe it is the process of exploring that I love, the journey and its intricacies – the details of transporting myself and my food and equipment, of setting a route and keeping to it, of making a camp.

*Maybe I'm not that bothered with the act of finding something or get-
ting to anywhere in particular. When I read of Fawcett and Costin
travelling through the forests of the Caupolican and the details are left
out, I feel cheated. So they travelled from Rurrenabaque to Apolo – but
how did they do it? How did it feel to punt a balsa raft up through the
canyon of the Bala? And what was the overland trek like after that?
Where did they camp? How did they camp? Did they use hammocks or
lie on a groundsheet with a mosquito net over them as I did? And who
went with them? History often fails to mention the servants and retainers, those who travelled along for the ride, except if, like Harvey the
gunfighter, they made a particular impression. Fawcett often employed
many Indian paddlers, but at no point says how they fitted into the team
as a whole, how their characters affected the mood of the expeditions, or
how he and his companions felt when their retainers left them to fend for
themselves alone in the vastness of the forest.*

*What did those 'classic' expeditions feel like? That's what I wanted to
know, even more than if some giant monkey lived in those ridges. To trek
through the Bolivian montana must surely feel no different now. With
largely blank maps and radio signals for our navigation equipment
blocked out by millions of trees, the terrain is as unknown as it has ever
been. Our trail cutting, making camp and hunting or fishing for our food
is essentially the same. Apart from the fact that our rucksacks and some
of our clothes are made of synthetic fibres, Julian and I are even kitted out
with equipment that the explorers we idolized would have recognized.
Like them, we had sweated our way over Serranias and seen marimonos and tapirs. We had eaten jochi and mutum, and in turn fed
countless marahuisas and mosquitoes. We too had felt the thrill of riding
the rapids and the heady mixture of fear and excitement you get when
you send your porters back and set off into the forest alone.*

*And now, soon enough, we would be setting off on foot through the
forest again. One last bit. We had arrived at the Madidi, but sometime
we would have to ready ourselves for the journey back. We would have
to canoe the river out of the last ridges of the mountains and then there
would be no choice but to walk. Contouring around the base of the
Serrania del Tigre, the Jaguar ridge, we would be skirting the swamps
of the Madidi where Fawcett had been convinced there were monsters.*

*Whether or not he was right, the area was still unknown, unexplored.
Julian and I both knew that the journey back would be an expedition in
itself.*

#

Nevertheless, the realization about the *Ucamari* put me in a foul
mood. I became irritable and surly with Julian and Irgen, putting
pressure on them to paddle longer and harder each day, even if this
meant missing some of the fantastic wildlife that we all wanted to
see. When we did see animals – more giant otters or tapirs crossing ahead of us in the river – I wouldn't let us linger; we had to get
on. When we came across the signs that a large herd of white-
lipped peccaries (the famously dangerous ones that Julian said he
had always wanted to see) had just crossed the river, I couldn't
even be bothered to go and look for them.

'Wah! it stinks like a fat man's armpit', Irgen snorted, wrinkling
his nose and sniffing the air. 'There could be a hundred or more.'
He pointed to a patch on the bank where a swathe of vegetation
about three metres wide had been trampled down. 'They forage in
huge circles. It might have been years since they were here last.
Shall we go and look for them?' He was already standing up as we
nudged the boat towards the gap where the peccaries had entered
the forest. Julian looked keen to go too. But not me. I had only just
got dry after dragging the canoe across several waterslides, and
now I was feeling warm and cosy, I didn't want to go through the
rigmarole of 'kitting up' and putting my wet boots on. But my real
reason was the time it would take.

'You're becoming obsessed with getting down the river as
quickly as possible', said Julian when I whined that it would be a
waste of effort looking for the peccaries. 'You agreed yourself that
the headwaters would be the best bit. The river's already getting
much bigger. Soon we'll be out of the Serranias and we'll have
missed our chance to really explore them. I say we stay around
here for a while. We can make up time later, put in longer days,
paddle faster.'

He knew his argument was weak and I seized on it. 'We have no idea of what happens next. Let's face it, the map is crap. It doesn't show anything. There could be bad rapids, a *curiche* even. That would totally finish us, stuck in that shit with no way back or forwards.' Julian tried to protest, but I pushed the point further. 'And this road that we've drawn on the map, this Carreterra Alto Madidi – what if it doesn't exist? What do we do then?'

'It does exist!' Julian blurted out. 'Negro said so. Chichito is logging just near it . . . and besides, even if the road's not finished, there'll be a trail where it's going to be. Two days maximum, I reckon. We'll get back to Ixiamas weeks early and miss all the good stuff.' I knew he had a point, but what if he was wrong? My tone was vicious, bullying.

'Negro could have just told us what we wanted to hear. Everyone else has', I said. 'There's no guarantee that there is a road or that Chichito will be waiting for us in three weeks with his jeep. Nothing is certain. We have come here to explore the Madidi river, not to hang around and take in the jungle.'

'All right', said Julian resignedly. 'We go on.'

I had won. I should have felt good about getting my own way but I didn't. I sniffed the air. Nothing new; just damp and stale sweat. Perhaps, I decided, I stank as bad as the peccaries.

❀

It rained so hard next morning that it hurt. It was like being pelted from above with gravel. Soaking in the boat, we paddled with an amazing ferocity, not out of any sudden desire for speed but out of the need to keep warm. The only way to do that was to keep our muscles working. The river ahead was a foaming mass of splashes, frothing up into true white water at the rapids, which we slid over with unexpected ease now that the river was starting to rise. Most of the falls were just the usual waterslide arrangement of boulders that we'd scoot down, only to row hard against the suck-back of the whirlpools at the end. But some of the rapids were bigger, and in our desperation to keep paddling we were nearly swamped more than once by the great waves that bounced off half-submerged tree trunks and swept us down chutes of churning water. Each time we'd be spewed out, soaked but exhilarated and amazed that we'd managed to come through without completely filling the canoe or capsizing. Any control we had was minimal. We were largely at the mercy of where the flow wanted to take us and, thankfully, there was often such a huge wave of water ahead of us that we'd be swept away from imminent collision with rocks or trunks, just at the time we had given up fending off and were bracing ourselves for impact.

The river eventually flattened, splitting to flow around islands of shingle. All we had to do was to make sure we were on the route with most water and keep paddling. Once we passed a pair of king vultures standing bedraggled and forlorn-looking on one of the islands. Their huge white wings hung at their sides like wet sacks, naked heads hunched close to their bodies. They looked as cold and pathetic as I felt.

After two hours we had had enough. Though Julian felt marginally better under his raincape, Irgen at the front and I at the rear of the canoe were so cold that our hands and feet were starting to go numb. We needed to dry off, warm up and get some hot food inside us. The curassows that we saw in a tree at the shore stood no chance. Big black turkeys on an open branch were too inviting a meal to be passed up. The thought of spitted bird roasting over the fire was fully in mind as I silently slid the rifle from its position alongside the food sack and carefully passed it to Irgen. He could make the kill. This wasn't a time for me or Julian to go wasting bullets. Scarcely rippling the paddle above the water, I steered the canoe towards the shore.

When the boat grounded, Irgen took up the rifle, aimed and shot. He missed. Against the pelting rain the noise from our small-bore gun was hardly audible. The *mutums* hadn't noticed the noise. Irgen shot again. This time he was successful, sending one of the birds tumbling down through the branches while its companions sped for the security of a nearby thicket. Irgen retrieved the carcass and we set about it in almost desperate haste, pulling off the feathers in handfuls, stripping the bird completely in little more than a minute. Then we re-launched the canoe back into the current. Next bend, next beach we would make camp, get a fire going and eat hot food. There was a stand of *chuchillo* cane that we could use to make poles for our 'tent', balsa saplings for making bark string and a good supply of driftwood for a fire. The beach wasn't very high above the water level, but we felt so cold and wretched that it would have to do. Though the rain was by now starting to ease off, none of us could face carrying on. We were ruthlessly efficient in making the camp, moving energetically to bring our cold muscles back into life. While Irgen dashed off into the *chuchillo* thicket to cut poles for the tent frame and some large fan-like fronds to make a shelter for the fire, I tied up the canoe to one of the paddles which I sank, handle first, into the mud. Then I went to help Julian find some firewood. By the time we had returned to our camp Irgen had already made the two tripods plus cross pole that made up the frame over which we'd hang the plastic sheet, as well as a wind-break for the fire. I helped him tie the tarpaulin over the frame and we were heading towards the canoe to pick up the ruck-sacks when Irgen suddenly swore and started sprinting for the river. The paddle that I had sunk in as an anchor was dragging slowly across the mud. I watched it slipping into the water. The canoe was floating away.

CHAPTER THIRTEEN

Barbaros

IRGEN AND I dashed for the boat, which by now was edging towards midstream. I saw its blue, nylon rope uncoil from the fallen paddle/anchor and snake across the sand. The tip slid into the mud-coloured water just as I reached out to grab it. I heard a sharp crack on the other side of the river. Stones tumbled and splashed, the bank falling as the current scooped it away from underneath. There was a loud 'tear' as roots sheared and a palm tree swung out at an improbable angle from the edge, held for a second, then slid down into the flow where it was instantly swept away. I waded in up to my waist, lunged for the end of the rope, and missed. A wave caught my chest and I was suddenly aware of mud-reddened water, the hiss of surf and of my gasping breath as I struggled to keep myself upright. I saw Irgen some yards downstream. He had hold of the rope and was leaning back so far that he was nearly level with the water as he tried to pull the canoe back to the shore. I could see the canoe bucking in the current, then bending as Irgen grabbed the side and heaved it fully onto the sand. A moment later and it would have been caught in the main flow along with the ripped off branches and beach debris that jostled down the middle of the river. Then it would have been lost. That was too terrifying to contemplate.

Irgen's comment as he started back up the beach was like a slap across the face. 'Learn how to tie knots, Simon', he said. 'That was too close.'

'It wasn't my knot', I snapped back. 'The river is rising.'

We each took a side of the canoe and hurried over the already much-narrowed beach towards Julian. The lower parts were starting to fill up. A narrow trickle was forming a shallow bay between where we had sited our fire and a five-foot high bank, where Julian was now shifting the food sacks. I dragged the canoe as far up as I could and tied it firmly to a tree trunk. Julian and Irgen, meanwhile, pulled the food bags, rifle and rucksacks up as the water got to our camp, dousing the fire we had just lit and swamping the floor of our shelter. The water surged on towards our sandbank and just ahead, in an unbroken line, came a tide of tiny frogs and long-legged spiders that had been driven from their holes in the beach. As the water arrived, they skittered through our equipment and swarmed over us in their escape to the higher ground.

When everything was out of the way of the flood there was nothing we could do except watch as the water rose and hope it wouldn't overflow our section of riverbank. The Madidi was now a churning, mud-coloured torrent. The central section, where we had canoed just twenty minutes earlier, now surged with white-topped breakers. Whole trunks, uprooted from the banks, crashed and spun in the turmoil. There was even a pair of giant otters that stretched their necks out of the water and snorted at us as they too were swept past. The river continued to rise. Within minutes, it had fully submerged the beach and was lapping against our bank. By the time an hour had passed its level had risen five feet and our sanctuary had almost become an island in the flow. As the current undermined the edges we pushed our equipment further up the roots of a couple of small trees just in case we were flooded out entirely. Luckily, the Madidi rose no further. By early afternoon the water was subsiding. On what had been the beach, we could see ripples and protruding dorsal fins where shoals of trout-sized *sabalo* fought against the current. They made slow progress, the weaker ones slowing to a halt, then suddenly being swept away by the force of the water. Catching them was a game we all joined in, whacking them with the blunt side of a machete then scooping them out with our hands before they could swim away or were lost in the current. We had to be quick to catch them as, once stunned, they soon disappeared in the opaque water. We hit many but landed only three. Later we roasted them, wrapped in large leaves, and ate them with the *mutum* that Irgen had shot on the way downriver.

As the water drained out of the pools that had been created, the fish made their last dash for freedom before they were cut off. Already at the other end of the beach I could see magpie plovers and egrets pecking at the bodies of fish marooned on the mud. Quite abruptly, the clouds evaporated. The midday sun's rays smacked against the sodden beach causing it to steam visibly. The sudden wave of sauna-like heat and humidity made my pores pop out sweat so that my shirt was instantly peppered with wetness.

With the river still running high there seemed little point continuing in the canoe that day, and so I set about what I always did whenever we made camp and got the GPS out to find our position. Its carrying bag was misted with condensation and when I pressed the 'on' switch nothing happened. After several more tries without result I became really quite worried. I felt my pulse quicken, tasted sick at the back of my mouth at the realization that we didn't know how far downriver the flood had taken us. We wouldn't know when to start looking for the way out. Or which way to go. My fingers were shaking by the time I levered off the battery hatch. Inside was dry but the ends of the cells and their spring contacts were speckled with mould or corrosion. I shook them out, dabbed them with some toilet paper and scraped the oxide off the metal with my penknife. Then I snapped the device back together. Still nothing. I pressed my finger so hard on the button and kept it pressed, willing the device back into life.

'INITIALIZING . . . SAT STATUS . . . SEARCHING'

The words gave me such relief that I laughed out loud. The bar chart of satellite signals flashed onto the screen and within seconds I had our position. I found my diary and wrote the co-ordinates down quickly, just in case the connection broke. Then I carefully repacked the navigator in my reserve clean pair of socks and sealed it inside two plastic bags in the middle and safest part of my pack.

When I checked our co-ordinates on the map, our position came as an intense disappointment. We had made 15 kilometres in two hours, about twice that distance if I included the meandering of the river. My plot on the map put us way beyond the Madidi's headwaters; we were still paralleling the line of the Serrania del Tigre ridge, but at a place where, within a day or two, the river would swing towards the north-east and beyond the mountains for good. The realization hit me; in letting ourselves be taken by the flow, in paddling so hard to keep warm, we had come too far. We had left the Serranias behind and were now onto the flat of the flood plain. All that lay ahead was slow, looping meanders and uninspiring stands of bamboo and cecropia trees. There would now be no way of going back to find out if there really was a *Mono Rey*, or even to look for an *Ucamari*. We would not be able to investigate the large *marimonos* again and show if they were truly some new species. Julian was devastated. He commented that I had got my own way again and should be happy now that we were that much closer to home. I tried to appease him by suggesting that we might explore up one of the Madidi's small tributaries, but he looked unenthusiastic. Our whole sense of purpose had gone. Now there would be nothing to do except make our way back.

⚜

When we set off the next day we were all in a sombre mood. The water was so full of mud it was undrinkable. No fish would take the bait on our hooks. The weather stayed dreary, and as any *mutums* we could have shot stayed away from the river's edges, our food (rice with lentils) was dreary too. I was depressed that we hadn't actually found anything that might justify our expedition, and Julian was depressed that all I wanted to do at that moment was to go back. I had three weeks until my flight. Getting that was now my priority. But, I realized, for the present we would have to go forward. We could not even consider trying to walk out while there was still a Serrania in the way. We had to continue with the river until it had got us around that last ridge. Then we would walk. We would find Julian's 'Madidi Highway' and take that back to where Chichito would be waiting with his jeep. Providing the canoe made it that far. The hull had now sustained so much damage riding the rapids during the storm that the keel strip was hanging off. The only tape that I had left to hold it on with had lost its stickiness in the humidity that had built up since. The leaks were so bad that we now sat in six inches of water as we canoed down the river; even then someone constantly had to bail. Another set of shallows or a snag would have the keel stripped off and the decision about when to start out overland would be made for us.

Irgen said we had to continue with all speed. He seemed edgy. The reason for this revealed itself when we rounded a meander and saw a clearing on the riverbank.

'*Barbaros*', he whispered. 'We will travel on the other side now.'

As we approached, we could see that the clearing had long grown over with a mass of creepers. Secondary-growth trees coated the river edges on either side. There were more open areas further on, and growing in them were the paddle-shaped leaves of what looked like banana plants.

'Bananas', Irgen confirmed my thoughts. 'Those must have been their *chacras* – their plantations. Looking at the size of those plants', he added, lifting himself half out of the canoe to get a better look, 'they must be at least ten or twenty years old. Strange. I was told that all the Indians had headed towards the Rio Colorado long before that.'

'Maybe some stayed', said Julian, who had definitely perked up since the word '*barbaros*' had been mentioned.

Irgen shrugged. 'Not that I knew of', he said. 'There are maybe small groups on some of the other rivers – Ignacio found some tracks by the Suapi a year back – but the Colorado is where most of them are now. My father used to trade caiman skins with the Pacaguaras over that way 20 or 30 years ago. He said they were true savages, fierce, with bowl haircuts and feathers through holes in their noses.'

'What about the Tacana?' I ventured. 'I thought some of them still lived in the forest like they used to.' Irgen shook his head. His answer put me in my place.

'The Tacanas, they're farming Indians', he said dismissively. 'They live in the forest, yes, but they cut it down to grow crops. They've been settled like that for centuries with towns and missions and Catholic priests. My own mother is Tacana. We know some of the ways of the forest – some of the medicines and how to hunt – but nothing like as well as the Indians who planted those bananas. Those people plant a few crops but they soon move on. They live much more from the *selva*. Those people, the Pacaguaras, the Echojas, the Toromonas', he reeled the names off with a look of admiration, 'are the real thing, the true *barbaros*.

'But they shouldn't be here. I thought they had all gone', Irgen continued, a look of concern spreading across his usually impassive features. 'This worries me.'

'Can we get out and look around?' Julian asked. I could tell he was excited at the possibility of meeting 'real' Indians. Irgen's glance cut him short.

'Simon, Juleen', he said gravely, 'Listen to me seriously. We must be quiet and we must watch the banks. And Juleen, don't get any ideas about meeting these *barbaros* and learning to be like one.' Julian looked offended. Irgen continued. 'The fact these are old *chacras* doesn't mean there aren't newer ones behind. If we see anyone – even a child – we must not smile or say "hello". We just paddle past. *Muy tranquilo*. You understand?' We both nodded dutifully, but I couldn't help noticing how Julian suppressed a smile each time he caught my eyes during the rest of the morning. I knew he'd be quietly imagining himself in the place of one of his heroes like the German-American adventurer, Fritz Up-de-Graf, who had tapped rubber and searched for gold in the territory of Jivaro headhunters (in Amazonian Ecuador) around the turn of the twentieth century. His exploits riding the rapids of the 'Pongo de Manseriche', travelling in the Jivaro war canoes and describing in lurid detail how they shrank the heads of their victims by prising out the skulls and pouring in heated sand (after first sewing the eyes, lips and nostrils up to prevent seepage), formed the basis of Julian's daydreams. Alright, it was unfortunate that Up-de-Graf had later shot his canoe-full of Indians when he had mistakenly taken the sound of a gun firing around the next river bend as a warning from his companion. But barring errors like this, such were the sort of adventures that Julian wanted to have. He was proud of the fact that he had trained hard before the trip so that he was at the peak of fitness. After the disappointment of his detention at the village in Surinam, he was determined to be ready if ever the chance of travelling with 'real' Indians should present itself again. That was probably why he had hired Irgen to take us on to the Madidi after Charlie had decided to quit. Perhaps it was the Guarayos not the *Mono Rey* that he had sought all along, though admittedly it was hard to tell; he still kept many of his thoughts on the matter very much to himself. Certainly the Madidi had once been 'Indian country', even if it wasn't today; a river historically feared and untravelled while so many others were having their banks exploited for their precious rubber resources.

In 1888 a priest, Padre Armentia, who would later become bishop of La Paz, wrote of the river in his report of the Franciscan missions of the Caupolican, 'Today, both banks of the Madidi are occupied by the ferocious Guarayos who make its navigation extremely difficult if not impossible.'

Evans too spoke of the Guarayos or Guacanaguas. He said that they had been Christianized and formed the mission of Santiago de Pacaguaras near the Madidi (though he did comment that it seemed strange for their mission to take the name of another tribe). Following a feud with the inhabitants of Ixiamas, where they had mutilated a Guarayo brave as punishment for desecrating their church or violating one of their women (nobody was sure any more), the tribe professed 'an undying hatred for the Christian Indians. . . . Their war cry is said still to be an imprecation against Ixiamas. They carry banners with the form of a monkey or other animal woven into it.'

Evans did, however, accept that not all the murders attributed to wild Indians were the fault of the Guarayos. 'Guarayo', he added as a footnote in his report to the RGS, appeared to be a general term for 'fighter, murderer, ferocious savage or outlaw'.

Fawcett went on to further justify the hostility of the Guarayos of the lower Madidi. He said that it was the fault of the rubber estates, and his sympathies lay fully with the Indians:

> Slaving raids on the savages were a common practice. The prevailing idea that the *barbaro* was nothing better than a wild animal accounted for many of the atrocities perpetrated on them by the degenerates who were the straw bosses of the *barracas*. I met the Guarayo Indians later, and found them intelligent, clean, and infinitely superior to the drink-sodden 'civilised' Indians of the rivers. True they were hostile and vengeful, but look at the provocation.

The owners of the rubber concerns along the rivers viewed the forest Indians as little more than animals to be rounded up and used as slave labour in their rubber collecting enterprises, or to be disposed of if they were in the way of their business. Slaving expeditions were common. So were revenge raids by the Indians. Fear of wild savages in the remote rubber settlements was intense, and when the Indians in a rubber area were rumoured to be hostile, estate bosses often pre-empted any trouble and attacked first. Fawcett noted one particular raid on a Guarayo village led by a Swiss and a German from an estate below the confluence of the Madidi with the Beni. He wrote,

> A village was destroyed, men and women butchered and children killed by dashing their brains out against trees. The raiders returned proudly with a prize of eighty canoes and boasted of the exploit!

This had been triggered by the fear of a raid on their *barraca* since 'a few timid Indians had come into camp'.

When Fawcett encountered the Guarayos[1] it was not on the Madidi but on the Rio Heath, further to the north-west. Under a

---

1   Fawcett called all the 'wild' Indians of the Rios Madidi and Heath, Guarayos or Guacanaguas. These were a distinct tribe from the Christianized Guarayos of Eastern Bolivia. The Indians that Fawcett wrote about may have been separate tribes; the Guarayos on the Rios Heath and Tambopata, and the Guacanaguas on the Madidi. From Evans's report its seems that both may have been branches of a tribe which had earlier been called the Tiatinaguas.

rain of arrows from across the river, the explorers had amazingly managed to resolve the situation peacefully by singing 'Swanee River', 'Bicycle made for two' and other popular tunes of the day, whilst one member of the party, Todd, sat on an open sand bar accompanying them on his accordion. (Fawcett commented, 'he was an expert with the accordion, which was one of our principle reasons for bringing him'.) When the presumably bemused Indians stopped shooting, Fawcett and the expedition doctor paddled across the river and were taken off down a forest trail to meet the Indians' chief. The Guarayos were intensely interested in the strange people that had come into their lands and provided a feast of fish for them that night, after which six of them stayed the night on the river beach with the expedition who, for once, felt so at ease that they set no guards.

Fawcett recognized that the numbers of the *barbaros* were declining. In his 1913 report to the RGS, he commented:

> The Madidi and its tributaries harbour only five small tribes of not a dozen souls in each, a terrible indictment against the rubber industry, chiefly responsible for their disappearance.

What happened to the Guarayos-Guacanaguas – whether they moved on, perhaps to the Rio Colorado, or died out – is unclear. 'Guarayos' was now just a name on one of our La Paz military maps, a settlement, possibly a Christian mission, further down the Madidi. 'Guarayos' was a name Irgen said he hadn't heard of. He said he thought the Indians that had cleared the *chacras* we were passing had been Pacaguaras, which to me seemed strange as the Pacaguaras were a tribe that had traditionally lived far down the Rio Beni. One thing was sure though: whoever had cut those clearings had done so much more recently than our guide had expected. Ten to twenty years ago, it may have been by his reckoning, but that was still recent enough for him to stay distinctly on his guard for the rest of the day until we had long passed that part of the river.

Julian and I stayed in a state of alert all day too. We scanned the banks, not just for wildlife now, but also for signs of *barbaros* – a dugout canoe, a clearing with a palm-frond round hut, a long-haired figure in a bark cloth shift, watching us silently from the waterside. But we saw nothing out of the ordinary, not until two days later when we arrived at a wide expanse of shallows where a mud-brown tributary fed into the Madidi.

I saw the hut first. Straight lines like those don't occur in nature. I knew it looked out of place before I recognized what it was, or the fact that this was not Indian-built; the wood along its walls had been chain-sawed. The hut was perched, partly overhanging a red mud bank, behind some riverside rocks. It was obviously abandoned. Much of the ground underneath it had caved away and now the building was on the point of falling into the river. When we beached the canoe, we saw immediately that there were people around, or recently had been. A squeezed-out toothpaste tube lay discarded on a rock. It couldn't have been washed up there by the river. It was too high up. Nor could it have been left there for more than three days. The rain on the day of the flash flood would have swept it away.

The thought of meeting people on the Madidi disappointed me. Our untouched river no longer felt so unexplored, so pure, so unsullied. I also felt scared. This was obviously not some makeshift loggers' camp. What would anyone be doing out here? From my position on the rocks below the hut I could see the bushes on the bank were machete-cut into a path that led back from the river. I followed Julian and Irgen up it to a clearing in which stood a large, sturdy-looking house made from sawed planks. Two colourful towels had been left out to dry over one of two window ledges on the right side of the building. In the middle there was a doorway through which we could see another opening at the other side. We shouted our greetings at the unseen owners but there was no answer. We went in.

To the left of the entrance, the house appeared abandoned. The room on this side was dark and smelled of damp and rot. The two rooms to the right were tidier. In the front one with the towels was also an old pair of jeans (folded), a row of blue and yellow 'Ray-o-Vac' batteries lined up along the windowsill and two pairs of plimsolls placed next to each other in a corner. The back room contained a bunk bed. On the top bunk there was a folded photocopy of a map of northern Bolivia; several paths or streams had been marked.

'Loggers?' ventured Julian, poring over the map. 'Who are these people?' Irgen ignored him, preoccupied for the present with examining the shoes. He had accidentally set light to his two days before when he had left them to dry by the fire. He was obviously eyeing these up as replacements.

'*Cocaleros* – drug runners?' I suggested, feeling suddenly paranoid. I did not want to be here. Irgen put down the shoes and pointed at some blue paint marks, an eagle perhaps, daubed on one of the walls.

'Military', he said. 'I've seen this sign tattooed on soldiers' arms. Maybe this is a border post. We're very near to Peru here, you know?' He picked up the jeans, measured them against his legs and then dropped them on the floor. Too small. 'All this stuff's fairly dry. The people here can't have been gone that long – a day or two at most. If they've got a boat they could be down the Madidi or up that tributary we've just passed.'

'I think we should go now', I said. The others looked up.

'Why?' I couldn't explain. I felt terrified. My mouth tasted sour and my pulse was racing. It was an ambush. I knew it. This was a cocaine lab. There were *cocaleros* probably hiding around the hut even now, sizing up who we were, ready to shoot us when we came out. Maybe we had been lucky enough to arrive when they were away. Now we had to go before they came back.

'We should go now', I said again. Julian ignored me and went out of the back door. Irgen examined the other pair of shoes, then followed him.

My mind raced on. If they were soldiers, that was just as bad. Bored witless at such a remote spot, what would two heavily armed men do with us to keep themselves amused? They would hold onto us for a start. We had no permission to be here. This was a sensitive border zone. They'd probably try for a bribe but once they had seen our stuff it would be easy to get it all. We had one small-bore rifle and three machetes. Against two soldiers with automatic weapons we wouldn't stand a chance. We should go now. We had to get a head start before they could catch us up in their motorboat. If we left everything as we had found it, they need never know that we had been here.

Irgen reappeared. 'There's a grown-over airstrip back there', he pointed out. 'I think I know what this place is now.'

'Tell me later. I really don't want to stay any longer. Let's go now', I said.

Irgen ignored me. 'There's no reason to stay', I continued. 'We might have trouble if we meet people.'

Julian reappeared at the doorway. 'Get a grip, Simon', he said. 'You're getting paranoid. It's that Lariam[2] you're taking – it's screwing up your brain. These people could be really helpful. They might know of a track back to Ixiamas. We should wait for them to come back.'

'I'm not going to risk that. I'm going.' I started walking back towards the river. 'Are you coming?'

'At least we should take their map', Julian said.

'No. Leave it. Don't touch anything.' I got to the canoe and started sliding it back into the water. Julian and Irgen followed reluctantly. They were muttering. I made out the word '*loco*' (mad). Irgen had one of the pairs of plimsolls in his hands. I glared at him. He looked at me as if I had lost any sense that I had and tossed the shoes into the bushes by his side. He and Julian sullenly got into the boat. I pushed it off and paddled us straight for the midstream where the current was fastest.

After we had been paddling for about an hour, Irgen broke the silence. 'I think that was the prison', he said. 'The government used to send its political prisoners there – generals, politicians, anyone powerful who disagreed with them. This was

---

2 Lariam, a brand name of Mefloquine anti-malaria tablets which have received a lot of publicity due to their side effects, including feelings of paranoia and hal- lucinations.

in the 1950s, in the days of President Enstoresso. There were lots of coups then. Whenever they had one they would fly the troublemakers, along with their families, down here. They'd get taken back to La Paz when the government changed again, which it did quite often in those days. They say that the prison was quite luxurious. The prisoners had nice houses to live in. They had guards, of course, but stuck out here there was nowhere to escape to. The soldiers fought a lot with the *barbaros*. There was lots of trouble with the Nabajas who lived here at the time. They've since moved on to the Rio Heath. As for the prison, I believe it fell out of use in the 1960s. The government was more stable then.'

We continued paddling and, as we started to put some distance between us and the house, my anxiety lessened. With the addition of the water from another tributary the Madidi had grown to nearly a hundred yards wide now, and was deep enough that grounding and further ripping the hull was no longer a problem. However, the canoe was still leaking badly. During the next two days, as we rounded the final out-croppings of the Serrania del Tigre, we all became concerned that we should pack up and start walking soon. We would try to find the Carreterra Alto Madidi, a road, which though proudly referred to as 'our link with Peru' in Rurrenabaque, was a highway that no one was quite sure really existed, least of all Irgen. His opinion, which he stated over a miserable supper of lentils boiled in muddy water, was that we should continue for four or five more days and head for the San Antonio logging camp, an idea which filled Julian and me with horror; we still had bad memories of the place from the start of the trip. We looked at each other and decided that the time had come to produce 'Plate 120', photocopied from the greatest, most definitive atlas of them all, *The Times Atlas of the World*. It had been carried in Julian's rucksack top pocket for the past two and a half months, our trump card if ever we were lost.

Julian reverentially unfolded the scrap of paper and laid it on the sand. He pointed to a dot marked Ixiamas and to a dashed line that led to the Peruvian border. 'The Carretera Alto Madidi.' He beamed with satisfaction.

'Our way back.'

※

The problem was that we didn't know where the road crossed the river.

※

'Chainsaw', said Irgen, pulling his paddle clear of the water and nodding towards the left bank. 'Don't you hear it?'

I had to admit I couldn't. Against the lapping of the water and the quiet buzzing from the jungle, any extra machine-made hum was indistinct. But I knew Irgen was right. He always was about things like that. We had already come across cut tree trunks lying by the riverbank, a commercial timber called *Roble*, Irgen had said. It was waiting for collection to be taken downstream. I knew it was only a matter of time now before we met loggers. Then our adventure alone on the Madidi would be over. As we rounded the next meander, the noise became clear, a high-pitched, motorbike revving that grated unnaturally against the murmur of the forest.

At an opening stretch of riverbank sat a small red and white tractor. At least that's what Irgen called it. To me it looked like the front-half only, an engine with two tractor wheels. The device was controlled from handlebars behind. Irgen said that one of these could pull whole tree trunks. The driver steered the engine whilst walking behind or sitting on the logs that the tractor was chained to. I was surprised anything this big could be put in a dugout *lancha* and brought this deep into the jungle, but Irgen said it wasn't so unusual. *Roble* was an expensive wood. People would go to a lot of trouble to extract it.

'I'm going to ask for directions – see if they know anything about this Madidi highway', he said, steering the canoe towards the shore. 'You two wait here with the gun and guard the stuff. I won't be long.' He jumped out of the canoe and trotted up the bank and along the path that led into the forest behind the tractor. Julian and I waited and listened as the sawing stopped and, after what seemed like an age while we speculated wildly about what had happened to our guide, it started again and Irgen reappeared.

'There's just one guy', he informed us as he pushed the boat off and got back in. 'The rest of his team are deeper in the forest. They've come up the Madidi from near the San Antonio camp. It's about three days' paddling to get to the road there. This man knows of no other tracks, but he says there's another group of loggers camped a couple of river bends down. We could ask them.'

Their camp turned out to be huge, a virtual shantytown (in our eyes) of wood and bamboo shelters, roofed in the ubiquitous blue plastic tarpaulins that everyone here used. Two battered dugouts lay beached on a wide stretch of mud in front of the encampment. There we could see several children and five or six women; they were in a flurry of activity since they had spotted us.

'I think they're hiding animal skins', commented Julian. We beached the canoe and waded across the mud to meet them.

The place was squalid and the women were sullen and uncommunicative. They all had the Mongoloid features of forest Indians, and said that they and their men had come over from the *pampa* beyond Rurrenabaque over a year ago. At the moment the men were cutting timber in the forest.

They were filthy and surrounded by their own waste. Bones, bits of plastic and tin cans that wouldn't degrade littered the floor. Close by was their food. A stick of plantains hung from a roof beam of one of the shelters. There were the remains of several monkey limbs, the hair singed off, and tucked in a corner was the 'live meat' – a large tortoise which was tied into a crude wooden frame to prevent it escaping. The place reeked of rotting meat and piss. The flies were terrible. The women and children obviously had no defence against them. Their arms, legs and faces were mottled with tiny blood blisters where countless *marahuisas* had bitten them. The legs of one young woman, who was washing some clothes in a bucket of dirty water, were particularly alarming. They were covered in small nodules from the knees down.

'*Espundia*', whispered Irgen. Leishmaniasis. I grimaced. Transmitted by sand fly bites, lesions on the wrists and ankles were the start. Then the infection would affect the mucus membranes around her nasal cavities. Left unchecked, the woman's face would eventually be eaten away. She would be left with a gaping hole where her nose was, if she survived that long and infection didn't kill her first. The cure used by the doctors in the towns here involved ingesting arsenic. I doubted that she would have access to a doctor though. Her only hope, it seemed to me, was that there was some local herbal cure.[3] If not, and my diagnosis was right, she would deteriorate in a particularly horrible way.

The woman with the infected ankles stopped her washing and stood with the others. They did not talk bar the monosyllabic answers given in response to Irgen's enquiries. They stared at us, occasionally exchanging glances. Even their children had stopped moving. They were clearly uneasy with our presence, perhaps afraid. It was obvious they were desperate for us to go – these three intruders, two of them gringos, with prying eyes scouring their camp (yes, there were skins hidden under some bedding, from at least two jaguars). No, they knew of no track except the one from San Antonio. That was the only way back to Ixiamas that they knew of.

'Now, could we go?' I could feel them willing us away.

'Yes, just go', their eyes said. Irgen took a last look round their huts, picked up some of the plantains and led us back to the boat.

They were the last people we saw on the Madidi. After that, we came across a couple more camps but they turned out to be deserted. At one the ground was churned up with peccary tracks and we saw a troop of spider monkeys that noisily took flight at our approach. There was a road of sorts with tractor tyre marks leading into the forest. Irgen said it wasn't worth taking. It would just lead

---

3   Bernardino had shown me a tree fern whose new shoots were used against *espundia*.

to a tree stump. If the women had been right and there was no Carreterra Alto Madidi, he said he would just as soon carry on down the river instead of striking out overland. It was by far the easier option in his opinion.

But Julian would have none of it. 'The road does exist', he stated. 'I'm sure of it.' Personally, I wasn't so convinced. After all, the trail on his map was just a line on an atlas from home, hardly convincing in that much of the other information, like the position of the river (according to the GPS), had turned out to be wrong. However, I sided with Julian. For me, a trek, even weighed down with all of the gear, seemed preferable to the other option. I didn't want to spend three days paddling down such a wide and now boring river, followed by days of hiking up a hard logging road to the cesspit settlement of San Antonio. No, I decided; I would happily trek out through the forest rather than doing that. Even if we found no track, how difficult could it be?

CHAPTER FOURTEEN

Through the Swamps of the Madidi

WHEN WE MADE our last camp on a stretch of golden sand next to the river, our spirits were high. We were buzzing with excitement at having just seen a puma sitting on the riverbank. As we floated past, it watched us from the shade under a balsa sapling. Because the puma was still, it was hard to tell it was there at all until it stood up and moved away. Having spotted the cat early on, I cursed myself for taking my eyes off it and so losing its position while I fumbled in my dry-bag for the camera. Julian assured me not to worry; everything was on video.

We were also excited to be going back into the forest again. If Julian was right about the Carreterra Alto Madidi, we would soon find a track and the way back would then be rather easy and pleasant. Irgen was all for scouting ahead for a day to find the road before we set off with all of the gear. He reasoned that even if there were no sign of it immediately, it would be less arduous to carry everything in relays, exploring ahead with light packs to cut a trail first. We re-sorted the food and packed the canoe ready for our reconnaissance.

To begin with, the forest close to our camp was sheer perfection: easy to trek across with relatively sparse undergrowth through which large animals (most likely tapirs) had opened wide enough tracks for us to follow. Our progress with the light packs was quick and we soon surprised some black spider monkeys and a group of saddle-backed tamarins that clung to the tree trunks and chirruped at us as we invaded their space. Then we came to a *curiche* and any more hope of rapid progress ended.

Curiches are oxbow lakes, bits of river marooned in the land when parts of a meander bend around so much that they end up meeting. The flow then uses the short cut and the redundant loop is left as a long, curved lake that dries up over the years, going through various stages of 'swampy-ness' and eventually being absorbed back into the main dry-land forest. '*Curiche*' is the name for the wet swamp stage. This one was beautiful but impassable for us on foot, a tangle of twisted tree trunks and stilt roots, inter-twined fig trees, laden down with gardens of epiphytes and trailing creepers that dangled into still, tea-coloured water. Close by, the air was silent apart from the whine of mosquitoes. Beyond, deeper into the swamp we could hear the screeches of parakeets and the chesty wheezing of hoatzins. The sun shone through the low canopy, dappling leafy shadows on the tea-water. I had to admit it looked idyllic. I would have loved to spend more time there but right now we wanted to go on and there was no way through.

Irgen led us along one side of the *curiche* for a while until the lake ended. Here, at the end of the oxbow, he called this vegetation '*chaparral*'. This was a more dried-up state of swamp – a mess of vines, thickets of palms and large-leafed heliconias, sticking out from ankle-deep water and mud. Compared to the *curiche*, this was passable. We cut our way through with the machetes, wading and slipping forward until the dry land started again, then continued on a compass bearing, unable to get a position fix with the GPS as the forest was so closed in. We made four hours forward, failing to come across any track or signs of people. The highway had to be close, we reckoned, provided that we were still going in a reason-ably straight line and had not deviated that much in getting around the oxbow.

Eventually we decided to dump the equipment we were carry-ing for collection the next day and head back to our camp. By then I was feeling rather sorry for myself as I had twice been bitten by *viente-cuatro* (twenty-four hour) ants. My arm and left calf muscle hurt a lot. They were hard and swollen and I felt slightly feverish. I had trodden right in a nest of ants on seeing a tapir at one of our rest stops. I had been edging forward as silently as I could to get a better view of the animal when I had felt a needle spike into my left bicep with a sudden wave of pain that had filled the entire muscle and made me gasp out loud. I glanced down to see an enormous ant, over an inch long, wrestling its mandibles through the cloth of my shirt and into my arm. Meanwhile, its body was doubled over as it jabbed its tail sting through too (this sort of ant has a sting in the tail like a wasp's). The pain had been awful. I pulled the ant off and threw it to the ground, just as another bit my leg. Fortunately, the second attacker had not bitten as deeply. I had smacked it off and set to sweeping more *viente-cuatros* off my trousers, then jumping away from the tree that I had been leaning against.

Julian was not sympathetic. All he could say was, 'Thanks for scaring the tapir away.'

I felt grim for the rest of the afternoon. By evening the pain had receded into a dull throb. I decided that I had been lucky (comparatively speaking) in just having discovered the 'three-hour ant'.

❦

When we arrived back at our camp on the beach, there were decisions to make; whether we carried on bit by bit, scouting then carrying like we had started today or whether we opted to carry everything in one go. As we pored over the maps, trying to work out how far we had travelled that day, I stated my opinion.

'I say we go at it like *burros*. We carry everything. None of this backwards and forwards. One direction only.'

Irgen didn't seem so keen. 'But you know how slow it is with the packs', he said. 'I ask you, on that first day when we set off – how much distance did we make?'

'More than today', I countered.

'In that first day maybe, but later? If we go on and there's no road . . .'

I leaped in with my idea. 'I think we should decide if there are things that we don't need.' My mind raced for examples. 'We don't need all the salt. Dump some of that. And the tape for the boat. We've got three rolls – get rid of two. My tent's useless. If I chop it in half so I've just got the plastic groundsheet; that'll lose us a kilogram. The life jacket – we don't need that.' I looked to Julian for support.

'There's not a great deal I don't need', he said, 'maybe some dead batteries.' Still, he agreed with the plan. 'It's better than messing around like we did today.'

So it was settled. I cut off the material from my tent[1] and made a pile of the stuff we no longer needed – the food sacks, the suntan cream, a bag of lentils, some salt, the pole for Irgen's paddle. We burned most of the junk, but the sun cream I placed upright on a sandbank next to the river. The bottle with its English writing and price tag would make an intriguing find for some passing group of loggers.

Next we divided the packs. Irgen had the bulk of the food in his rucksack. It was a heavy but compact load. Julian had some food, the video and its associated equipment like the solar panels. He also had the cooking pots in a small, green rucksack, tied to his main pack. I had the canoe, all of it; the poles, the frame, the skin and the paddles, as well as my own stuff – camera, diary, spare clothes. My pack was huge. It stuck above my head. I knew it would catch all the vines and branches that I passed, but there wasn't any other way to carry the rolled-up boat. The rucksack was so heavy I could hardly lift it. When we set off into the jungle the following morning, I sat down virtually immediately. I had too much. I knew something was going to give. It would be my back. Irgen took a

1   The netting 'windows' on the tent sides had once been part of the gauze petticoats of my mother's wedding dress. She reckoned sewing this in was bound to bring me luck on the trip.

small bundle of my spare clothes. That reduced the bulk but I knew it still weighed too much. We set off.

❦

The trek was hellish. The heat and humidity were terrible. Even before we had left the relatively easy trail that we had already cut for ourselves the day before, I was soaking with sweat and suffering badly under the excessive load. Soon we were machete-cutting every bit of the way. The terrain got worse. The ground dipped down into swampy *chaparrals*, muddy systems of foot-deep trenches between raised tree roots. With no slope to flow down, it seemed as if the water had nowhere to go and instead had carved this maze of channels into the soft mud. We sloshed and stumbled forward as the ground gave way again and again, each time the mat of leaves and dead branches covering the mud broke under our weight, sending us reeling forward from the momentum of our huge packs. Tough, woody vines looped out to ensnare heads, rucksacks, feet. My high load caught on every-thing. Every few steps, I had to hack back with my machete and, when that became blunt, just extricate myself as best I could. Often I just gave up and pulled with my full weight, dragging a mass of vegetation behind until it finally snapped and I lurched forward, catching myself on some tree trunk to stop from tum-bling in the mud again. We blundered onwards in our increasing tiredness, ripping our clothes, scratching ourselves on branches and thorny palm roots. Then mosquitoes would home in on the bare skin. Their high-pitched whine became the all-surrounding sound of the swamps.

Soon I was lagging behind. With no trail, the best I could do was to follow the person in front, hoping his route would be more battered down and easier to push through. But as I became sepa-rated further and further from the others, I often could find no way and became ever more stuck in the tangles.

'Don't you understand!' my mind yelled out. 'The more you leave me behind, the slower it will be for all of us.' I screamed ahead, 'If you slow down, I'll see where you're going and I'll keep up.' But they ignored me. It was 'every man for himself' now.

Julian was suffering too. He had also been bitten by an 'ant twenty-four'. All I could think was, 'Good. Now he's in pain too he'll have to slow down.'

When we came to the first real dry land at the end of the afternoon, we stopped. Julian and I lay flat out, oblivious to the mosquitoes, only vaguely aware that Irgen was off scouting ahead. He was jubilant on his return a short while later. He said the stream close by led to a larger river where there was sky overhead and a stretch of sand where we could lay out our groundsheets. 'Follow my machete marks', he said, eagerly heaving up his rucksack and snatching up the rifle.

We followed.

After the closed in forest, the river was paradise. Only about 10 feet wide with a blockage of logs, which we crossed to get to the sandy beach on the other side, it was enclosed by high trees, yet open enough for the humidity to be far lower than in the forest. There were scarlet macaws shrieking overhead and the late afternoon sunlight flooded in. We used our machetes to shovel a flat patch out of the sloping sand on which to lay our groundsheets. Then we gathered firewood and washed. It was so good to feel unencumbered and clean again. In the relief, I toyed with the idea of us building up the canoe and continuing down this river. It wasn't marked on my map (what was?) but if the track was where we thought it was, this river would cross it fairly soon. We need not walk through the *chaparrals* again. Irgen was less than keen. He said it was a stupid idea.

'All it would do is waste time. And what if the carreterra doesn't exist? What do we do then? Come back up or carry on with this river back to the Madidi? Then we'd be right back at the start.

'I had a look around the bend and it's blocked up with logs, anyway', he added.

❦

A jaguar came into our camp that night. It roared from the bushes across the stream not 20 feet from us, a long, low, trundling growl that cut right through the tranquillity and left me shivering with a mixture of fear and excitement. Irgen and I sat up under our mosquito nets, torches at the ready, for when it showed itself. Julian slept on. The bushes shook but no *tigre* appeared. In the morning Julian didn't believe us when we told him. 'Piss off', he said. 'Your jokes about my snoring are just not funny any more.'

❦

The trek got no better over the next three days. The *chaparrals* continued. The slippery mud, the vines and jutting branches were just as bad as before. The oars I carried caught on everything. My pack seemed to be even heavier. I got left behind again. More of my shirt ripped off and my shoulders started to become very sore from where the rucksack straps were cutting in. The skin was rubbed through in places, and it was painful each time the pack jolted as I tripped or got caught on a branch or vine. I padded my shoulders with some spare clothes but it did little good since the wounds were oozing and damp with sweat. We walked for around nine or ten hours each day, trying to maintain the south-east compass bearing that surely would eventually get us to the San Antonio stream and the road where, hopefully, Chichito would be waiting with his Landcruiser. There was no way of knowing how far we had gone. The GPS wouldn't pick up any satellite signals under the forest cover. We plotted our position through the blank part of our map largely through guesswork.

Each afternoon, just as my spirits were lowest and I felt most like just sitting down and going to sleep where I was, Irgen would find something to give us hope: old machete cuts (the sure sign of a trail), a clear water stream, a patch of open sky – sometimes this was even large enough to make it worthwhile activating the GPS. We would spread out the groundsheets and hang the mosquito nets, cook up pasta and needle out the splinters of the day. We would praise Julian on his choice of extra-virgin olive oil with the macaroni then laugh at how one of his trouser legs had been eaten by *sepe* ants the night before (for some reason Julian did not find this as amusing as Irgen and me). In the morning we would start again. Irgen would launch himself into the *chaparrals* and I would follow. Soon I would feel just as wretched as I had the day before.

By noon on the fourth day of walking I had had enough. I rifled through my rucksack and threw on the ground everything I thought was non-essential; the remainder of the 'duck' tape, my binoculars (they were misted up with fungus and useless in any case), my shorts. I didn't leave the canoe – things weren't that desperate yet – but the paddles went. No longer, I decided, would I be burdened with such useless items. We would make some more or improvise somehow if ever the need arose. Irgen propped the paddles up on a tree trunk and hung the shorts over them, along with the binoculars.

'For those who follow us to find', he said. He got out a pen and on the shorts he wrote, 'Here is the last resting place of Coronel Jose'.

'Who's Coronel Jose?' I asked.

'That old, English explorer you keep talking about', Irgen answered. 'The one that was here before.'

⁂

By late afternoon we were lost again and I felt wrecked, both emotionally and physically. I stepped down to the streamside that Irgen had started clearing for our campsite in such a trance-like state that I scarcely noticed the troop of spider monkeys that had followed us and made their night's nest in the tall tree above. All the hope I had felt at the beginning of the day had dissolved when a line of machete cuts Irgen found had ended in a *curiche*. The trail had looked so promising too. A freshly cleared line along which every sapling and palm had been cut at waist height, it had led dead straight into the forest, not even deviating for swamps or streams.

Irgen had said this 'had to mark the route for the new road'. We had eagerly followed him for two hours until the cuts ended and our guide had sat down with his head in his hands and admitted he didn't know what to do now. Later, when we had found a clearing full of fallen trees, I had climbed up as high as I could to get a GPS position fix and found that we had only made 15 kilometres from our starting point on the Madidi. Irgen had been visibly upset that, for all his guiding, the device's mapping mode showed we had spent the past three days walking a semi-circle. Now I just felt so angry. I was angry at being left behind, angry at having the tallest, heaviest pack, at having the video shoved in my face for filming when I least felt like it. My shoulders were bleeding from being rubbed so badly, and all Julian could do was tell me I was whining too much and that I should have got fitter before the trip.

The next morning Irgen took the canoe frame and gave me back my bundle of clothes. It wasn't much, but it was a gesture. At least, I felt, he had taken notice. The spider monkeys above us, upset at having been woken up so early (around 6.30 a.m.) threw down sticks at us. We set off.

The terrain was starting to become less swampy. The under-growth appeared slightly sparser, perhaps because of the shade of the thick canopy of leaves above. Our progress felt faster. There was less machete hacking; now we could just push our way through. The land, though flat, was crossed in places by deep, square-section trenches where streams had eroded into the underlying clay. Sometimes we would find fallen trees to clamber across, but mostly we had to slide down the steep banks, eight feet or more, into the water at the bottom, wade across, and laboriously scramble or haul our way back up on roots that dangled down the opposite bank. It was then that the packs weighed most, first jarring into our shoulders at the descent then pulling back, unbalancing us as we clawed against the mud banks to get out.

Senses dulled by dehydration or lack of salt, I hurried on in a daydream, looking up occasionally towards where I could see the swaying undergrowth that marked the others' passage, and, if they weren't in sight, scanning at waist height for their machete cuts. At times the marks were so infrequent that I would simply follow the line of least resistance through the undergrowth. More often than not, this would be the same way that Irgen and Julian had come. This was probably roughly the same route, I mused, that Fawcett's great friend, Colonel (later president) Pando of the Bolivian army trekked through to Ixiamas in 1897, after exploring in the region of the Tambopata River in modern day Peru. His party had accessed the area from the eastern edge of the Andes, travelling down the Rio Cocos, first on foot, then on rafts that they had constructed once the river was navigable. The journey was arduous and, after being attacked by Guarayo Indians on 5 August, the party's morale broke. The decision was made to trek overland to Ixiamas, a journey that would have taken Pando and his men across the Heath, Madidi and Undumo rivers. From the Madidi to Ixiamas, they would have paralleled the Serrania del Tigre, just as we were doing now.

Evans wrote that the party suffered 'great privations. . . . For thirty-six days they had no other food than what they could find in the forest or in the *chacras* of the *barbaros*.'[2] Pando later told Fawcett that his group had rolled up their mosquito nets and left them nearby in decoy campsites while they slept; the bedrolls were often found in the morning 'riddled with arrows'.

'We never experienced a direct attack', Pando had recounted, 'but all the time they harried us from the bush and remained invisible.' I made a mental note that it was a century ago almost to the day. For a while it made me feel there was something epic about our trek, then I remembered my headache and how wretched I felt.

☙

My arrival at another trench stream knocked me back into wakefulness. I didn't bother checking for cuts as it was obvious which way the others had gone. There was a cleft in the bank and skid

2   From a footnote in Evans's RGS report.

marks where they had gone down. Steadying myself on an overhanging branch, I swung over the bank and slid, landing hard on
the wet, gravel bottom. Under the great weight of my pack, I sank
to my hands and knees and pawed up several mouthfuls of cool,
clear water from a pool where the stream dribbled over a dam of
sticks and pebbles. I paused for a few seconds, absorbed by the play
of the leaf-dappled sunlight on the surface ripples and by several
tiny hover flies that hung in front of my face, flitting off, then back
into position whenever I moved. There was a cluster of tadpoles in
the pool and, behind the overhanging fern fronds that brushed
against my face, I half-imagined that I could make out the outline
of a small tree frog. For a moment, I was quite entranced and I
knelt listening to the tickings and whirrings of the forest insects re-
establishing themselves over the sound of trickling water. Then I
gently parted the fern fronds to see if there really was a frog there.

I wanted to linger but I had to keep going, I told myself. I
pushed myself upright and turned to find the tracks on the opposite bank where the others had crossed. There were none.

CHAPTER FIFTEEN

Green Hell

D READ. I FEEL sick at the back of my throat. My mind already knows what this means.

'Downstream – you have to check.'

I follow the twisting trench, running as fast as I am able, sloshing through shallow water, pulling away the fallen branches that bar my way. I make about a hundred yards but there is still no exit so I return and try upstream. My progress is blocked virtually immediately by a fallen tree which, when I hack into it with my machete, sends up a cloud of tiny flies.

'Shit.

'Shit. Shit. Shit.' I am aware of my own rapid breathing, the high-pitched scrunch of my feet on gravel, water splashing. I return to the mudslide and reach up for the branch that I held onto when I slid down. Too high.

I shuffle back to the opposite bank for a run up and rush forward. My feet slip then find purchase on the slope. My right hand grabs the branch but the momentum of my pack hurtles me forward. The poles tied to the back swing slightly, shift my balance and my face hits mud. I swing around with my machete in my left hand and stab it in like a dagger. I hold for a second panting heavily. Mud and sweat drip down my face, into my mouth, down my neck. I pull and hear myself grunt/scream as I get a leg over the rim and scramble over to lie at the edge with my rucksack pulling me sideways like an upended cockroach.

Looking down, I see some tapir prints in the stream that I hadn't noticed before. Above, the twigs of 'my' trail, I notice too, are broken back, not cut. Some dangle with withered leaves.

'How far back did I lose Irgen's cuts?' I pull myself to my feet and try to trace the tapir trail back, but my route of least resistance no longer looks so clear and I soon give up. I have taken no 'landmarks'. There is no one tree that I can point to and say with any certainty that I walked this way; not in any direction. I don't know what to do. I just know I have to be quick with whatever I decide to have any hope of catching the others up.

I shout. I scream. But the sound is absorbed by the vegetation and I get no response. I feel a wave of heat sweep over my face then a fit of trembling that seizes my entire body.

'Stupid. Stupid. Stupid. What do I do?' My breathing is broken, sobbing, as wide-eyed I slowly scan around for any sign. Nothing – just trees, palms, undergrowth, a stream.

'Cross the stream. Follow the direction we were heading – south-east.' But I have no compass. I lent it to Irgen. And I can't use the sun to navigate because of the cloud. My mind fixes for an instant on using the GPS. 'Find a clearing and find your position.' But what's the point if I don't have a compass and Julian has the map. I must mark where I am now. I must mark my start point. Then I must cross the stream.

I follow the line of the trench up to the point where it was blocked. A small tree has fallen across. Its roots lie unearthed. They are covered in yellow toadstools mottled with black veins that make them look like little parasols. The trunk bridges the gap. It's only a foot or so wide and shoots have grown over it since it fell. They all stick straight upwards like the bristles on a gigantic brush. Between the new growth the surface is covered in moss and dead leaves. I edge across, sliding my feet sideways along the slippery cylinder, my hands reaching out to hold the new shoots more for the sense of comfort they give than for any true support these handholds offer. Leaves and debris fall. It's a 10-foot drop. A mass of branches below would break my fall. I unclip my rucksack's waist belt and slide my left arm through the shoulder strap so that, though it's still held close to my back, I feel I can jettison the pack if I slip.

I slide my foot forward, stripping off a long sliver of moss which dangles for a moment then falls into the foliage below. Where it had been is slick with moisture. Termites scurry across. As I near the middle of my bridge, I feel a slight shudder through the wood as the trunk shifts. The sticks below clatter as their positions change. I crouch and grip my hands onto the trunk and, sloth-like in my movements, I inch forward again until, at last, I am once more over firm ground. I swing off the trunk, slamming my feet down and lurch sideways, grasping for handholds in the spiky stilt roots of a small palm. Ignoring the prickles on my hands, I lever myself partly upright. And stop. A thin, mottled, green creeper slides out of the roots, traces a gently curved arc and stops right in front of my face. I can see eyes, yellow with black, slit pupils, and a grey-pink forked tongue that tests the air, samples my odour as the head hangs motionless. My breath is held. I keep myself totally still. Tensed muscles scream at me to move before they cramp. I stare at the snake. Eye to eye. It flicks its tongue at my face, as it sweeps down from my eyes to my chin, tasting the air, sensing my body warmth – forever, it seems. Then it slides away, arcing back along exactly the same line into its pyramid of rootlets.

I slash with my machete at the roots and at every bit of foliage in my way until I reach an area of comparative openness between the buttresses of an enormous tree – a ceiba, silk cotton. I can tell from the downy white fuzz that coats the floor. I slump down, freeing myself from the rucksack straps, leaning back and panting uncontrollably until my pulse has slowed. I'm still shaking. I feel sick, but somehow there is no more room for panic. My terror has hit some sort of plateau and can't get worse. I know what I have to do. I click open the rucksack's bindings, upend it and tip out the rolled-up canoe. This I carefully place with the poles in the crease of the roots. Then I take the yellow plastic bag that holds my clothes and cut it into strips, which I tie to the saplings around the ceiba trunk as a marker. I will return if I find the others. I lay the pack and all of its contents in front of me. It calms me down as I check through my equipment. Apart from my clothes, I have my survival tin with its line and fish hooks (keep), my medical kit (keep), washing stuff (leave), sleeping bag and net (keep), my diary and my camera (I keep both of these). I have no food except for a packet of glucose tablets that I have hoarded since the start of the trip and a plastic bag, half full of yesterday's left-over rice and lentils. I have no salt. I could possibly find a stream and catch fish, but how long would I survive? Not to mention the time and effort I would spend in catching the fish would probably prevent me moving far in a day. My pack is light now. I decide it's better to press forward while I can. I will continue on the same route and try to deviate slightly south when I see the sun and can fix my direction. That way, I should avoid going back into the swamps. I shoulder my pack and set off again.

⚜

'You must see past the trees. You must look for the little differences. Then you see everything', Bernardino told me when he got me lost so many weeks before on the Undumo.

I cut the sapling then pulled the top half over so that it pointed towards the spiky palm that I had chosen as a 'landmark'. Cutting only to ease the way, I skirted between several narrow-leafed bushes and sliced at some bright, fleshy stalks that sprouted from the leaf litter. The diagonal cuts glistened with sap welling up. I looked for my next marker and chose a wide straight trunk with lichen-mottled bark. It oozed crimson sap when I cut it. That was good; easy to find if I had to retrace my route. Each mark I knew had to be clearly visible to the next. Where I altered my course to avoid thickets or streams, I would find a trunk and slice the bark like the hands of a clock – a big slash to show where I had come from and a smaller cut to show where I was going. Any deviation had to be made up, though. When the undergrowth was clear, I would try to make sure all of my markers lined up.

'You have to have patience.' Irgen had told me that.

Over what felt like hours, I had made what I judged to be good progress since I had left the canoe at the ceiba tree. Twice I had crossed streams. At the second I had startled a pair of guans. They had 'galumphed' into the air honking wildly and landed on a low branch; a certain kill if I had had the gun. I had thrown a stone, hoping that a lucky shot might get me a meal, but I had missed and the birds had flown off. There was no point following them. I would need food. I was acutely aware of that. But right now, while I was strong, it was more important to make some distance. Without the weight of the canoe in my pack, I could walk quickly and quietly. I did not waste energy hacking or pushing through vegetation. I sought out the gaps, wound between the saplings and small palms, cutting only to mark, not to clear my way.

I was in a state of hyper-awareness, my consciousness fully concentrated on the route ahead. I dodged the hooked thorns of the cat's claw vines, hopped over the motorways of leaf-bearing ants. I noticed the spiders' webs slung between the saplings and the caterpillars on the leaves. I saw the algae-speckled foliage of the trees-in-waiting, ready to growth-spurt to the sun if a forest giant should fall. And I saw the agents of their destruction, the fungus that ate away at the roots, the vines that grew so thickly and pulled down with such weight that a well placed gust of wind in a storm might bring down an entire section of canopy. In the gallery space in between, I saw the floating seeds and butterflies, the small birds that occasionally darted across. I saw an eagle.

A black and white hawk-eagle. Shaped like a sparrow-hawk for chasing through treetops, it dived from the canopy, fanning out its huge white wings and lunging with hooked talons as it slammed into a mass of leaves at the top of one of the under-storey trees. Monkeys scattered in all directions; squirrel monkeys – yellow with clown faces and black skullcaps – as well as some tougher, brutish-looking brown capuchins. Some of the squirrels leaped into the bushes close to my head and screamed out from behind the branches, their faces contorted like little devils. Some others were still on the main tree. They slid down its limbs and onto the ground as the eagle swooped again, its claws ripping through the foliage as it beat back the air to stop itself. With heavy wing-beats it pulled itself back to the cover of the canopy. The monkeys close to my head were still agitated. They screamed and chattered. Death had come close but they had each other to console their fear. Already I could hear their kissing calls as the troop reunited itself. I felt very alone as I marked the tree where the eagle had swooped and continued on my way.

Not long after, in a marshy thicket of stumpy palms, I was suddenly aware of eyes on all sides; the pointed raccoon faces of a pack of coatis, sniffing the air with their moist muzzles and making quiet grunting sounds. As I passed between and underneath them, they scurried along the spines of the fronds. Some jumped to the ground and accompanied me, their ring tails held high like fluffy radio aerials. They stopped when I stopped and moved when I moved. Their attention seemed nosy rather than hostile. One of their number had been killed, perhaps by an ocelot or a hawk-eagle. I came across its skull and spinal column underneath a palm a little further on. The corpse (what was left) was so freshly dead that it did not even smell yet. No turkey vultures with their one-part-per-million smell sensors had come to loot the remains. Nor had any flies or sweat bees. The bones were still moist and some blood on the spine had not fully congealed yet. A few ants crawled over the skull. They entered the nostrils and the eye sockets. They walked over the tendons that still held the jaw in place.

I picked up the head and shook the ants off. The jaw hinged open into a wide grin and I saw that the tongue was still whole. For some reason, I found it sickening. I dropped the skull and wiped my hands on the leaves of a nearby bush. But they still must have carried an imperceptible scent of the dead flesh because they attracted sweat bees each time I paused to consider my way. So did the parts of my T-shirt nearest to where my shoulder straps had rubbed. I noticed that they stank like dead meat when I stopped to rest later in the day.

I eased off the straps and tried to remove my T-shirt but it was stuck. The inside edges of the straps were outlined on the cloth by yellow stains of dried lymph and blood. This started another wave of self-doubt. 'You're going to die here and no one will find you. You should have stayed where you were. The others would have come back. Go back now.'

'Don't', some other voice tried to argue back.

'Go back!'

I pulled myself to my feet and mentally retraced the route. I pictured the trees I had marked on the last stage, the clearing where the hawk-eagle had swooped, the *chaparral* where I had found the coati skull, two streams, finally my *ceiba* with my rolled up canoe placed neatly alongside one of its buttresses. The poles were still there, lined up next to it. In my mind I could see them. I might still make it back before dark if I went now. Even if the others had returned and I wasn't there, they would have cut a trail for me to follow.

'Go now. Go back now', half of me said.

'No.' I spoke the words out loud, forcefully, but not shouting. 'I've made my decision. I will carry on.'

❦

Fear: an inchoate scream that bubbles up to the rim of your sanity, a jabbering of conflicting instructions – Run! Stop! Scream! – that you know if it spills over will gush out uncontrollably, leaving you babbling for your mother and curling in on yourself like a newly born baby. You can see and hear the terror rising, feel it as your body goes into paroxysms of punctured breaths. You know the only way you can check it is with the power of your will, but that is surely as impossible as willing a stream to stop flowing or moving rocks with your mind. Quick death is easy. There is no thought involved, nothing you can do about the sudden snakebite or the fall from a cliff. The terror is in the lingering downward spiral of dehydration and fever, of seeing your strength ebb away until you end up lying on the damp sand of some gully with a column of ants marching across your face, exploring the tender cavities of your nose and eyes, while your hand twitches feebly, unable to brush them away.

I see the face of my wife. She is cupping my face in her hands as she did the night before I set off. I fix on the image, on my promises not to be stupid, not to die. I fix on her blue eyes, flecked with hazel, and on the curve of her cheeks; I imbibe the inflections of her voice to the exclusion of all else. Comfort. Quiet. Calm. I linger on her features and I am aware the terror, which though not dispelled entirely, has subsided from the rim enough so that, at least for now, I can function.

❦

I entered a *chaparral* and tangled myself in a looping *una-de-gato*. When I had extricated myself and my pack from the liana, I tripped on a root and fell to my knees in the muddy water. Why had I carried on? I should have gone back. I could start now. There would be no chance of getting there before dark. I could make camp at one of the streams. I pulled myself upright on the narrow tree trunk in front. A small brown ant stung me; a fire ant – the tree was a *palo diablo*. A bird in its branches called out a raucous 'chik chik chawww' and flew off. It was a call that for some reason I knew sounded out of place in the forest. My mind flicked through the possibilities, then locked on where I had heard it before.

'Red-faced Caracara, a buzzard-sized scavenger of river edges.'

'A river, open sky.'

'Chik Chik Chawwww.'

I sloshed forward, ignoring the bites of enraged ants as I pushed through the leaves of the *palo diablo* and into the light.

❦

It was the biggest view I had seen in days, a wide expanse of shingle with a clear stream zigzagging over it. Beyond that the forest restarted and further on, partly shrouded in mist, were the mountains: the Serrania del Tigre. Our route, my route, had taken me right around them since we were on the Madidi, and now I was looking at those peaks from the other side. I was out of the swamps at a higher level where the river ran over stones instead of cutting deep into mud. I felt such relief sweep over me. I threw down my pack, ran across the shingle and dunked my head in the cold water.

'What now?' It was still light; there was maybe one hour left. I would travel upstream. That was what we had all agreed on. If we found a river we'd walk up it and follow any tributaries that headed to the left. That way would take us along the bottom edge of the mountains, maybe with luck to the old logging road that we thought we had found three days before.

The gravel of the riverbed was firm and flat and wide like a motorway. There were no obstacles except for the puny stream, which I had to cross occasionally, and I walked at a furious pace. I activated the GPS. It said that I had made eight kilometres since the previous fix taken the day before. Ixiamas (its location was already stored in the unit's memory) was 42 kilometres away. I could make that. No problem. I just had to keep going. I lifted my eyes to check out the view ahead. And I saw smoke.

There wasn't much, just a thin wisp that spiralled up into the still air – one, maybe two river-bends ahead. Irgen and Julian? Or loggers? I broke into a run, splashed across the stream and jogged along the wet sand at the edge, rounded an island of cecropia and *chuchillo* and there they were – Julian and Irgen. They were sitting by an enormous pyre, across which it looked like half a balsa tree had been dumped. Smoke billowed everywhere as flames engulfed the branches and shrivelled the leaves. Julian and Irgen were sitting between the fire and the stream prodding something flat and round with sticks. They leaped up with a start when they saw me running towards them.

'The wanderer returns', Irgen grinned and raised his arms wide as I flung myself into the camp.

'Where the hell have you been?' said Julian. I hugged each of them.

'Oh God. I'm so glad I found you. I thought I was lost for good. I lost the trail, got stuck down a gully, then I came face to face with a snake. I thought I was going to die', I ranted without pausing for breath. I spilled out the story. Once started, I could not stop. Irgen laughed at all the dangerous bits.

'Ah, Simon. *Que aventura* – just like your Coronel Jose!'

'You only were gone for about six hours', said Julian.

Was that all? It seemed like days. It felt as long as I could remember.

'Weren't you worried about me?'

'We knew you'd turn up sometime', Julian answered. 'That's why Irgen lit the fire. When we hadn't seen you for an hour or so, we figured you would head south-east.'

'Irgen had my compass.'

'Oh', said Julian. 'The GPS?'

'You had the map.'

'So I have.' I could see it beside him. Irgen cut in.

'Don't worry, Simon. We would have come back and looked for you – tomorrow for sure – if you hadn't arrived. Your trails are like a railway line. Even Julian can follow them.'

'Anyway, we found a track', said Julian. 'An old logging road. It's totally overgrown apart from a path along one side, which Irgen reckons is in fairly regular use. He says some of the cuts are only about a week old. I think it's the track marked on my map.' He unfolded one of his La Paz military maps and pointed to a dashed line in an otherwise green and featureless sheet, on which Ixiamas and several roads were marked on one of the corners.

'Or at least', Julian continued, looking perplexed at the map, 'our track will join this one when we get onto this sheet.'

'It's near here?' I asked, slightly distractedly as the round, flat object by Irgen's feet had started to quiver and was now wafting a spiny tail over its back.

Irgen leaped to his feet avoiding the stingray and stood so that he faced across the streambed. He held his arms outstretched.

'This is it', he said.

'Where?'

'Here', he stated, his arms indicating patches of shade in the vegetation on either side.

'Oh.' In the half-darkness of early evening the track could have been anywhere. 'So what's with the stingray?' I tried to sound casual.

'He stood on it', said Julian.

'Shit.' I noticed his leg. What looked like chunks of tree bark had been stuck on with surgical tape.

'From a garlic tree', said Irgen.

'So its tail got you?'

'No it didn't', Julian replied.

'But I had to make extra sure', added Irgen. 'Tomorrow, I will go back and get your boat, then we will rest. Julian's gone all weak.' I looked to Julian. He nodded.

'I don't feel so strong it's true, but that's not the real reason we rest tomorrow. It's just in case we get to meet people and Irgen sees a woman.'

'A menstruating woman', Irgen corrected. 'Everyone knows that. If you get stung by a stingray and a woman who is on her period sees you, then you have so much pain that sometimes you die.'

'But I thought it didn't get you', I said.

Irgen sucked in a long, deep breath. 'No, but it was a very near miss and I don't want to take any chance at all.'

☙

We rested for the next two days. The GPS showed that we had indeed reached Julian's good map. The stream was the Aroyo San Juan. Our stream, the San Antonio, lay only one long day's walk away.

Irgen went back for my canoe as he had promised. I took him down the streambed to where my trail started and from there he walked alone. He was back in three hours, returning on the logging track, which he said must have only been a few hundred metres parallel to where I had walked. He came back with a Spix's guan that he had shot. We cooked it over the fire that night, then we slept like the dead until past dawn. Irgen said it was a shame that we slept so deeply. In the morning, there were heavy, scraping tracks alongside our camp that Irgen said belonged to a *pejiche* – a giant armadillo – an animal so rare that even he had only ever seen one once.

The two days of rest were glorious. We spent our time replete with bush turkey, sleeping, writing our diaries and trying to entice (without success) five saddle-backed tamarins that lived in the trees behind our camp to take some rice that we put out for them. But we were keen to go. We were so near to the finish that we felt that staying here was just putting off the inevitable. One more day would see us at our rendezvous with Chichito, or if he wasn't there (I doubted he would be), we would soon arrive at the start of the new highway. There would be tractors, lorries and people working on the road. We would appear out of the jungle and when we told them we had come from the Madidi, they would be so surprised. One more stream, we told ourselves, five hours maybe and we would be there.

But it didn't work out like that. One stream passed, then another. The old logging road remained closed in with vegetation. We hacked and pushed forward through the masses of vines that blocked the way and clambered over the trees that had fallen across the road. My rucksack weighed down again, the straps ripping where the wounds had started to heal. We were making progress but every stream was the same; no road, no people and no sign of Chichito, even though by now we were well onto the good map and past the river marked 'San Antonio'. Finally, at around midday, our spirits lightened. Footprints – and they were fresh! Irgen reck-oned they could be no more than a day old. We carried on with extra speed after that, certain that we would get to the road before nightfall. And we did, though it was little like what we had been anticipating.

The start of the Carreterra Alto Madidi was an anticlimax. There were no people, no vehicles, no sign that the road had even been worked on for a long time. We were hacking our way through the thickets of the track and then we burst onto open ground; it was 10 metres wide, levelled, stretching away into the distance. It was a road, certainly, but overgrown with a dense mat of grass and strewn here and there with branches that had been blown down from the trees above; it was not a road that anyone used.

We threw down our packs for a moment, lay back in the grass in a pool of sunlight that illuminated the end of the 'highway'. There was nothing here. We were still as much in the jungle as we had been before. There was no Chichito waiting for us, no San Antonio stream, nobody here at all. But it was a road and that had to be an improvement. Disappointment merged into relief. Those other things might exist after all. Presently we hoisted our packs and continued on our way, ticking off streams on the map as before until at last we got to one that fluttered with hundreds of yellow butterflies. It wasn't the butterflies that caught our attention, though, but the boulders in the middle of the stream. Strewn across them was a mass of multicoloured shapes: towels and T-shirts left out in the sun to dry.

CHAPTER SIXTEEN

Jungle Heaven

'CIVILIZATION'. A CAMP consisting of a wooden shelter with a blue plastic sheet roof, a fireplace under a lean-to of palm fronds and racks of fly-covered meat hanging out to dry. The flesh stank. It was spider monkey. Two or three sinuous arms dangled alongside the other strips of drying meat – '*charque*'. Close by, above a burnt-out fire was another rack, this one loaded with the charred remains of a dismembered tapir. A tortoise tied into a square of bamboo batons, a future meal, tugged on a rope that held it to the shelter. The ground was littered with bones, tin cans and food packaging.

A crew-cut boy of around fifteen who had been left to tend camp was taunting a baby spider monkey with a string tied around its neck. The monkey scrabbled up into a tree as far as its cord would allow and squealed pathetically. In the way of bored teenagers everywhere, the boy appeared disinterested at our sudden appearance from out of the forest. His answers to our questions were mostly monosyllabic and uninformative: Yes, this was the Arroyo San Antonio. Yes, this was Chichito's camp. Chichito was with the other woodcutters hauling logs with his Toyota. They would all return at nightfall. We soon gave up asking and the boy walked off to tease the monkey again. As if to emphasize that we were right at the cutting edge of human expansion into the rain-forest, a chainsaw started up in the distance.

I walked back to the river to wash. It was so good to take off all my clothes and immerse myself fully in the cool, clear water, to wash away the jungle grime and clean the wounds on my shoulders in the knowledge that no more would I have to carry that load. Away from the camp there were few *marahuisas*, thus I took my time working the soap into a lather and examining the scratches and insect bites that covered much of my body. Then I stretched myself out over a large round boulder and dried off in the sun while clouds of yellow butterflies flitted around me and a group of monkeys trilled from the trees across the water. *Mono lucachi* – dusky titi; I knew the wailing call well by now, though I had only seen this type once before. I decided the monkeys could wait, and continued sunbathing.

When I got back to the loggers' camp, Irgen asked me if I would like to go and see the *lucachis*. Julian, relaxing in his hammock, said he wasn't that bothered. Nor would I have been, except that I could see that Irgen was quite keen and I might as well go with him while I had the chance, even though it would mean getting dirty and sweaty again. I took my time getting dressed while Irgen took my camera and started out for the river. Then I picked up my sketch pad and, not bothering to fasten my sandals, shuffled after him.

It's strange how things work out. If I hadn't been so slow, we would have got to the river too early, and if I had taken longer, we would have been too late. As it was, our timing was perfect. We arrived to find a puma bathing roughly at the same spot where I had been not ten minutes earlier. It was only 30 feet or so upstream of where we stood and totally unaware of our presence. The late afternoon sun made its coat glow a golden orange colour as it slowly picked its way through the shallow water and up onto the sandy beach on the other side. Irgen handed me the camera and I pulled in the zoom lens to get the largest picture I could, snapping off six shots before I ran out of film. The puma noticed me on the last one. I splashed forwards into the water to get a better view and it spun its head around to face me. It hunched low as if ready to spring. I clutched my camera as if it was a defensive weapon. For a few seconds we faced each other off. Then it relaxed its muscles, turned and calmly slunk off into the riverside undergrowth.

❀

When Irgen and I returned the loggers were starting to arrive back for the night. There were eight of them, mostly of Indian descent but two, who appeared to be brothers, looked distinctly Semitic or Middle-Eastern (Fawcett had commented on how many Syrians worked the rivers). They were very interested in our arrival, chatty and genuinely keen to find out what we had been doing. One old Indian with a world-weary expression and a dead spider monkey slung over his shoulder greeted me warmly as if he knew me already. Maybe we had met at San Antonio camp or in Tumupasa. It wasn't that unlikely. With so few people travelling in these jungles the chances of meeting the same ones again was fairly high, I suppose.

The two 'Syrians' were particularly keen to try out our rifle. They joked with Irgen and flattered him until one of them plucked up the nerve to ask if he could have a go with it. Irgen said yes. I wish he hadn't. The Remington Speedmaster with its high rate of fire was like a new toy. The two quickly whizzed off, coming back a few minutes later with a Spix Guan. After that we asked Irgen if he could get the gun back before they destroyed the entire fauna of the area. It was hardly as if they needed any more meat and there was no way they could store their food even if they did kill more animals. Without being asked, the man gave back the rifle and the chatting and general banter continued.

Just before sunset Chichito turned up in his red and yellow Landcruiser. He was fatter than I remembered him. His paunch peeped out from under a small, light green vest. He locked my hand in a bone-crushing handshake.

'Simon. You're early. I wasn't expecting you for another week yet. You didn't get lost again did you? That last time I took you to the Undumo – I heard you guys got stuck and had to come back.

Weren't you out in that really cold *surazo*?' Chichito kept up a
tirade of questions and comments that almost left us lost for words.
He hugged Irgen warmly and gave Julian an enormous slap on the
back that nearly sent him reeling. He shouted some instructions at
the crew-cut boy and food was produced – enamel plates of rice,
tapir meat and plantain. Three cut-log seats were placed in the
middle of the feasting loggers. We were handed mugs of fruit
drink. The storytelling began.

'Tell it right from the start', demanded Chichito. 'Tell us the
story of the Madidi and the "Expedition *Mira-Palanca*".'
Surrounded by the forest, lit by the glow of an open fire, it felt in a
way like some scene from an epic medieval tale. All three of us took
turns telling the story. We told of how we had got lost down the
Undumo with Bernardino, how we had gone up the Rio Hondo
without him and how we had lost Charlie. Then we told him about
the Madidi, of Justino and his penance and how we had crossed the
Serrania with Ignacio making silly comments all the way. We told
them about the rapids, the candiru and the giant *marimonos*. We
told everything. Chichito chipped in comments from time to time
to clarify various points to the audience – why Ignacio had called us
'The Expedition *Mira-Palanca*', and about my fantastic canoe. He
also filled in various things that we didn't know.

'Ignacio and the others got back to the Tuichi in just one day. . . .
And, without anything to carry, Justino was the fastest one
back. . . . That puma you saw this afternoon; he's been hanging
around for the last few days. He's after the meat. There's a *tigre* that
comes by as well.' The stories stretched into the night. When they
were done, it was time to talk business.

'So you want a ride back then. How much will you pay me?'

At least Chichito was direct in his approach.

⁂

We set off early the next morning. I sat up-front in the cab of the
Landcruiser with Chichito as he steered through the deep ruts in
the mud road and avoided the fallen branches that were strewn

across it. It wasn't long before the untouched forest ended and we came to a clearing on one side where the forest had been chopped down and burned. The burning hadn't been very effective here – perhaps the cut wood hadn't been left to dry for long enough – and the charred earth was a mess of blackened logs and tree stumps. There were traces of green where new growth had already started, but no crops had been planted as yet. It was a dismal scene after the verdant rainforest, a jagged picture of greys, browns and black. In the centre stood a rickety shack made of crudely sawed planks, plastic sheeting and pieces of corrugated iron. On the road nearby was an Isuzu truck, up to its axles in mud, around which clustered a gang of men 'tooled-up' with shiny machetes and axes. The men were lighter skinned and less sturdy looking than the loggers we had been staying with.

'Argentinians', said Chichito, knocking the van down a gear and easing to a halt beside the stuck lorry. 'The government has sent them down here to "forge a new life".' He chuckled at his last words. 'They are Bolivians who were living across the border in Argentina and the Argentinian government decided it didn't want them and sent them back; no matter that they had been living there for generations. Our government doesn't know what to do with them, so it gives them some tools and this new truck and sends them down here. "Go and cut down some jungle and start a farm", it says. "This land belongs to no one. You can have it".'

He stopped the Landcruiser and leaned out of the window to shout some instructions at one of the 'Syrians' who had come with us in the back of the van. The man started passing down chunks of the tapir carcass that we had in the camp the day before. The Argentinians eagerly grabbed at the hams, trotters and head that were handed down. One was talking with Chichito, pointing out items on a shopping list: wire, nails, some more torch batteries. Money changed hands. Chichito folded the list over the wad of notes and carefully placed it next to several similar lists on his dashboard. Then he put the van into gear again and we lurched for-ward down the muddy track.

'They haven't got a clue', he said after half a minute's silence.

'They're from the mountains. They don't know how to hunt animals or farm crops here. They wouldn't survive without us giving
them meat. God knows what they'll do when their crops fail –
starve, go back to La Paz most probably.'

The Carreterra Alto Madidi started at a wide but shallow river that
the Landcruiser forded easily. Beyond were several huts with government signs on them and the forest had been cleared back a
hundred feet or so on either side of the road. Now the track was
wider but just as slippery and full of potholes as before. At one
place we had to stop and wait while two big yellow bulldozers with
protective cages around their cabs pushed away some trees that
had fallen onto the 'highway'. There were more settlements. The
first we came across were covered with the ubiquitous blue tarpaulins and looked temporary. This was where people had recently
laid claim to the land. These were replaced further on with more
permanent-looking thatch-roofed houses with crops of yucca and
plantains growing between the stumps and logs that littered the
ground. Chichito explained that the people here were mostly high-
land Quechuas. In his opinion, they had little more idea about
farming the jungle than the Argentinians, though he said they
were hardy people and had come here by choice. If these small-
holdings did not work, they would clear more forest and start
again.

Not long after that, we were back in Ixiamas, civilization proper,
with a grid plan of streets, power lines and concrete buildings. We
stopped at a restaurant and bought a meal of chewy beef and rice.
Pop music blared out from loudspeakers in the corners and the
walls were adorned with posters of women in swimsuits advertising
beer and chainsaws. We drank Coca-Cola and cold beer and
decided that, though they tasted good, they did not live up to the
expectations of the last three weeks. How long would it be, I wondered, before the settlements we had passed that morning had all
this? And Chichito's logging camp: when would they run out of

mahogany and move onto the next stream? Soon the Carreterra Alto Madidi would reach the idyllic Aroyo San Juan where Irgen had nearly trodden on the stingray, and not that much further on it would arrive at the Madidi itself. People would come; first loggers who would find an abundance of nearly tame animals to hunt, then settlers, whether they were Argentinians or Quechuas. They would destroy the wildlife and their crops would start to exhaust the soil. Chichito reckoned it would take two or three years for the road to reach the Madidi, possibly less, depending on the attitude of the government. But it would, he thought, take much longer for settlers to make much of an impact. The river, which had proved such a headache to us navigating down, would also stop the spread of people up it.

Chichito's opinion on the fate of the forest was typical amongst most Bolivians that I met. 'The *selva* is vast', he said. 'People nibble at the edges but they can't destroy it all. Look', he added, pointing to a clump of cecropia and balsa saplings at the edge of one of the farm plots. 'The jungle grows back as fast as they cut it down.'

'What about the mahogany and the cedar, the true rainforest?'

'Ah', he conceded. 'That takes longer.'

The Madidi's headwaters and its valley down to roughly where we had left it to trek overland were protected, at least on paper. The Madidi National Park joined to several other reserves in Peru, in theory creating the largest preserved area in the entire Amazon. The Madidi had been recognized as one of the areas of highest bio-diversity on the planet, with a 'complete Amazonian faunal assemblage'. Attempts were being made to keep the 'core' pristine and the areas around villages like San Jose 'zones of integral management', where limited timber extraction and eco-tourism would bring in money to the local economy. The intention to shield the Madidi from the worst of the exploitation was at least there.

I felt that what would ultimately preserve the ecosystems of the Serranias was their very inaccessibility. For the moment they still seemed to be safe. At the top end of the Madidi we virtually could have picked any direction and walked for weeks without coming across signs of other people. Up there in those parallel ranges of mountains were ridges and valleys that had never been explored and, even if they had been walked over once or twice, the forces of erosion and growth re-sculpted them year by year, continually rendering them 'unknown'. Here there were still the *maras* and the *roble*, the curassows, peccaries, and ocelots, and the *marimonos* of the mountains, waiting to be discovered. On the highest ridges there would still be the *Ucamari* – the spectacled bear, pulling up palm trees and ripping into the pulp inside. If a giant monkey, the *Mono Rey*, really did exist, then here would be the place to find it.

⁂

After I arrived home I did an internet search for the *Mono Rey* and 'Loys' Ape'. I wanted to see if there was anything that I had missed, find out if anyone else had made a connection between de Loys' photograph and the king monkey, or see if that link was just a construction of my imagination. I tried the various search engines and found out that 'Mono Rey' was a computer game in Mexico (it had numerous tips and 'cheats' posted for it). I also found one of my own letters, posted on the website of the canoe company, outlining my expedition and requesting some spare parts.

Searching for 'Loys' Ape' gave me more addresses to visit. I tapped into a rich vein of cryptozoology; the 'Loys' Ape' story was usually tagged onto sites about Bigfoot. I visited the 'Hairy Hominid Archives' where Loys' Ape was pictured along with an artist's impression of Mothman who amazingly flew with no discernible flapping of his 10-foot wings through the Maine countryside. I skimmed through 'Cryptozoology and Palaeontology News', 'Jimmy the Brain's Bigfoot link page', 'Stan's stories of Bigfoot and El Mono Grande' and 'Crypto land', where a seemingly rather 'spaced-out' author had written,

> . . . this photo really used to freak me out when I was a kid. Anyway,
> while I agree the ape in question bears some resemblance to a spider
> monkey, the face does not resemble any spider monkey I have seen.

This was fairly typical of the descriptions. Every reference I
found as I trawled through the pages turned out to be just a rewrit-
ing of de Loys' story, usually reworded in a way that showed how
the 'ape' could not possibly have been a spider monkey. None of the
sites provided any information that I didn't already know. None
listed any more sightings or proof and, rather disappointingly, none
mentioned the name '*Mono Rey*'. I ended up with the impression
that there were a lot of people who really wanted to believe in
giant apes wandering the wildernesses of the world and didn't
require a great deal of proof to convince them they were there.

There was, however, one exception with the sites I found, one
that gave me the jolt of discovery that the idea for my expedition
might have had some justification after all.

'Giant Primates of the New World', by the Yerkes Regional
Primate Research Center, was sandwiched between an article on
two oversized razorbills sighted in 1835 and one on 'the Dequincy
Louisiana Chupa roadkill', which told how a strange baboon-like
creature had been run over by a car there in 1996. 'Giant Primates'
was well written and serious. It outlined the story of de Loys' expedition and listed original papers by Montandon, de Loys and their
contemporaries that supported or refuted the evidence. But it
wasn't the information that thrilled me (I had already read the
documents); it was the subtitle of the article, the only time I had
ever seen the same link that I had made between the photograph
and the existence of a South American Ape.

'*Ameranthropoides Loysi* or the Mono Rei.'

Here at last was confirmation that somebody else had the same
ideas as me.

❦

At about the same time, I received a letter from Charlie. He said he
had tired quickly of Brazilian beaches and returned to the Bolivian

jungle. He had hired a guide and set off with two other backpackers up the Rio Hondo towards the Serrania Chepite. He got as far as '*Pacu* Pool', but became ill and turned back. During his return, he macheted himself in the leg and ended up spending five days on a drip in a clinic in Rurrenabaque. Later, doctors in Australia dug out two half-inch long bot-fly maggots from his back. Another was extracted from his leg.

His enthusiasm was undimmed. This is what he wrote:

> What can you say but 'WOW!' as the photos rock back and you have to say 'Shit – we were really there' – And as bitten and as physically knackered as we were, I had to admit, it was fucking unreal!
> Madidi – The Return – It's got to be done!

❦

Like him I want to go back, to experience the power of the raging rivers and see the macaws light up in the sun at dawn. And I want to believe in the *Mono Rey*. I know the *Ucamari* is just a bear and that for all the information written about it, there is only one real account of de Loys's discovery. But an element of doubt still remains. It was triggered by something that Irgen's father said to me after Irgen, Julian and I had returned to Rurrenabaque. Irgen had insisted that I should meet him as he had come downriver from his *chacra* on the banks of the Beni on one of his infrequent visits to sell his surplus produce and stock up on provisions like bullets and fish hooks. It was unlikely I would get another chance. We met for breakfast at the Club Sociale, on the patio that overlooked the Beni, the same place, in fact, where Charlie had talked his way onto the expedition nearly three months previously. On the river there was the usual bustle of motorboats ferrying back and forth to San Buenaventura on the other side. The Serrania Susi ridge rose up behind. It was early enough in the day for the peaks still to be obscured in the morning mist, but I could just make out the pointed summit of the largest one, Cerro de Brujas – 'Witches Mountain'. Legend said that you could climb for as many days as you liked but you would never reach the top.

Leoncio Janco, Irgen's father, was a gnome-like man of around 70 years. The thing I noticed immediately was his enormous ears which stuck out like flanges at the sides of his head, and his age-lined, leathery face which was not unlike Negro's. In contrast, his body looked almost young. Under his T-shirt, the muscles were still supple and though barely five feet tall, Irgen's father looked like he was, or once had been, immensely strong. I explained that what I was most interested in was the *Ucamari*, as Irgen had said that he might have seen one.

'It was during the war that the Americans fought against the Germans', Leoncio Janco said, sipping at his tall glass of black coffee after we had exchanged pleasantries and Irgen had told him all about the 'fantastic canoe' that could be carried in a *mochila* and yet rolled out to be five metres long.

'Rubber, quinine; there were good prices then. I was up in the Beu looking for cinchona bark. I was around fourteen. We came across this *Ucamari* ripping up palms and we shot it. It had black fur, no tail. It would have come up to my chest when on all fours. It had a face like a dog. Maybe it was a bear.'

I nodded despondently. 'That's what I thought.'

'Another time', Leoncio Janco continued, staring into space, slowly drawing out the memories, 'twenty of us paddled a dugout all the way up the Madidi from Puerto Cavinas at its mouth. We were taking machetes and fish hooks to the Pacaguaras, who at that time were moving towards the Colorado. It was 1951 and they had killed some locals – eaten them too.' His eyes widened. He continued without looking up. 'The army went in for revenge and shot some of them, and the *barbaros* moved deeper into the jungle. But', he added, 'we had no argument with them. They gave us cinchona bark and herbs in return for metal items and some of our clothing. They liked the clothes. Some wore things – what remained of them – left by missionaries. A few wore shirts made of natural fibre from the *selva*. They had painted faces and feathers stuck through holes in their noses.'

Leoncio Janco and I talked on and I paid the bill. When I was about to go, the old man leaned over so that his face was close to mine and said, 'You still haven't asked me about the *Mono Rey*.'

'The *Ucamari* . . .' I started.

'. . . is not the same thing.' Leoncio let the sentence sink in while he sipped the remainder of his coffee. Did he mean the large *mari-monos* we had seen in the Serranias? Were they, as Bernardino had suggested, like the *Mono Rey*?

'They are just one of many animals that people say are undiscovered', Leoncio answered. He reached across the table and gripped my arm, looking up into my eyes for the first time in our conversation. 'Did you notice how the *maneches* were different too?' His eyes glinted as his face cracked into a grin. 'They are more orange than the ones around the Tuichi. Or the tapirs? The ones in the Serranias are bigger and blonder.

'With the *Mono Rey*, I'm not so sure', he continued. 'But, I was told there are two sorts. One is black and is a bit smaller than me. The other has brown hair and is two and a half metres tall. Now that is not the *Ucamari* I saw. All that *selva* – the Beu, the Chepite, the Madidi.' He pronounced the names deliberately, almost as if intoning a prayer. 'No one has been to most of it.

'Anything could be there', he said, his face raised momentarily in the direction of Witches Mountain. 'You might even find your *Mono Rey*.'

Glossary of Spanish Words

bagre a large catfish
barbaro literally 'barbarian', 'savage' – 'wild Indian'
barraca rubber estate
bibosi fig tree
burros donkeys
cargador porter
chacra 'slash and burn' farm clearing
chaparral rough ground or shallow swamp
charque dried meat
cholos Indian peasants (from the highlands)
chonta a type of palm with very hard wood
chuchillo riverside bamboo
cocalero drug runner
cuchillo knife-edge ridge
curiche deep swamp, oxbow lake
dorado golden, a type of fish
espundia leishmaniasis, a disease that affects the mucus membranes
and 'eats' away your nose
estradas a 'round' or lane of rubber trees
feio ugly
hombre de la selva man of the jungle

jatata a tough palm whose leaves are used for roofing

jatoba a tree whose bark is used to make canoes

jau a catfish

jochi paca, a type of large rodent

jodas fuck, bugger, an expletive

lancha canoe dug out from a large tree trunk, often built up at the sides with planks, powered by an outboard motor

madidi a type of forest ant

mamore a salmon-like fish

maneche howler monkey

manso tame

mara mahogany

marahui riverside midge

marimono spider monkey

mochila rucksack

mono monkey

mono lucachi dusky titi monkey

mono oso 'monkey bear', another name for the *Ucamari*, spectacled bear

Mono Rey king monkey, mythical giant monkey

mono silvador whistling monkey, brown capuchin

montana jungle of the Andean foothills

motorista boatman who steers the outboard

mutum curassow, a type of bush turkey

negrito small black, stingless 'sweat' bee or a type of spider monkey

oso bandera giant anteater

pacu large river fish with nut-crunching molar teeth

palanca gear-stick, penis

palo diablo devil's pole; tree with fire ants living in it

pampa area of grassland

papas de la selva jungle potatoes, edible tubers

pejiche giant armadillo

pintado a type of catfish

pucarara bushmaster, a poisonous snake

rico rich (eg. food); 'yummy'

roble timber tree

sabalo a type of fish

sausa a tree whose bark, boiled up, makes a diarrhoea remedy

seguro sure, certain

selva rainforest

sepe leaf-cutter ant

seringuero rubber tapper, also a type of bird with an annoying
   whistle

serrania mountain ridge

sierra mountain range

sur, surazo Antarctic weather system, usually around June, that
   brings very cold temperatures

suribim a type of catfish

tabano like a horse-fly

tejon a coati – like a racoon

tierra firme hard ground

tigre jaguar

tigrecillo ocelot

tojo orependola – jackdaw-sized bird, which constructs pendulous
   woven nests

tujuno a type of catfish

turista tourist

Ucamari spectacled bear

una-de-gato cat's claw; a type of barbed vine, also used as a herbal
   'cure all'

uruci palm nut

viente-cuatros 'twenty-four', a type of large ant with a sting in the
   tail, reputed to give you a twenty-four hour fever

wiche kinkajou, a tree-living animal

yoporobobo Fer de Lance, a poisonous snake